Also by Mordecai Richler

HOME SWEET HOME

HOME SWEET HOME

My Canadian Album

MORDECAI RICHLER

McClelland and Stewart

Published in Canada by
McClelland and Stewart Limited
The Canadian Publishers
25 Hollinger Road
Toronto, Ontario
M4B 3G2

CANADIAN CATALOGUING IN PUBLICATION DATA

Richler, Mordecai.
    Home sweet home: my Canadian album

ISBN 0-7710-7488-3

1. Canada—Addresses, essays, lectures. I. Title.

FC60.R53   1984   971   C84-098249-6
F1008.3.R53   1984

Excerpts from this book have appeared, sometimes in a different form, in the
Atlantic Monthly, Canadian, Harper's, Life, Esquire, New York magazine, *The
New York Times Magazine, The New York Times Book Review, The Ultimate
Baseball Book, Geo, Inside Sports, Signature, Encounter,* the *London Spectator,* the
New Statesman, Saturday Night, Maclean's, and the *Toronto Star Weekly.*

Manufactured in the United States of America
First edition

For JACK MCCLELLAND
Without whose encouragement this book
might never have been written

Contents

HOME SWEET HOME

Home Is Where You Hang Yourself

DON'T KNOCK FLATTERY.

Increasingly, during the latter part of my all but twenty-year sojourn in England, visiting Canadian professors and even Ottawa mandarins, their manner solemn, said to me, "You ought to come home. We need you in Canada."

Oh, isn't that nice, I thought. But shortly after my return the question I was confronted with again and again was, "Didn't things work out for you in England?"

"Yes. Certainly."

"Oh, come on. If that's the case, what are you doing here?"

Actually, avarice played its part.

On a flying trip home in the late Sixties, I learned of a writer, minor by Canadian standards, minor even by Ontario standards, who, though still in his late thirties, had already sold his collected letters and manuscripts to an Ontario university for several thousand dollars.

I was, to begin with, appalled. But, being far from incorruptible myself, my second thoughts were shrewd ones. Plunging into my mother's cupboards, I unearthed my first parochial school report card. Early, but *significant*, high school compositions. A tattered Yo-Yo badge. A novel begun when I was fourteen, not to be despised, if only because it showed that I had since shed the influence of Alexandre Dumas. Which is to say, I no longer believed that I was the last of the Romanoffs, Czar Nicholas's Number One Son, temporarily abandoned to St. Urbain Street, but, if only my uncles knew, one day to be Czar of all the Russias. All these enormously valuable manuscripts I stored in a fireproof box, not because I was venal, no sir, but because like that minor Ontario poet, I had come to appreciate my debt to unborn generations of Canadians.

But what really impelled me, after years of vacillating, to finally pack my bags was a recurring fear of running dry, a punishment, perhaps, for luxuriating all those years in London, not paying my Canadian dues. Literary London had been uncommonly hospitable. It was still exhilarating. But, looking around—counting heads—survivors—it suddenly seemed to me that too many other expatriate Commonwealth writers, writers I respected, had been driven in exile to forging fictions set in the distant past, the usually dreaded future, or, indeed, nowhere. Which was sufficient to frighten me into trying home again, going back to Montreal.

And so, blessed with a family loyal, yet justifiably resentful at being uprooted, I booked passage on the *Pushkin* in June 1972. The 19,860-ton M.S. *Alexander Pushkin,* flagship of the Baltic Shipping Company, launched in 1965 and charged with an electric generator that could in a pinch supply a town with a population of 50,000. What I had anticipated were days filled with herrings, borscht, pirozhki, and shashlik karski, and nights awash in duty-free champagne and caviar. A sort of floating communist pleasure palace on which my cozened family, beguiled by tales of my Montreal boyhood, would learn to look toward the coming Canadian plunge with delight. Six grueling months of benumbing winter; in the absence of spring, a thunderbolt proclaiming summer, overnight as it were; and then our finest season, the autumn, achingly beautiful, the Laurentian hills ablaze with color, the skies a hard deep blue.

In 1951, I had left Canada, a cocky nineteen-year-old, foolishly convinced that merely by quitting the country, I could put my picayune past behind me. Unpublished but hopeful, I sailed for England, fabled England, all my possessions fitting neatly into one cabin trunk and, in my breast pocket, a letter from the managing editor of the now defunct *Montreal Herald,* saying I had been a loyal, industrious, and (the clincher, this) sober employee. I was returning with a wife, four children (a fifth, our eldest, staying behind to complete his O-levels), two budgerigars, two ring-necked doves, eighteen wooden cases, and a mountain of suitcases and doubts.

Determined to take leave of old friends in Twenties style, I had arranged for a party in our cabin, even as the *Pushkin* lay in Tilbury Docks, and it was there I had my first intimation of Russian appetite, not to say duplicity. I had personally passed a case of liquor onto the ship for our farewell party, but on the hazardous journey from lower to upper deck the sailors, who had graciously accepted the case, managed to empty a bottle of gin, a bottle of scotch, and a bottle of cognac.

Our first dinner on board was a disaster. Spaghetti followed by tough boiled beef. After the horse reins, the saddle. The *Pushkin* was purportedly a one-class ship, but it was immediately made clear that in the *Pushkin*'s nomenclature it was not each according to his need, but every comrade in relation to his connections. While we struggled with our overcooked spaghetti, at the officers' table they brazenly washed down smoked sturgeon with iced vodka, followed by steak with claret, salad, cheese, and strawberries.

Wandering the sun-filled decks, picking my way between boiling bodies, largely German—immense of thigh, broad of belly—sprawled everywhere like beached whales, I took to brooding about home. I wondered if I had left matters too late, if my return was ill advised, a sentimental and potentially costly form of self-indulgence.

Once before, in 1963, I had been on the point of returning, when a misadventure with the CBC television drama department in Toronto was sufficient to make me change my mind. With Joe Melia, a British actor fluent in Russian, I had done a new translation of Isaac Babel's play *Sunset,* adapting it for BBC-TV, where it was directed by Ted Kotcheff. This was, albeit only on television, the first production of Babel's play in the West. It attracted some flattering reviews, as well as letters from as far off as Harvard. I was, and remain, absolutely convinced of Babel's greatness and was never so presumptuous as to write "additional dialogue" or tamper with the script. My role was modest. I served as a respectful carpenter. But when the script was sent off to *Festival,* CBC's cultural showcase of the time, it evoked an astonishing letter from one of its resident producers. He had, he wrote, had strange doubts while reading the play. "The reason for this is that both my father and mother come from Russia and from the general time this story was written. I felt that somewhere along the line, some of the Russian characters had been changed into Jewish people and that they had not been rewritten or changed organically, but only in name. . . . The story is reminiscent of 'Taras Bulba' by Maxim Gorki [sic] and is more believable if it deals with Cossacks of that time than the Jews of that time. No cantor would ever shoot a gun in the synagogue! No Jewish son would ever hit his father with a gun butt! No Jew would ever say he ceases to be a Jew when he gets on a horse . . . and no Jew was that wealthy in Russia at the time. These are points I corroborated with my parents. . . ."

Had the producer's parents been born Greek, and had I submitted an adaptation of *Oedipus Rex,* I daresay that script also would have been rejected with the rejoinder that no Greek boy, especially a prince, the king's *kaddish,* would bed his mama.

In any event, the producer's letter was a jolting reminder of many of the reasons why I had left Canada in the first place, and I took to rereading it, an antidote, whenever I was overcome with nostalgia. A longing, striking me at 3:00 A.M., to see big Jean Beliveau carry the puck all the way down the Montreal Forum ice one more time. Or the need, overtaking me with equal suddenness, for a smoked-meat sandwich from Schwartz's incomparable delicatessen on the Main. I missed the *Montreal*

Star's page for septuagenarians, "The Best Is Yet to Come," and each fall's flood of "In Canada" books: say, "The Battered Child in Canada" or "Not So Gay in Canada."

Nostalgia, to come clean, had become a problem. With immense excitement, I read of Montreal's historic 1972 blizzard, a two-day humdinger, cars abandoned everywhere, downtown streets impassable; the men, unable to make it home from their offices, consoling themselves in hotel bars; and snowmobiles displacing ambulances. Instead of being grateful to watch it on the telly, snug in my Surrey home, I felt deprived. I had also come to pine for sweltering summers and the mountain lakes of my boyhood. I sent home for seeds and planted Quebec Rose tomatoes in our greenhouse. They failed to take. Surely, an omen.

O Canada!

On a visit in 1961, it was my privilege to drive to Brantford, Ontario, to pay tribute to Pauline Johnson, who had been born there a hundred years earlier and was now to become the first Canadian writer to appear on a five-cent stamp. The program got off to a rousing start with some tribal dances by Chief Red Cloud, a most engaging man, and his grandson Little White Bear; a Miss Rosalie Burnham, who was in Indian costume, treated us to her own rendition of Tommy Dorsey's arrangement of "Indian Love Call." Then the deputy minister of citizenship and immigration, Dr. George F. Davidson, rose to speak. "Though highbrow critics tilted their noses high in the air," he said, "Pauline Johnson was the most truly Canadian poet of them all. It's not high-class poetry," he allowed. "In fact I don't know if it's great or good or what, but ordinary Canadians, like ourselves, liked it. Miss Johnson," he concluded, "wrote for our boyish enjoyment. Like William Shakespeare."

Certainly I had sailed away from Canada without regrets in 1951. Like many of my contemporaries, I was mistakenly charged with scorn for all things Canadian. For the truth is, if we were indeed hemmed in by the boring, the inane, and the absurd, we foolishly blamed it all on Canada, failing to grasp that we would suffer from a surfeit of the boring, the inane, and the absurd wherever we eventually settled. And would carry Canada with us for good measure.

My friend Robert Fulford, the editor of *Saturday Night,* once observed that the trouble with our generation of Canadians, the cultural-internationalists of the Fifties, was our conviction that the only thing for the talented to do was "to graduate from Canada." Yes, possibly. But what many an expatriate felt on return visits was that those in the arts who had stayed behind were chickenhearted, middle-aged before their time, settling for being big fish in a small pond. A decidedly unfair judgment of Northrop Frye, Morley Callaghan, and Robertson Davies, among others. But, certainly, others in the arts who stayed at home did so out of necessity, not without self-apology, promising themselves that next year, or the year after, they would try London or New York, testing their talents against the larger world. Alas, next year or the year after (graduation day, as it were) never came, and a decade later many felt themselves compromised, self-condemned, a big noise on campus forevermore, until, with hindsight, they redeemed themselves by becoming the most impassioned of nationalists, declaring that for all seasons there was nothing like home.

Home, where some of the younger nationalists, ironically, suddenly turned against leading literary figures, men who had served well for years with little recognition: Callaghan condemned for saying, "Forget all about the words 'identity' and 'culture,' just never mention them. Seek only excellence and in good time people all over the world will ask about Canadians." And Frye and Davies rebuked for being "internationalist." In a review of Robertson Davies's *Fifth Business,* in the *Canadian Forum,* the author was adjudged a rotter because, in his novel, he was nasty to Canadian ladies. "Why," wrote reviewer Anne Montagnes, "should the beautiful girl whose idea of love is 'a sweet physical convulsion shared with an interesting partner' be South American? Why must all those book subscribers know contemporary Canadian women under forty only as two school girls, one pimply, the other spoiled? And why oh why, dear school master, when you even date your last page as recently as 1970, must you still locate the simian androgyne and the big spiritual adventures outside of Canada? Canada, while you've been expiating, has come to abound in a passionate pagan temperament."

What we had here was a new critical direction—the Canadian school. Its strictures, if applied to British or American letters, would have obliged us to repudiate E. M. Forster for writing about shenanigans in a Malabar cave when, as we all knew, there were just as many holes in the British Isles, and it would have utterly dismissed Hemingway, a loutish cosmopolitan, for setting *The Sun Also Rises* in Paris when it was just as easy to lose a generation in Milwaukee.

But, to be fair, come the early Seventies, the nationalists had acquired an editor not only concerned but also intelligent, the poet Dennis Lee, and a gifted writer and spokeswoman, Margaret Atwood, who were then active in a lively new publishing house called Anansi. And, furthermore, for all my complaining, I was often pulled back to Canada during the Sixties, twice for a year's duration and, more often than I can count, for stays of three weeks or more. Venturing onto Ottawa, Toronto, the West.

Studying the fever chart.

Taking the pulse.

Karsh of Ottawa

I MET KARSH AT HIS HOME, A HANDSOMELY APPOINTED COUNtry estate on the Rideau River, about fifteen minutes' drive out of Ottawa. 1960 that was, the year the National Gallery in Ottawa had invited him to give a one-man show. In the eighty-year history of the gallery, Karsh was the first Canadian photographer to have been so honored.

Karsh was born in Mardin, Armenia, in 1908, and was brought to Canada by his uncle in 1924. "This country has been kind to me from the very beginning," he said. "I would never leave it."

With us in the garden were Madame Karsh and Marsh Jeanneret, director of the University of Toronto Press. A tape recorder stood on the table next to the publisher. I asked Karsh about the little statue of St. Francis of Assisi standing on a mound under a tree.

"But this is a bird sanctuary," Karsh said, "and St. Francis, of course, is the patron saint of the little creatures."

"We call our house 'Little Wings,'" Madame Karsh said.

"Oh," Karsh said, snapping his fingers, "I just had a thought."

Jeanneret sprang quickly to his feet and turned on the tape recorder. "Karsh has just had a further thought," he said into the microphone before handing it to Karsh.

"Excuse me," Karsh said.

"Go right ahead."

Karsh cleared his throat. "This is Karsh with a postscript," he said. "When we first came out to this lovely place we saw a blue-bird light on the ground—"

"Not a blue *bird*," Madame Karsh said emphatically, "but a *blue*bird. The bluebird of happiness."

"—and we thought," Karsh said, "this was a very good omen. If this site was good enough for the bird, it would certainly do for us."

Jeanneret flicked off the tape recorder and explained that he had been staying with the Karshes for two days, recording anecdotes for an eventual biography.

"Yousuf Karsh," Madame Karsh said, "has taken so many great portraits of so many great men—"

"He doesn't just take pictures," Jeanneret said, "but captures the quintessence of a man."

"—that eventually the world will want to know who he was and what he was like."

Many of Karsh's portraits of the great have appeared on the cover of *Wisdom*. This magazine, published by the Wisdom Society in Beverly Hills, California, makes an annual Wisdom Award, a twelve-inch-high replica of Rodin's *The Thinker*. If, however, you take out a lifetime subscription, you too can have the Rodin statue, with your name engraved on the pedestal. *Wisdom* had recently devoted almost an entire issue to Karsh's work. "Of all contemporary artists," the editor wrote, "Karsh is the most likely candidate for immortality."

Karsh offered me another drink. "This is the only home outside the United States," he said, "that Ed Murrow has ever visited on *Person to Person.*"

We drifted inside for lunch. One dining-room wall was dominated by a portrait of Karsh in a prayerful pose. He wore a monk's habit. A bluebird flew overhead. "It's very artistic," Jeanneret said, "isn't it?"

"When I first met Yousuf Karsh," Madame Karsh said, "I asked him what it was he wanted, fame or fortune, because you cannot have both. Karsh told me without hesitation he wanted fame. I was the first one to realize," she said, "that he had genius."

Marsh Jeanneret, Karsh's publisher, felt he should talk about the photographer's most recent book, *Portraits of Greatness.*

"This book is my life's work," Karsh said. "It represents a dream come true."

The first printing of the book, Jeanneret said, had been sold out on publication, and the book had since gone into its third printing. More than 40,000 copies had been sold round the world; 7,000 of these in Canada. "At first," Jeanneret said, "we thought we'd have to subsidize publication of the book." He explained that the University of Toronto Press was a nonprofit, strictly cultural organization. "We don't publish cookbooks or novels, for instance."

"I see."

"Have you seen Karsh's magnificent portrait of Churchill?" he asked.

It had been published three times by *Life,* twice on the cover, once inside. Prior to taking Churchill's portrait in 1941, Karsh was the most sought-after society photographer in Ottawa, but still had no international reputation. By 1960, however, he had little time for personal commissions. "The Churchill portrait," he said, "was the turning point in my career."

"That portrait came to symbolize Britain's determination to fight," Jeanneret said. "It helped win the war. It was a great influence on morale."

Another Karsh portrait, this one of the Dutch Royal Family in exile in Ottawa, was parachuted by the thousands to resistance fighters in Holland during World War II. He made no charge for this, Karsh said, and he also waived all royalties on his portrait of Pope Pius XI that was produced in an edition of 6 million copies.

I asked Karsh if he contemplated a sequel to his *Portraits of Greatness.*

"Find me ninety-six more great people," he said, "and I will gladly do it."

Karsh said that it had been no easy chore to narrow himself down, from the many studies accumulated over a ten-year span, to ninety-six portraits of the truly great, among them Audrey Hepburn, Norman Rockwell, and Their Serene Highnesses Prince Rainer III and Princess Grace of Monaco.

"I've never read any reviews of the book," Karsh said. "It would mean taking the bitter with the sweet, and . . ."

"It's mostly sweet," Jeanneret said quickly.

A Real Canadian
Success Story,
or
What You Dare to
Dream, Dare to Do

"YOU'LL FIND THIS IS A GOOD STORY FOR YOU," HE SAID.
"A real Canadian success story."

The party at the other end of the line was Ben Weider, president of the International Federation of Body Builders, who was sponsoring the Official Combination Contests to Select Mr. America and Mr. Universe at the Monument National Theatre, in Montreal, in 1960. The competition, according to advance publicity, was going to be the "Greatest Physical Culture Contest ever organized any place in the World!"

"I've been to eighty-four countries in the last six years," Weider told me, "including Red China. But I'm not a communist, you know."

Weider was a man of many offices. He was, with his brother Joe, the Trainer of Champions, with outlets in cities as far-flung as Tokyo, Rio de Janeiro, and Vienna. He was president and director of Weider Food Supplements (makers of Super Protein 90 and Energex) and the Weider Barbell Co., and managing

editor of *Mr. America* and *Muscle Builder,* among other magazines. He was the author of such books as *MANGEZ BIEN et
restez svelte* and *JEUNE toute sa vie.* In one of his many inspirational articles, "The Man Who Began Again," he wrote, "True
sportsmen always cheer for the underdog . . . for the guy who
has come up from down under—the hard way," and that's certainly how Ben Weider had risen to eminence as manufacturer,
publisher, author, editor, world traveler, and number-one pur-
veyor of muscle-building equipment and correspondence courses
in North America.

Weider was only thirty-six years old. His brother Joe, who ran
the American end of their various enterprises out of Union City,
New Jersey, was thirty-nine. They had both been brought up in
Montreal's St. Urbain Street area during the Thirties. Skinny,
underdeveloped boys, they first took to body development as a
form of self-improvement. Then, in 1939, they began to write
and publish a mimeographed magazine that would tell others
how they could become he-men. To begin with, the magazine
had a circulation of five hundred copies. Enthusiasts began to
write in to ask where they could get the necessary equipment to
train themselves. And so, from their modest offices on Colonial
Street, the Weiders began to supply the desired equipment and
correspondence courses until, Ben Weider said, they became the
acknowledged leaders in the field. *Muscle Builder* and *Mr.
America,* no longer mimeographed, now appeared monthly in ten
languages with, Weider claimed, a total circulation of a million
copies.

In May 1960, Ben Weider moved into his own building on
Bates Road, from which he overlooked his widespread empire in
the comfort of a most luxurious office. For inspiration, perhaps,
there hung behind Weider's desk a painting of a resolute Napo-
leon, sword drawn, mounted atop a bucking stallion. It was here,
amid trophies, diplomas, and the odd bottle of Quick-Wate (Say
Goodbye to Skinny Weakness), that we had our first chat.

"Why don't you send me a chapter from your next novel," Weider offered, "and we could shove it into *Muscle Builder* or *Mr. America.* It ought to win you a lot of new readers."

Yes, possibly. But, alas, I had to let on, I had never been considered A BIG HITTER by the muscle-building set.

Weider looked at me severely.

Later, once I had read some of his correspondence courses, I realized that he had probably spotted my inferiority complex. I was not thinking BIG, *positive* thoughts. "DON'T BE ENVIOUS OF SOMEONE ELSE'S SUCCESS," brother Joe advised people who felt inferior. "MAYBE SOMEONE ELSE ENVIES YOU! They are bald . . . *you have a head full of hair.* They are fat . . . *you are building a he-man body.*"

Weider was a soft-spoken, courteous, ever-smiling man ("YOUR TEETH," Joe wrote, "ARE THE JEWELS OF YOUR FACE") with a high-pitched voice. A conservative dresser, he had surely grasped, just as Joe advised in BE POPULAR, SELF-CONFIDENT, AND A HE-MAN, that it was necessary to MAKE YOUR FIRST IM-PRESSION A GOOD ONE! Why? Because, as Joe said, *your packaging is your appearance.* Another thing was that Ben had chosen his hairstyle wisely. *It fit his face!* He was not the sort of birdbrain Joe complained about who wore his hair in, say, a Flat Top Crew Cut, just because "it's what everybody else is wearing now."

Weider, married in 1959, had recently become a father. His boy, he told me, weighed ten pounds eleven ounces at birth. *He was also twenty-three inches long!*

"CONGRATULATIONS!!!" I said, grasping his hand *firmly.* And, even as we parted, I made a note to remember his name, for . . . "People like to be called by name. . . . You can make yourself a real *somebody* by being known as the *one* man who never forgets names."

At home, I had time to read only one of Weider's correspondence lessons before going to bed. My choice was *Secrets of a Healthy Sex Life.*

Choosing the right girl, brother Joe wrote, was vitally important. *"Is she sports-minded?"* he asks. "Would she frown on you
having your own home gym? DOES SHE LIKE WORKING OUT
WITH YOU?"

Weider also suggested that young couples should pray together, use a good deodorant and positive thinking, and keep
their weight *normalized.* He offered sensible advice to young
husbands. "Wear clean pajamas each night . . . and be sure that
you have a variety of patterns in pajamas. You would not expect
her to retire in a torn nightgown with cold cream daubed over
her face . . . hence you should make yourself as attractive as
she."

All in all, *Secrets* gave me plenty of food for thought. It
seemed a good idea to absorb its message before plunging into
other, more advanced lessons, like *How to Get the Most Out of
People,* although this particular pamphlet looked most intriguing.
The illustration on the cover showed an assured, smiling young
man grasping piles of dollar bills, coins, and money bags. I was
keen to learn from him how to use people, but one BIG, *positive*
thought was enough for one day. So, putting the lessons aside, I
turned to *Muscle Builder.* There I read that Chuck Sipes, a recent Mr. America champion, had built his TERRIFIC muscles by
using the Weider Concentration Principle.

A couple of days later I met Sipes at the Mount Royal Studio,
where he had come to train for the approaching contest.

"Been in weight lifting a long time?" I asked.

"Yeah."

"Like it?"

"Yeah."

"Enjoying your stay in Montreal?"

"Yeah."

Sipes managed a gym in Sacramento, California. He told me
that when he started lifting weights eight years ago he had been
just another puny guy of some 165 pounds, but now he weighed

in at 204. I wished him luck in the contest and went on to chat
with Mr. Ireland, Mr. Bombay, and Mr. Hercules of India, all
fine fellows. But the man who made the greatest impression on
me was Mr. Scotland Sr., otherwise known as R. G. Smith, of
the electricity board in Edinburgh. Smith, who was to become
my friend, had come to Montreal both to visit his children and to
enter the contest—not that he had the slightest chance of winning. Smith was fifty-four years old. He had begun to practice
body building at forty-seven.

The body builders' exhibition was held on Eaton's fourth floor
on the Friday night before the contest. There was a good turn-
out. Some 300 to 400 people, I'd say. An associate of Weider's
introduced me to Dr. Frederick Tilney, who had flown in from
Florida to be one of the contest judges. "Dr. Tilney," the man
said, "has seven degrees."

The doctor, a sturdily built man in his mid-sixties, looked surprisingly young for his years.

"Can you tell me," I asked, "at what colleges you got your
degrees?"

"What's the difference what college? A college is a college.
Some college graduates end up digging ditches. It's what you
make of yourself that counts in this world."

"What exactly do you do, Doctor?"

"Oh, I lecture on health and success and that sort of stuff."

Suddenly Ben Weider was upon us. "Sorry to interrupt your
interview," he said, "but the show must go on."

A young French Canadian body builder mounted the platform
to introduce Dr. Tilney. "The doctor," he said, "has traveled all
over the world and is one of the most famous editors and writers
in it."

"Well, then," Dr. Tilney said, "I'm sure all you washed-out,
weak, worn-out, suffering, sickly men want to renew your youth
and delay that trip to the underground bungalow."

A body builder came out and struck a classic pose.

Dr. Tilney beamed at us. "We have assembled here some of

the finest examples of manhood in the world. We are building a new race of muscular marvels, greater than the Greek gods. We're doing it scientifically."

Mr. Ireland assumed a heroic pose.

"You too," Dr. Tilney told us, "can develop a physique like Bill Cook's and overcome constipation, hernia, hardening of the arteries, diarrhea, heart disease, tuberculosis, rheumatism, and so forth."

We were introduced to Ed Theriault and his eight-year-old son, who demonstrated the Weider Chest Expander.

"This man here," the doctor said, "is the strongest short man in the world. He can do it—so can you! And look at this boy here. Isn't he sensational? Body building is one of the finest means of overcoming delinquency. If the kid's in the gym he's not in the poolroom. Why, I'm sure none of you want your boy to grow up a skinny runt—puny! You want him to be a real Weider he-man!"

Some other men came out to demonstrate weight lifting.

"And just look at the fine equipment, Weider equipment," the doctor said. "Guaranteed to last a lifetime. No parts to break. Isn't it something? And I have news for you. Eaton's is going to make this beautiful equipment available to you on their wonderful convenient time-payment plan. Isn't that something?"

Ben Weider applauded.

"You men out there," the doctor said, "want to have the bodies the Creator meant you to have, don't you?"

Mr. Scotland Sr. asked if he could say a few words.

"Sure."

"I just wanted to tell you," he said, "that I'm glad to be in your city, it's a wonderful opportunity, and I think body building is marvelous."

"Isn't that sensational?" Dr. Tilney said.

Chuck Sipes, the former Mr. America, came out and bent some enormous nails. He asked for a hot-water bottle and blew it up and exploded it just like a child's balloon.

"He's demonstrating wonderful lung power," Dr. Tilney said. Chuck said he'd like to tear a telephone book for us.

"You'll notice," the doctor said, "that he's starting on the real tough end, the bound end of the book."

Chuck pulled, he grimaced, he grunted, he pulled again.

"A lot of you folks have heard body builders are musclebound. Well, you just watch Chuck here demonstrate . . ."

Chuck couldn't tear the book. He apologized, explaining that his hands were still greasy from having rubbed so much olive oil on his chest before posing for us.

"See you on Sunday at the Monument National," Dr. Tilney said.

The crowd began to disperse. I went home to study Weider's magazines and correspondence courses and to read up on Dr. Tilney, in anticipation of the grand contest on Sunday.

The pinups and articles in *Muscle Builder* and *Mr. America* appear between advertisements for Weider equipment. In one advertisement in *Muscle Builder*, Weider offers his readers $50 worth of personality courses FREE—with each order for $21.98 worth of equipment. Otherwise, his booklets sold for $1 each. They included *How to Make Women Like You, How to Develop Leadership Qualities,* and *Sex Education for the Body Builder.* "WHAT YOU DARE TO DREAM," one booklet advised, "DARE TO DO."

All the personality-course booklets were signed "Joe Weider, Trainer of Champions," but Dr. Tilney assured me that he was the actual author. The doctor, who had been in the health business for fifty years, also claimed that he had written the original Charles Atlas courses in the Twenties and, to his regret, sold them outright for $1,000.

Tilney was a doctor of philosophy, divinity, natural law, naturopathy, chiropractic, and food science. I am indebted to Armin Mitto-Sampson of Trinidad for this information. Mitto-Sampson, author of *Meet . . . Dr. Frederick Tilney,* writes, "He stands like a Colossus, a God-propelled Titan, floodlighting the

cosmos with his inspirational thunderbolts. He has zoomed up
the voltage of more downtrodden souls than most all the Teachers, Adepts, Masters and Leaders of Men put together. . . . Most
of Dr. Tilney's articles are stunners—torrid capsules. . . . His
word-arrows are the language of TRUTH, not the piffle of intellectual witch-doctors. . . . At his lectures truth-starved souls gulp
his gems, eager to utilize the Jewels of his Thoughts."

The next time I saw the doctor it was backstage at the Monument National Theatre on the day of the Mr. Universe and Mr.
America contests, and all around me body builders were busy
rubbing olive oil on each other's backs and chests, posing for
photographers, and trying out difficult postures before a full-
length mirror. Ben Weider flitted anxiously from group to
group, like a bad-tempered schoolmarm on scholarship day. I
spotted my friend Mr. Scotland Sr. standing alone. He was, like
so many of the body builders in the contest, an unusually short
man. "If you ask me," he said, "it's going to be Mr. Guadeloupe
and Mr. France. They can't be beat."

Joe Weider, who had flown in from Union City for the contest, wore a dark suit, a conservative tie, and a pleated dress shirt.
A romantic drawing of him appeared in almost all Weider advertisements and bottle labels. The drawing showed Joe with enormous arms folded over a massive bare chest, his expression
manly, commanding, but of course it could give no indication
that in real life he also suffered from a nervous twitch.

"You all get into a circle now," Joe ordered the bashful contestants. *"Did you hear what I said?"* And he began to strut
around them like a ringmaster. Meanwhile, Ben, followed everywhere by a sad, nearsighted photographer, grabbed Mr. Guadeloupe. "Take my picture with him." Briefly, Ben smiled. "Got
it?"

The photographer nodded.

"Where in the hell's Mr. France?"

I took a seat in the orchestra pit with the judges and noted that
the contest had attracted a full house. Ben Weider welcomed us

on behalf of the IFBB. The master of ceremonies came out and told us, "I will announce each contestant as Mr. So-and-so from here-here in English and French. Then I'll tell you his weight, height, and measurements of chest and biceps. That's biceps," he said grinning, "not bisex. I will also tell you where each contestant has flown in from for the contest."

The boys began to appear onstage. The former Mr. Eastern Canada Jr., Mr. Calcutta, the Most Muscular Man from the Middle Atlantic, Mr. Hercules Jr., Mr. Montreal, Mr. Northern Quebec, and Mr. Muscle Beach. One by one they stepped under the spotlight, assumed a series of manly poses, and showed some spectacular muscle control. The last activity includes throwing the shoulder blades astonishingly far apart, jerking breast muscles, raising shoulder humps, and revolving still other muscles.

During the intermission, between the Mr. America and Mr. Universe contests, the activity backstage was frenetic, what with cameramen competing to get shots of the likely winners. Ben Weider, here, there, and everywhere, attempted to gather his body builders into a corner. "Now listen to this! Will you come here and listen, please!"

Slowly the contestants gathered around.

"There will be no more gum-chewing or muscle control. And I'm not kidding, guys. Anybody who does chew gum or do muscle-control stunts on stage will lose points."

I was, I must say, taken aback by Weider's behavior. Only the other day I had read, in *How to Develop Leadership Qualities,* "*Avoid shouting* . . . BE FIRM—BUT DON'T BULLY. The most commanding people I've met were the gentlest and the kindest. Only the weak individual becomes a bully." But this, I felt, was not the right time for reproaches.

The second half of the program, the Mr. Universe contest, moved along more quickly than the first, and after the lads had done their bit Ben Weider summoned them into a corner once more. "O.K., we're soon going to announce the results. Now listen, you guys, *will you listen please.* EVERYBODY'S GOING TO GET

A MEDAL. But you have to be ready to go on as soon as your name is called. *Understand?* Be ready when your name is called. And just don't come crying to me afterward and say you didn't get your medal. *Because you won't get your medal afterward."*

Before the results were announced, Weider, once more composed and soft-spoken, came onstage to present an award to Dr. Tilney for his tremendous contribution to the cause of body building. "The Doc," he said, "is a real O.K. fella."

Then, one by one, the contestants' names were called, and, just as Weider had promised, there were medals for everybody. Mr. Guadeloupe and Mr. France both won bigger trophies than the rest, but the grand prize of all, Mr. Universe, went to Chuck Sipes. He burst into tears.

Then it was off to the City Hall in the rain for the official reception. Dr. Tilney and the other judges had already arrived by the time I got there. Heaps of sandwiches and glasses of fruit juice were laid out on a long table. Finally, the boys began to turn up. And after a short delay, Ben Weider rushed into the hall, carrying diplomas in both arms. Tony Lanza, one of the judges, went to summon the mayor.

Sarto Fournier, then mayor of Montreal, told us how much he admired body builders. "I have been told," he said, "that you boys have come from twenty different countries."

Weider summoned his photographer to take pictures of himself with the mayor. Shuffling through diplomas, he began to call the boys forward. "And this," Weider said to the mayor, "is the young man who won the Most Muscular Man in America Award. *He's a fine French Canadian boy,* your worship."

The mayor grasped the boy's hand and smiled. Photographers drew nearer. Weider, also smiling, stepped between the mayor and the boy, thrusting his wife into the picture as well.

"And this, sir, is Bill Cook. MR. IRELAND!"

Cook wore a green jacket.

"I can see," the mayor said, with a twinkle in his eye, "that you are Irish."

Weider shook with laughter.

Then, as more and more boys came forward to collect diplomas, the mayor glanced anxiously at his watch. Weider began to speed things up. "The mayor," Weider said, "has taken off valuable time from his work to greet us here. Well, I think everybody will agree he's a jolly good fellow."

As Ben Weider and his wife, brother Joe, and Chuck Sipes gathered around, the mayor got out his Golden Book. Everybody smiled for the sad, nearsighted photographer. "No, *no, NO,*" Weider protested. "I want my wife to sign the Golden Book too."

Toronto, Ont.

To THIS DAY, WHEN I TRY TO CONJURE UP AN ILLUSTRATION of the uniquely, endearingly Canadian, one of the things that springs to mind immediately is the Toronto production, in 1961, of *The Connection.* The play was about junkies, if you remember, and, in those relatively unpermissive days, was taken to be very outspoken indeed. The original setting was a squalid Greenwich Village pad, the dialogue bristling with obscenities. But in the Canadian production, reset in Toronto, all those freshly scrubbed local kids didn't seem to feel right in a pad. It was a clear case of good Canadian breeding (summer camps, McIntosh apples) triumphing over New York depravity. For, as my wife pointed out to me, even as the boys desperately awaited their fix, flinging abuse at the bourgeois audience, they were never so rude as to flick their cigarette ashes on the floor. Always, they sought out an ashtray.

I was in Toronto again two years later.

In 1963, it seemed all but impossible to get an honest drink served in a well-lit place. Coming in out of the afternoon sun you stumbled through bars that were in almost total darkness to be served by girls in long black net stockings. In something called the Bombay Bicycle Room, for example, the waitresses wore saris and offered young men in horn-rimmed glasses, their breast pockets brimming with ball-point pens, the loan of a pith helmet to go with their gin. Then there was the Ports of Call. Once a sleazy hotel where sour men met for a beer, this place had been rebuilt as a sexy but safe fantasyland. Genet made palatable for

Orangemen. Outside the Ports of Call there squatted a wooden South Seas idol whose stomach flap lifted to reveal a telephone. Inside, among other wonders, there was the Bali Hai, complete with ship's bridge, waterfall, and Rotarians; a Gay Nineties room; and a Last Chance Saloon, where the sheriff showed the B'nai B'rith badmen to their tables and the inevitable girl in tights served the drinks. But just to show you that British cultural influence was still a living force there was a pub, the Dickens Room. According to the original Ports of Call publicity release, the Dickens Room was "furnished in the style of his period, Tudor." And, damn it, so it was.

Toronto, September 1970.

Only three hours after I had landed in the city, still woozy from a transatlantic flight, I found myself in the thin front line of the newly joined battle for Canada's soul, at a press conference, in the Royal York Hotel, knocking back drinks with other reporters. One of them, long on appetite, short on a sense of occasion, whispered to me, "After this, the Niagara Society is having a winetasting upstairs."

I had come to hear the spiritual great-grandsons of the Fathers of Confederation; a witness to the formation of the Committee for an Independent Canada. Under the klieg lights, TV cameras whirring, sat co-chairman Jack McClelland, the country's leading English-language publisher, and Claude Ryan, then the distinguished editor of Le Devoir. "We believe," they declared, "that Canadians today share a surging mood of self-awareness. . . . A society has evolved, unique in its quality of life—a kind of civilized resistance to the similarly blessed but much more violent land to the south of us."

Immediately this statement was made, a sagacious reporter bobbed out of his chair. "What," he asked, "does, um, Washington think of your plans?"

Québec Oui, Ottawa Non

IN MAY 1964, I WAS IN MONTREAL FOR QUEEN VICTORIA'S birthday, a national holiday in Canada. A thousand policemen were required to put down a French Canadian separatist demonstration. Flags were burned, a defective bomb was planted on Victoria Bridge, and a wreath was laid at the Monument aux Patriotes, which marks the spot where twelve men were executed after the 1837–38 rebellion.

The last time I remembered such excitement in Montreal was when Maurice "The Rocket" Richard, possibly the greatest hockey player of his era, was suspended and could not play in the first three games of the all-important Stanley Cup finals. Richard's suspension led to a riot. A French Canadian hero, he had been disciplined by the president of the National Hockey League, a Scot named Campbell, and that didn't help. On the contrary: It illustrated yet again that in Canada, at that time, it was almost without exception the Scots who were the managers and the French who were the clerks. The French, though they made up nearly a third of Canada's 1964 population of more than 19 million, held something less than 15 percent of all responsible federal jobs. Furthermore, a survey showed that while four-fifths of the directors of 183 major companies in Canada were Canadian-born, 90 percent of them were of British origin. Less than 7 percent of these positions were held by French Canadians. Commenting on this already inflammatory situation in 1962, Donald Gordon, president of Canadian National Railways, said that he had never appointed any French Canadian vice-presidents because they lacked the necessary university training. French Canadian students responded by burning Gordon's effigy in Montreal's Place Ville Marie. Then an enterprising Toronto reporter discovered that of the thirty vice-presidents employed by Canada's two railway systems, only seven had actually been to university. And furthermore, Mr. Gordon himself had not.

Suddenly, QUÉBEC LIBRE was painted on many a Montreal wall; students fixed stickers that read QUÉBEC OUI, OTTAWA NON to cars, and there were bombing outrages. After one of the most successful dawn lootings of an armory (62nd Field Regiment in Shawinigan), John Diefenbaker, leader of the opposition, asked in Parliament what was being done "to protect the armed forces."

Parti Pris, an intellectual separatist monthly with a circulation of 3,500, came out frankly for revolution right now: ". . . we are colonized and exploited. . . . Quebec society has entered a revolutionary phase. It is ready to take all means, not excluding violence. . . ."

All this should have been disturbing, but as a returning native I must confess that what I felt was a certain childish glee. In New York, a week earlier, my editor Bob Gottlieb had told me that he and his associates had recently compiled a list of twelve books with which to start a new publishing firm that was bound to fail. Leading the list of unreadables was *Canada: Our Good Neighbor to the North.* Well, now something was happening. At last something was happening in what our most notable gossip columnist still called "Our-Town-with-a-Heart."

One night an old schoolmate told me, "I was going to buy a place in the Laurentians this year, but the truth is I'm now thinking of looking for something in Vermont. I hate to say this, but if I was going to buy a place in Montreal I'd get myself the biggest possible mortgage. Let somebody else get stuck if there's trouble."

One of the most responsible journalists in town said, prophetically, as it turned out, "The men on the fringe are dangerous.

Honestly, the next step could be an assassination, and don't think the RCMP isn't worried. It could be Vanier, the French Canadian governor-general. That would certainly provoke Ottawa. They might have to send in troops and then the whole thing would blow up."

Again and again I was asked, "What are people saying in London? What do they think?" I had to tell them the truth. Nobody was saying anything.

"If this was happening in Africa," a friend said, "or South America, everybody would be excited. Another Cuba, they'd say. But Canada, hell, we're always taken for granted."

Another journalist, an old Montrealer not generally given to hyperbole, told me, "You know what I'd like more than anything? To be twenty and French Canadian. My God, it must be exciting." He went on to say, "All my sympathies are with the French in this. They're the best people in the country, aren't they? I mean, the Protestants are so guilt-ridden and joyless. The French have such a damn good case too, but it's emotional, not rational. I mean, you can't sit down at a table and say I want this and I want that, you can't bargain. . . ."

Off to visit an old friend the next morning, I spied a lonely and defiant Red Ensign, then our semi-official flag *manqué*, fluttering in a garden in affluent Westmount, a suburb where only a year earlier FLQ (Front de Libération du Québec) terrorists were planting bombs in mailboxes. My friend, a faculty member at Sir George Williams College, was unavailable. "Sorry, he can't be disturbed now," I was told. "He's having his French lesson."

In English-speaking boardrooms all over Montreal it was the same, the Berlitz school running company programs. I got a picture of a lot of big boys doing penance. Why, there was now even a French-language column in the *Canadian Jewish Chronicle*.

The previous autumn, André Malraux had come to town to open a "France in Canada" exhibition. "France needs you," he told the sapient aldermen of the Montreal City Council. "We

will build the next civilization together." Malraux added that he
brought a personal message from General de Gaulle. It was that
"Montreal was France's second city. He wanted this message to
reach you. . . . You are not aware of the meaning you have for
France. There is nowhere in the world where the spirit of France
works so movingly as it does in the Province of Quebec."

Opening the exhibition the next day, Malraux said, "For
France, Canada is not the past. It is not Jacques Cartier. . . . It is
what we will do together."

Four days later the Montreal *Star* replied with "The Malraux
Story: If Quebec Belonged to France." "If Quebec belonged to
France," the story began,

> the big policy decisions would be made by a super-president
> three thousand miles away in Paris. Every man would have
> to spend at least eighteen months in the nuclear army.
> There would be better schools—but fewer universities—
> and education would be in the hands of the State, not the
> Church. All television and radio operations would be a part
> of the state propaganda machine. All citizens would enjoy
> liberal welfare benefits because Quebec—like the mother-
> land—would be a welfare state. Businessmen would have to
> accept a higher degree of planning. In the courts, an ac-
> cused would be presumed guilty until proven innocent. . . .

At a press conference the next day, Malraux said, "The mere
thought that French Canada could become politically or otherwise dependent on France is a dangerous and even a ridiculous
one." He added that his "utterances never implied anything beyond the historical and the artistic, even though as a cabinet
minister I might have been thought to be somehow politically involved."

But even as M. Malraux explained himself in Montreal, General de Gaulle sent a warm letter of congratulation to a Frenchman, Jean Cathelin, who had visited Canada twice and written a

book called *Révolution au Canada*. De Gaulle wrote that he'd "draw profit" from the book, and Cathelin, a member of the Comité International de l'Indépendance de Québec, a Paris lobbying agency for separatists, claimed official blessing. The Elysée Palace insisted that de Gaulle's letter was a formality and that he was not a separatist. Meanwhile the two French Canadians who started the Comité—and who, incidentally, had been compared by one Paris newspaper to Tom Paine and Benjamin Franklin—claimed that both Algeria and Senégal had promised diplomatic support for a free state of Quebec. *Carréfour,* a French Catholic weekly, ran a headline that read: FORTY-FOUR INDEPENDENT NATIONS SINCE THE WAR. WHY NOT FRENCH CANADA? And Jacques Berque, a professor at the Collège de France and a member of the Comité, wrote in *France Observateur* that Ottawa's imperialism "has not exercised the same rigors and crudeness as [imperialism] elsewhere but takes the more insidious form of fake bilingualism, economic pressure, and financial exploitation."

French intellectuals were not always so enamored of Quebec, a province which was largely pro-Vichy in sentiment during World War II and whose flag is still the *fleur-de-lis.* When Gomez, the Spanish republican in Jean-Paul Sartre's novel *Iron in the Soul,* finds himself in New York on the day that Paris has fallen, he sees only grins and indifference on Seventh Avenue. Then, on 55th Street, he spots a French restaurant, A La Petite Coquette, and enters, hoping to find solace. "Paris has fallen," Gomez says to the bartender, but only gets a melancholy grunt for a reply. Gomez tries again. "Afraid France is a goner." Finally the bartender says, "France is going to learn what it costs to abandon her natural allies." Gomez is confused until the bartender adds, "In the reign of Louis the Well-Beloved, sir, France had already committed every fault there was to commit."

"Ah," said Gomez, "you're a Canadian."

"I'm from Montreal," said the bartender.

"Are you now?"

And Gomez goes off in search of a *real* Frenchman.

Marcel Chaput, an early French Canadian separatist, said, "If Quebec still belonged to France, I should preach separatism just as hard as I do today." In his book *Why I Am a Separatist*, Dr. Chaput wrote, "The French Canadians form a nation. . . . There is no Canadian nation. . . . There is a Canadian state [which is] a purely political and artificial entity [while] the French Canadian nation is a natural entity whose bonds are those of culture, flesh, and blood."

The English Canadian response to Dr. Chaput was not always strikingly intelligent. An editorial first printed in the *Orillia Packet and Times* and then widely reprinted by Thomson Newspapers Limited was titled "The Canada I Love: An Unfashionable Testament."

> I love Canada. . . . a thousand critics inform me that there is no such thing as a Canadian, no separate and distinct Canadian identity. I am one. Politicians and pundits assure me that there is no Canadian flag, no national anthem, but I am content with our flag, a sort of red ensign . . . and I am always moved when a good band plays "The Queen" but I could learn to stand up for "O Canada" too. I love Canada. There are people like . . . Marcel Chaput who . . . assail me for oppressing my French Canadian brothers and threaten me with a promise to pull Quebec out of confederation, but I have been . . . drunk with the Van Doos and kissed Ghislaine Gagnon . . . and saluted George Vanier . . . and I know they're Canadians too. . . . I love Canada. Our politics are dull and our sports bush-league, but you can't beat the beer or the air. . . . I am a Canadian. Are there any more like me?

Unfortunately, yes. Lots. But there are others too. In a seminar on French Canada held in Montreal in 1963, Eric Kierans, then president of the Montreal Stock Exchange, said, "This feeling not of revolt but of assertion in Quebec is deep, all-pervasive, and it's not going to go away, and I for one don't think it should go away." He added that it was plain there had been a lack of any real direction on a federal level in Canada for the past ten years. "The Liberals," he said, "were used to running this country like a clock. . . . This country is too diverse to ever let it run like that. . . . So we have a vacuum, and in a vacuum all of the inherent differences in the country emerge."

A European refugee I knew in Montreal told me, "The separatists are right when they say Canada isn't a nation, it's a state, but if only they knew how lucky they were! They haven't seen our European style of nationalism and what it does. This isn't a country—but that's what I like best about it here!"

I was in Montreal for a lengthy stay, in 1960, when the Union Nationale was defeated in the Quebec provincial election. A year earlier, Premier Maurice Duplessis, leader of the Union Nationale, had died of a stroke. Duplessis's successor, Paul Sauvé, died four months later; and in 1960 the Liberals, led by silky Jean Lesage and prodded by a brilliant newcomer to politics, René Lévesque, toppled one of the most corrupt and deeply rooted political machines in North America. It was more than a heartening political upset. What amounted to a French Canadian revolution had begun.

By 1964, there was a sense of liberation everywhere in Quebec, a province that is, incidentally, twice the size of Texas. All manner of hitherto suppressed energies had been released, and the feeling at the time was that now anything could happen. And anything included the possibility that Quebec could separate to form an independent state. If Quebec seceded, it was assumed by many that British Columbia could follow quickly. Confederation, as we knew it, might collapse. Then it was not unfeasible that a number of provinces would sue for entry into the U.S.A.

A survey undertaken by *Maclean's* magazine in June 1964 showed that 29 percent of all Canadians, almost one voter in three, were in favor of political union with the U.S.A.; 42 percent wanted economic union only. A. M. Lower, a Canadian historian worried about the many young people who quit Canada for the U.S.A. (an estimated 50,000 in 1963), wrote, "It has tended to be the more able and especially the spontaneous who have gone. . . . Canada has retained those with the least energy and ability." One of those with ability who had stayed behind was Professor Frank Underhill, who, in his book *In Search of Canadian Liberalism,* wrote, ". . . if we allow ourselves to be obsessed by the danger of American cultural annexation, so that the thought preys on us day and night, we shall only become a slightly bigger Ulster. . . . If we will only be natural . . . we shall discover that we are very like the Americans, both in our good qualities and our bad qualities." An earlier *Maclean's* survey, conducted in 1963 when the Separatist movement was barely two years old, revealed that 13 percent of French Canadians were already convinced separatists. This group, the survey showed, was largely urban, young, and well educated; it included a number of influential journalists and many professional people and senior civil servants.

The French, the first to colonize Canada, are a conquered people. Jacques Cartier explored the St. Lawrence Gulf in 1534 and brought the Indian chief Donnacona back to France with him, where Donnacona spun the French court tales about "immense quantities of gold, rubies, and other rich things." In 1608, Samuel de Champlain founded the city of Quebec in New France and opened up the fur trade with the Iroquois. Maisonneuve founded Montreal in 1642.

> He sprang ashore [Francis Parkman wrote in *The Jesuits in North America*] and fell on his knees. His followers imitated his example, and all joined their voices in enthusiastic

songs and thanksgiving. Tents, baggage, arms, and stores were landed. An altar was raised on a pleasant spot near at hand, and Mademoiselle Mance, with Madame de la Peltrie . . . decorated it with taste which was the admiration of beholders. Now all the company gathered before the shrine. . . . They knelt in reverent silence as the Host was raised aloft, and when the rite was over the priest turned and addressed them:

"You are a grain of mustard seed that shall rise and grow until its branches overshadow the earth. You are few, but your work is the work of God. His smile is on you, and your children shall fill the land."

A century passed. More. Then, in 1759, Wolfe defeated Montcalm on the Plains of Abraham. Quebec City fell to the British. Montreal was taken a year later, and in 1763 France ceded its North American territories east of the Mississippi to Britain. New France—a few arpents of snow, as Voltaire wrote so contemptuously in *Candide*—was no more. But according to the Quebec Act of 1774 the boundaries of Quebec Province were enlarged and freedom of religion for Catholics was confirmed under a combination of British and French law. The same year, French Canada's loyalty to the crown was first tested by uppity American rebels. The not-quite-Continental Congress invited the French to abandon their British masters and "seize the opportunity presented to you by Providence itself." But even when the American irregulars, taking the Ho Chi Minh Trail of their day, captured Montreal, the French, possibly remembering their earlier wars against the *Bastonnais,* stood aside. In 1837, however, *les Patriotes* rose in brief armed rebellion against the British. The rising was ruthlessly put down. Afterward Lord Durham wrote that French Canadians "brood in sullen silence over the memory of their fallen countrymen, of their burnt villages, of their ruined property . . . of their humbled nationality," and he anticipated "an indiscriminating and eternal animosity." In his famous report on Canada in 1839, he added, "There can hardly be conceived a nationality more destitute of all that can invigorate and elevate a people than that which is exhibited by the descendants of the French in Lower Canada, owing to their retaining their peculiar language and manners. They are a people with no history and no literature."

Twenty-eight years later, one of the veterans of the rebellion, George-Étienne Cartier, took French Canada into confederation—a bartered bride—pronouncing it the lesser of two evils. "We must either have a confederation of British North America or be absorbed by the American union." So, in 1867, the British North America Act was passed and the Dominion of Canada was created.

Quebec, from the beginning, put graft-ridden governments into office. Maurice Duplessis, who was first elected to the legislature in 1937, did not introduce corruption to the province, but under the Union Nationale, from 1944 to 1960, it just about defined the regime. A royal commission investigating the Union Nationale government in 1961 estimated that the graft paid out by companies doing business with the provincial government over a sixteen-year span came to about $100 million. Liquor licenses for nightclubs in Montreal, for example, sold for as much as $30,000, whereas later, under a "clean" Liberal government, they could be had for $100. But Duplessis himself, it's worth noting, did not acquire a private fortune. He ran Quebec as his private manor, and short of ordering his ministers to dance the Gopak he made sure that their public humiliation was complete. He contradicted and ridiculed them almost sadistically in the legislature and mocked them before journalists. Duplessis, a hysterical anti-Communist, time and again employed brutal strike-breaking tactics in the province and threatened townships blatantly when he needed the vote. From the platform, he would shout, "Do you want a new hospital? A new bridge? A new school? Then vote Union Nationale. I would hate to force gifts on you that wouldn't be appreciated."

Miriam Chapin, author of *Quebec Now*, writes that when she asked a farmer why he voted Union Nationale, he replied, "We've got to have roads. Look at Verchères. They sent a Liberal to Quebec six years ago and they haven't laid eyes on a bulldozer since. A woman down there, they tell me, died in childbirth last spring, the doctor couldn't get to her through the mud. We *got* to have roads."

Throughout Duplessis's reign the rich and powerful English-speaking community remained silent. In exchange, they were, in effect, allowed to run the province's economy. The banks. The trust companies. The brokerage houses.

Though Montreal is the second-largest French city in the world, as recently as 1956 only 3 percent of the English-speaking population was bilingual. Montreal was, and remains, a sequence of ghettos. Even though I was born and brought up there, my experience of the French was a pathetically limited and distorted one. During the war years St. Urbain Street families used to club together to rent clapboard cottages from the French Canadians in the Laurentian mountains. Then, suddenly, things went sour between us. One day we fished and stole apples together and the next there were signs painted on the highway, *A bas les juifs*. Adrian Arcand, the fascist leader, alarmed us. The Liberal government in Ottawa called for a plebiscite on conscription for military service overseas, and on a sleazy beach outside Montreal, French Canadians and Jews fought with clubs. A popular Jewish sportsman lost an eye.

Moi, aussi, je me souviens. Raised during the Duplessis years, I cherish memories of the era, among them the time one of his acolytes handed me, on the eve of an election, a pamphlet warning the people against the perfidy of Jewish financiers. It showed a bearded Jew with a bulbous nose, actually drooling as he gathered bags of gold unto himself. I also recall, during World War II, one of Duplessis's back-benchers standing up with impunity in the Assembly to protest that Jewish doctors were being allowed to handle naked Gentile flesh in army induction centers. The children of the *shtetl* goosing the progeny of *voyageurs*, asking them to cough in English. Such, such were the joys of cultural pluralism.

Looking back, I can see that the real trouble was that there was no dialogue between us. Under the confessional system, we went to one set of schools and the French Canadians to another. I'm sure many of them believed that there was such an order as the Elders of Zion and that the St. Urbain Street Jews were secretly rich. On my side, I was convinced all French Canadians were abysmally stupid. We fought them stereotype for stereotype. If the French Canadians were convinced the Jews were running the black market, then my typical pea-soup wore his greasy black hair parted down the middle and also affected an eyebrow mustache. His zoot trousers were belted just under the breastbone and ended in a peg hugging his ankles. He was a dolt who held you up endlessly at the liquor commission while he tried unsuccessfully to add three figures, or, if he was employed at the customs office, he never knew which form to give you. Furthermore, he only held this or any other government job because he was the second cousin of some backwoods notary who had delivered the village vote to the Union Nationale for a generation.

I believed Montreal was the second-biggest French city in the world, *but only because my geography books said so.* Aside from boyhood street fights and what I read in the sports pages, all I knew of French Canadians was that they were clearly hilarious. Our Scots schoolmaster could always raise a laugh in class by reading us the atrocious Uncle Tom-like dialect verse of William Henry Drummond: *Little Baptiste & Co.*

On wan dark night on Lac St. Pierre,
De win' she blow, blow, blow,
An' de crew of de wood scow Julie Plante
Got scar't an' run below—
Bimeby she blow some more,
An' de scow bus' up on Lac St. Pierre
Wan arpent from de shore.

St.-Jean Baptiste is still the patron saint of Quebec, but in the 1964 annual parade he was no longer played by a boy. He was, for the first time, represented by an adult, and the sheep that had accompanied him in former years was tossed out. A few days before the parade, the extremely influential Société Saint-Jean Baptiste de Montréal, with a membership of more than 300,000 throughout the province, presented a 125-page brief to the Quebec Parliamentary Committee on the Constitution. The Société said that Canada must consist of two equal partners—the Ottawa government leading the nine "English" provinces and a fully self-determined Quebec. The brief recommended, among other things, sovereign status for Quebec, including Quebec citizenship for its residents, and recognition of two nations in Canada. "This," Professor Michel Brunet of the University of Montreal told reporters, "is the answer to outright separation." He added that French Canadian nationalism was not a fad. "The 'contract' which was made in 1867 was one between an adult and a minor, but the French partner in the contract feels very much that he has come of age and he thinks strongly that he has been 'had.' "

Another indication, if it was needed, of how times had changed in Quebec was the recall from Swiss exile that summer of the Marist Brother Pierre-Jérôme. Brother Pierre-Jérôme, a legend in the province, was the author of a witty and engaging book, *Les Insolences du Frère Untel,* that was published anonymously in 1960 and sold an astonishing 127,000 copies in Quebec, making it the best-selling book in the history of the province. *Les Insolences* was one of those rare and timely volumes that became a factor in the making of a social revolution. It was the first book with a wide circulation to outspokenly criticize the church-run education system, the sloppy French (*joual*) spoken by the young, and the corruption of Quebec's political autocracy. "The whole of French Canadian society is foundering," Brother Pierre-Jérôme wrote in 1960. "We are a servile race; our loins were broken two hundred years ago, and it shows."

Shortly after *Les Insolences* became a *succès de scandale*, Brother Pierre-Jérôme was sent off to the Mother House in Rome by his Marist superiors. He lived there under strict discipline for a year before going on to teach at the University of Fribourg, from where he was finally recalled to Quebec.

Les Insolences was first published as a series of letters by André Laurendeau, then editor of *Le Devoir*, and a long-standing enemy of Duplessis. Laurendeau went on to serve on the Royal Commission on Bilingualism with Davidson Dunton, the president of Carleton University in Ottawa, and F. R. Scott, the dean of the McGill law school. It was Laurendeau who developed the theory of *le roi nègre*—that is to say, the real rulers of Quebec (the English) used a French-Canadian (Duplessis) chieftain to govern the province, just as colonial powers used African puppets to keep their tribes in order.

Laurendeau was not alone among French Canadian intellectuals who wanted to see Quebec's revolution develop quietly within confederation. On May 14, 1964, the *Montreal Star* reprinted a "Canadian Manifesto" that first appeared in *Cité Libre* and was signed by seven distinguished French Canadian intellectuals who called themselves the Committee for Political Realism. The committee called for social justice, a fairer distribution of the wealth, and a revised penal code, rather than more nationalistic heat.

To use nationalism as a yardstick for deciding policies and priorities is both sterile and retrograde. Overflowing nationalism distorts one's vision of reality, prevents one from seeing problems in their true perspective, falsifies solutions and constitutes a classic diversionary tactic for politicians caught by facts.

Our comments in this regard apply equally to Canadian or French Canadian nationalism. . . . We are not any more impressed by the cries in some English circles when American financiers buy Canadian enterprises, than we are by the adoption in the Province of Quebec of economic policies based upon the slogan *"maîtres chez nous."*

Separatism in Quebec appears to us not only a waste of time but a step backwards. . . . We refuse to let ourselves be locked into a constitutional frame smaller than Canada. . . . We do not attach to its existence any sacred or eternal meaning, but it is an historical fact. To take it apart would require an enormous expenditure of energy and gain no proven advantage. . . .

Among the authors of the manifesto was a then little-known law professor called Pierre Elliott Trudeau. Trudeau was a founder and editor of *Cité Libre,* a magazine once considered radical in Quebec. By 1964, however, it was being dismissed as timorous by separatists. For now the separatists had gone beyond abandoning the traditional sheep on St.-Jean Baptiste Day. The symbol of the RIN (Rassemblement pour l'Indépendance Nationale) was the ram's head. Young separatists were scornful of anyone over thirty—anyone who belonged to the generation that tolerated Duplessis. Governor-General Vanier, a French Canadian, was their Pétain-figure ("he speaks French with an English accent"), and even Jean Lesage, who had brought an honest government to the province, was considered a transitional figure.

"Duplessis isn't our problem," a separatist told me. "Lesage and the others pushed open the door and for that they deserve credit, but they were totally unprepared for the new release of energy."

Neither did the separatists take the many conciliatory gestures of English-speaking Canada, including the Royal Commission on Bilingualism, very seriously. "I never heard of anything so silly as bilingualism," an RIN member said. "Why should they speak French in Vancouver? It's stupid!"

I spent an afternoon in Montreal with two RIN members, both students at the University of Montreal, both articulate and middle-class. Jacques, referring to one of Montreal's largest department stores, said: "Now they advertise that nine out of ten people who work there speak French. Sure, only the tenth one is the president of the company."

André said: "We have nothing against English Canada, you know. We don't hate them. We want to run our own affairs, that's all. And if you ask me they'd be better off without us too."

I asked Jacques if he felt the standard of living in Quebec would decline if the province was to separate.

"English Canada," he said, "puts up with a lower standard of living in order to remain independent of the United States. Why don't they credit us with the same sort of pride?"

"Anyway, the standard of living would not go down," André said. "The Belgians would invest. So would the French and the Americans."

André and Jacques, both of whom professed to be against violence, claimed that they were often followed by the RCMP and photographed at demonstrations. I spoke to them about English anxieties. Quebec, I said, had an unfortunate history of corrupt politicians and right-wing demagogues. Many English Canadians feared a right-wing coup should Quebec become an independent state. Furthermore, several French Canadian trade unionists I had spoken to, men with a long and honorable history of fighting Duplessis, were also unhappy about the separatists. They feared that an independent nationalist government would necessarily support reactionary but indigenous capitalists against the unions. I also pointed out to the two students that the authors of a "Ca-

nadian Manifesto" had written: "Nationalistic policies in Canada
or in Quebec are generally advantageous to the middle class
though they run counter to the interests of the majority of the
population in general, of the economically weak in particular. . . ."

André and Jacques dismissed the manifesto as the work of
Anglicized French Canadians and claimed—correctly, as it
turned out—a broadening trade-union support. As for English
Canadian criticism, "Well," André said, "sure we had Duplessis,
but he was backed and kept in power by English Canadian financial interests."

This, of course, was an extension of André Laurendeau's theory of *le roi nègre*. Extending it even further, some French Canadian intellectuals began to fancy themselves as Canada's white
Negroes. *Les nègres blancs d'Amérique*. Well now, while I agree
that the role of the English-language press in Montreal during
the Duplessis era was, to say the least, disgraceful, the French
Canadians, unlike the southern blacks, had the vote; they were
not kept from the polls; and so if I was brought up in a notoriously backward and corrupt province it was—no matter how
artfully you slice it—a French Canadian electoral majority that
put the government in office, and kept it there and kept it there.
The English-speaking community may have been more than
pleased about it, and there is no doubt that they behaved slyly,
shabbily, even dishonestly, but the shame, such as it was, was
largely French Canadian.

André d'Allemagne, one of the leaders of the RIN, told me,
"As a French Canadian, I have no country." D'Allemagne, who
was thirty-four years old, used to work in the House of Commons in Ottawa as a translator. But, like so many other French
Canadian civil servants, some of them in the most senior positions, he had returned to Quebec. D'Allemagne said that the
RIN was opposed to violence, and would try to get its policies
accepted by direct appeal to the electorate. If, however, the RIN

were outlawed, they would have to turn to violence. "Like the *maquis*," he said.

Quebec, d'Allemagne was convinced, would ultimately opt for independence. If English Canada resisted, he had told a reporter a month earlier, "two sunken ships would block the Seaway. We don't want to do it. The Seaway is international. But we will if we have to."

The RIN, d'Allemagne said, was not precisely socialist, "but somewhat to the left of centre." It was for secular control of education and one official language in the new state: French. D'Allemagne looked to the next Quebec provincial election in 1966 as the big test—and he wasn't the only one.

If, in 1964, it seemed doubtful that Quebec would ever actually sue for separation, then it was largely because the movement still lacked a leader of sufficient stature. But there was just such a potential leader then active in the province—René Lévesque. At the time, Lévesque was the minister of natural resources in Jean Lesage's cabinet. He was also, as far as most French Canadian intellectuals were concerned, the conscience and most advanced thinker in that cabinet and, to the English-speaking community, anathema, the likely wild man. Lévesque had not entered politics until 1960. Once elected and in the cabinet, his first act was to prod the government into nationalizing all hydroelectric power in Quebec, a measure for which he was abused in English Canadian newspapers. "Why attack us now," he said, "for doing what a Conservative government of Ontario did in 1905?"

Before standing as a Liberal candidate, Lévesque was widely known and respected throughout Quebec as a television commentator who was outspokenly critical of Duplessis. "I am," he said, "not a separatist, but I admit my thoughts are running in that direction." He was described as "a last-resort separatist," i.e., if English Canada stood in the way of Quebec's social and economic development, then—and only then—would he bolt the Liberals. Speaking at the Empire Club in Toronto, Lévesque said, "Actually, I am a forty-year-old moderate. There are guys behind me who make me nervous."

Bedlam in Bytown

(The Canadian Football League is split into two divisions, East and West, the former composed of four teams, the latter of five. Once every autumn the leaders of each division meet for the Grey Cup game, which decides the national championship. This annual event, pitting East against West, is prized as a singularly important force for Canadian unity. The Grey Cup game, politicians in all parties agree, helps bind this country together. An interesting notion, this, considering the leading players on both sides are American imports, either not good enough or too old to play in the American NFL or, conversely, serving a well-paid apprenticeship in Canada before moving on to greater things in the United States.

In 1967, the Grey Cup finalists were the Saskatchewan Roughriders and the Hamilton Ti-Cats, who had taken the Eastern Division title by defeating the Ottawa Rough Riders.)

Sunday, November 26, 1967.

It was with considerable enthusiasm that I flew from England to Ottawa or—as Jack Kinsella's publicity release had it—Grey Cup-ville, where "the mild insanity launched inadvertently 58 years ago by Lord Grey [would] reach new heights of 'delirium puntens' " on the morning of November 27 when all nine Miss Grey Cup hopefuls would arrive at Ottawa's Uplands airport—a mass rendezvous that was contrived, Mr. Kinsella wrote, "at an altitude of 60 miles above Kazabazua Korners, an isolated hamlet in the heart of the Gatineau moonshine country."

Alas, on arrival in Ottawa on Monday, November 27, I found not mild insanity, but sour, disgruntled fans. The hometown Rough Riders had been eliminated 26–0 by Hamilton in the final Eastern Division game. Ottawa, contrary to expectations, would not be fielding its own team in the Grey Cup game. IT'S TIME TO CELEBRATE, ran the *Ottawa Journal* headline, BUT THE JOY IS GONE.

If spirits were sinking in Grey Cup-ville, duties were not neglected. At noon the intrepid boys and girls of the Fisher Park Junior School Band, shivering in their red capes, assembled in Centennial Square to welcome the nine Grey Cup girls and to watch Mayor Don Reid perform the official kickoff. Don Reid did not falter. He reared back and kicked mightily. Simultaneously, there was an exceedingly loud report in the skies. But Don Reid had not been resoundingly indiscreet. The loud report had been caused by a multigun salvo fired by the 30th Field Artillery.

Across the street, at the Château Laurier, I chatted briefly with a toothy matron as she sipped her Diet Pepsi. "We're all Miss Grey Cup chaperons," she said, "but we can't find the girls anywhere. Have you seen them?"

In one of the Château's many banquet halls, the girls were also being awaited at an official luncheon. Substantial-looking men drank patiently at the bar, wearing lapel badges that announced, "For a kickoff my name is . . . TUBBY." Finally, the girls, touchingly young, appeared in their miniskirted splendor. Gail and Bonnie, Marjorie Jean, Anne Louise, Leslie Jane, Su Lorraine, Julia, and Lucie. Out of so much candy, I selected Miss Saskatchewan Roughrider for a word, consulting my form sheet first. Anne Louise Kennedy (age 19, 115 lbs., 35½–25½–35½) liked tennis, badminton, volleyball, skating, and skiing. She came from North Battleford, Saskatchewan, where she was the Boosters Club candidate for Miss Grey Cup. "What will you do if you win?" I asked.

"I am accompanied everywhere," Anne said, "by a chaperon and a guard."

"A guard," I said. "Whatever for?"

Anne wouldn't say, so I confronted a uniformed representative of the Capital Guard Service. "What are you guarding the girls against?"

His expression severe, he replied, "You will have to ask the men who hired us."

I did not stay for lunch, which began—ominously, I thought—with tinned fruit salad, but retired to my room to study the Ottawa newspapers. RIDER FANS ASK WHY? Jack Koffman, *Citizen* sports editor, wrote on the front page. Bob Mellor, columnist with the same newspaper, opened with a damning quote on the home team (*They fail, and they alone, who have not striven*—Thomas Bailey Aldrich), and went on to say, "The burial was without honor. The battle had been without valor."

In the evening, at the B'nai B'rith Sportsman-of-the-Year dinner in honor of Jake Dunlap, a former Rough Rider star, I sat at a table with Ottawa and out-of-town sportswriters. My colleagues felt that so far Ottawa fandom had failed to show the proper Grey Cup zeal. Jack Koffman pushed his plate aside. "It's a crime," he said, "that we're not in the game this year."

This year, Centennial year, being the first time since 1940 that the game was to be played in Ottawa.

"The fans are cooling," Koffman said. "It's a shame."

Another sportswriter held up his hand, indicating a full mouth. We waited while he swallowed. He put down his knife. He put down his fork. He wiped his mouth. "It's human nature," he said.

Tuesday night the streets of our nation's capital continued to be muted. On Wednesday morning Mayor Don Reid, no

party pooper, "dropped a verbal bomb on city merchants."
He denounced their lack of Grey Cup spirit. Ottawa
responded smartly. The grizzled, middle-aged bellhops of the
Château Laurier broke out in rakish Grey Cup boaters on
Thursday morning. But no sooner were pagan high spirits
rumored than Presbyterian prohibitions were enforced. Glum
guards took up positions in bars and hotel lobbies. At the
Château Laurier, all unanchored lobby furnishings disappeared,
and barricades went up before the elevators. If I was still able to
enter the parliamentary East Block, where our prime minister labored, without being stopped by anyone, it now became necessary to produce a pass before stepping into an elevator at the
Château.

I made my way down icy, sober streets to the National Press
Club, where the rival coaches, Ralph Sazio and Eagle Keys, were
to reveal something of their battle plans. But Sazio, the Ti-Cat
coach, was to be with us in spirit only. He would pronounce by
long distance from Hamilton. "Now here are the ground rules,"
Jack Kinsella began. "You will ask questions in turn—"

"But I've already written my column," one sportswriter protested.

Another asked, "Do we get a translator for Eagle Keys?"

Finally, Mr. Sazio came on the line. "Hello, Ralph," Kinsella
shouted. Then, beaming at all twenty-two of us, he added,
"There are fifty or sixty of the boys here to ask you questions."

Alas, no questions immediately sprang to mind. The boys
were silent and hungover.

"Ha ha ha," Kinsella laughed, glaring at us. "The boys are a
little reluctant this morning. Um, how's Joe Zuger's nose?"

"Real good," Mr. Sazio replied.

A sportswriter asked, "Hey, Ralph, would you like a frozen
field on Saturday or a gooey one?"

Mr. Sazio did not hesitate or evade. "This is, um, a classic.
The Grey Cup. We will go real good frozen or gooey, that is,
um, even if the—ahm—weather rears its ugly head."

"You arrive at two o'clock from Hamilton, Ralph. What is your game plan for this afternoon?"

"Well, um, we won't practice. I feel it would be real good for the boys, um, to familiarize themselves with the feel, the electricity of the, um, Grey Cup spirit of Ottawa."

"They roll up the sidewalks here at nine-thirty, Ralph."

"We're going real good and we'll do a real good job."

A half hour later Eagle Keys, the Roughrider coach, drifted into the room. Keys, on first glance, had the look of a permanent army man, possibly the fellow in charge of the stockade. Words slid from his mouth slowly, painfully, as if speech were both excruciating and unnatural for him. This forbidding manner was leavened by a sly, cornpone humor to which the sportswriters responded with much knee-slapping and tribal shouts.

Following the conference, more confused than enlightening, I hurried to Wellington Street. This, after all, was Western Day in Ottawa, and a parade was promised. It turned out to be a paltry thing. Tatty. Forlorn. Paunchy men on horseback. Broad-bottomed girls wearing glasses with shell half-frames flinging their Stetsons in the air, crying yah-hoo and yippee to no visible effect. They rode their charges into banks and bars. "Let's go that-a-way."

That night I joined 1,600 other pleasure-seekers at the Miss Grey Cup Pageant, sponsored by Ottawa Kiwanis. The pageant had a distinct 1940s band-show flavor, the Kiwanis ladies in their glittering finery and mountainous hairdos being sufficiently out of date to enhance the illusion. A CBC orchestra, their violin bows seemingly Vaselined smooth, played the old tunes, the nice tunes, and then a group called the Swingers bounced breathless on stage. "Grey Cup time is a rooting time, a root-toot-toot-tooting time," they harmonized. Other wholesome, old-time acts followed, and finally there was Juliette, a dream in candy floss pink, singing, "When you're smiling . . ."

Once the show was done, all nine Miss Grey Cup contestants came onstage, cheeks glowing. A cynic in the row behind me said, "You can bet your bottom dollar the winner is Miss Ottawa Rough Rider."

Just so. The 1967 Miss Grey Cup was sweet, pretty Julia (Julie) May Dixie. Julia, the form sheet said, was 19 years old, 5 foot 1½ inches, 100 lbs., and 34-24-34. She had blue-green eyes and blond hair. "Julie is a public school teacher for Nepean township school board. She plans to work toward her BA in education and wants to travel in Europe. Her hobbies are sewing, baking, and being a majorette. On the sports side she likes skiing, football, skating, and swimming."

When the judge's decision was announced, Julie squealed with surprise. Her lovely eyes filled with tears. The other girls, good losers all, gathered around to congratulate her. Gum-chewing, sweaty photographers fell at her feet. Flashbulbs popped. Cameras churned. Microphones were thrust toward Miss Grey Cup's slightly parted lips. Tomorrow the world.

But when I rushed to retrieve my coat, all the hatcheck girl could manage was, "At least we won something."

Staggering drunks, rugged fellows, filled the lobby of the Skyline Hotel. "Anybody here from the West? My name's Hank. Where you from?"

Later, at the Riverside Hotel (home of Upstairs at the Rib; home of Downstairs at the Rib, with forty-five beautiful bunnies), I joined two carousing young westerners at their table. Jim and Bob, who went to the Grey Cup game every year, had left their wives at home in Regina. "You've heard of a freakout," Bob roared. "Well, this is a week out."

Jim knew all the bunnies by their first names. "Hey there, Betty," he hollered, "Hiya, Gail," as the harassed girls, their pinching bras discolored by sweat, zipped from table to table.

"Yahoo! Go, Riders, go," the men at other tables shouted each to each. Like Jim and Bob, they sat in pairs for the most part, without women.

"Enjoying yourself?" I asked.

"Yahoo!"

But Jim shook his head. "Hell," he said feelingly, "if I were only a girl, I could have such a good time here."

Friday morning I counted no fewer than seven uniformed guards standing before the elevators at the Château Laurier. Confronting the most intimidating of them, a man well over six feet, I asked, "What are you all doing here?"

"We're here to help people."

"What sort of trouble are you expecting?"

He seized me by the arm. "You better move along now, I think."

When I returned to the Château, at six the same evening, there was fresh blood splattered on the floor beneath the swinging doors that led into the lobby. "Oh, my God," a woman cried.

I had come for the 18th Annual Grey Cup Dinner, an event whose tone had been definitively set by Chairman John Wilkinson's program poem:

> *We hope you'll enjoy your visit*
> *with us,*
> *And later—if you should roam,*
> *You may not know when,*
> *But—come back again,*
> *And make yourselves at home!*

Among the forty-odd dignitaries at the head table, each fulsomely introduced by MC Terry Kielty, there was Mayor Don Reid, who was (according to my program) swiftly turning Ottawa into the "fun city of the north"; Lawrence Frieman, community leader ("a busy man—but—the first phone call is always from Lawrence. The conversation begins: "I'm in"); Lorne Greene (Ben Cartwright, perhaps then the best-known man in the world); and many, many more.

For an hour, maybe longer, the worthies at the head table

awarded each other plaques and scrolls, paid handsome tributes to each other, and applauded themselves. Then there was an invocation by Chaplain Ernie Foote, who prayed to the Lord for good sportsmanship in tomorrow's contest, asking for integrity of play, not forgetting to add that all of us were involved in a bigger game, the game of life. The competing coaches, Sazio and Keys, addressed us briefly.

"I'm real proud," Sazio said. And Keys said, "We're going to play real good."

When big Lorne Greene, born in Ottawa, was introduced, many people stood up and cheered.

"He's come back to us, all the way to Parliament Hill," Kielty said, "from La Ponderosa."

Lorne Greene grinned at us. "I would have brought Hoss," he said, "but I couldn't get a plane big enough."

We laughed and slapped our knees.

Again and again men stood up to say how proud they were to be in Ottawa, and that the Grey Cup game was the greatest unifying force in the nation.

Other, more brutalized nations were knit by civil wars or uprisings against tyrants, but Canada, our Canada, was held together by a pigskin.

Outside, the icy, bitterly cold streets were all but impassable. Roaming gangs of teenagers, armed with plastic trumpets, shouted Go, Riders, go. No car passed without going root-toot-toot. Men tossed Stetsons in the air. Squealing ladies in multicolored parkas waved Go Big Green pennants from the tops of cars. Everybody seemed desperately determined to have a good time, but, unfortunately for most of them, there was simply nowhere to go or nothing to do. You couldn't even get into a hotel unless you were staying there.

Shaking with cold, I retired to the Château Laurier, where I had been invited to the B.C. Lions' hospitality suite. This, like most other Grey Cup parties, did not lack for high spirits, but suffered from a shortage of girls. Any girls.

"How you doin', Chuck?"

"Great. Just great."

"Whaddiyu say, Denny?"

"In 1969, the Lions will shine."

Outside, men huddled in the cold, stamping their feet together, waiting to get into bars. Shouts of yahoo and yippee had become more forlorn. I was, however, reassured by Saturday's *Ottawa Journal.* OUR GREY CUP RUNNETH OVER WITH HIGH SPIRITS, the front-page headline exclaimed. "Ottawa's reputation as a staid, perhaps stodgy, civil service town may never be the same. It was sheer bedlam in Bytown Friday night. . . ." Increasingly, the Grey Cup festivities had become more stimulating to read about in Ottawa newspapers than to actually witness.

All the same, I did go to the game on Saturday. A punishing wind cut across the icy field, where the Roughriders were jumping up and down. One-two-three-four. Between exercises the imports from Florida and Texas blew on their reddening fingers and stamped their feet together. Wandering across the field, I stumbled on a milling group of pimply, bony girls in green-and-white tights, trembling with cold, teeth chattering, noses running. The Riderettes. Sex kittens out of Saskatchewan. A thoughtful bandmaster had provided them with woollies, sadly loose-fitting, to wear over their stockings. The fourteen-year-old girls, like the more warmly dressed men who would play in the game, kicked their feet together for warmth. Suddenly a TV camera came into play, the drums went boom, and the intrepid girls, after one last wipe of the nose with chapped hands, flashed radiant smiles and strutted away from me across the frozen field.

"Get 'em, get 'em," the Riderettes chanted. "Go-go, Riders." But the Riders were not going anywhere in 1967. A dreary game was enlivened for me only once, when a youngster leaped onto the field, seized the ball, and, evading players and cops, threw it into the stands.

"It's a weekend in the cooler for him," the man seated beside me said.

His companion was displeased.

"Now those fucken newspaper guys are going to make him fucken famous. If you ask me, they shouldn't even mention his fucken name."

Immediately after the game, a seemingly needless interruption of the Grey Cup week bacchanal, hotel-room parties were resumed. At the Skyline Hotel, where I had taken a room earlier in the day, the corridors spilled over with merrymakers. It would end in pushing and shoving, some tears, and a good deal of vomiting in corners. Meanwhile, everybody was overbearingly friendly. Lorne Greene, his white hair combed in a ducktail, his face tanned leather-wallet brown, emerged from a suite. A housewife squealed with delight. "It's Lorne Greene. Harry, go get Midge. Get Midge immediately or she'll never forgive me."

"Hey, Lorne, where's Hoss?"

Greene smiled benignly.

At 1:00 A.M., I was jammed into an elevator with yet another group of celebrants, groping for each other between the eighth and ninth floors, not so much compelled by passion as driven by a need to hold each other upright. On the ninth floor, we were joined by an immense, magnificently built black man, a Hamilton lineman with a champagne bottle in his hand.

"You related to George Reed?" a drunk asked.

The black lineman looked down at the fat little fellow in the raccoon coat. "We're all related," he said.

My Father's Life

AFTER THE FUNERAL, I WAS GIVEN MY FATHER'S *TALIS*, HIS prayer shawl, and (oh my God) a file containing all the letters I had written to him while I was living abroad, as well as carbon copies he had kept of the letters he had sent to me.

December 28, 1959: "Dear Son, Last week I won a big Kosher Turkey, by bowling, when I made the high triple for the week. How I did it I do not know, I guess I was lucky for once, or was it that the others were too sure of themselves, being much better at the game than I am."

February 28, 1963: "This month has been a cold one, making it difficult, almost impossible to work outside. Yes! it's been tough. Have you found a title for your last novel? What can you do with a title like this? 'UNTIL *DEBT* DO US PART'?"

His letter of February 28, 1963, like so many others written that year, begins, "Thanks for the cheque." For by that time we had come full circle. In the beginning it was my father who had sent checks to me. Included in the file I inherited were canceled checks, circa 1945, for $28 monthly child support, following the annulment of my parents' marriage. A bill dated January 15, 1948, for a Royal portable, my first typewriter; a birthday gift. Another bill, from Bond Clothes, dated August 21, 1950, on the eve of my departure for Europe, for "1 Sta. Wag. Coat, $46.49."

My own early letters to my father, horrendously embarrassing for me to read now, usually begin with appeals for money. No, *demands.* There is also a telegram I'd rather forget. March 11, 1951. IMPERATIVE CHECK SENT PRONTO MADRID C O COOKS WAGON LITS ALCALA NR 23 MADRID. BROKE. MORDECAI. Imperative, indeed.

I was also left a foot-long chisel, his chisel, which I now keep on a shelf of honor in my workroom. Written with a certain flourish in orange chalk on the oak shaft is my father's inscription:

Used by M.I. Richler
Richler Artificial Stone Works
1922
De La Roche Street
NO SUCCESS.

My father was twenty years old then, younger than my eldest son is now. He was the firstborn of fourteen children. Surely that year, as every year of his life, on Passover, he sat in his finery at a dining-room table and recited, "We were once the slaves of Pharaoh in Egypt, but the Lord our God brought us forth from there with a mighty hand and an outstretched arm." But, come 1922, out there in the muck of his father's freezing backyard on De La Roche Street in Montreal—yet to absorb the news of his liberation—my father was still trying to make bricks with insufficient straw.

Moses Isaac Richler.

Insufficient straw, *NO* SUCCESS, was the story of his life. Neither of his marriages really worked. There were searing quarrels with my older brother. As a boy, I made life difficult for him. I had no respect. Later, officious strangers would rebuke him in the synagogue for the novels I had written. Heaping calumny on the Jews, they said. If there was such a thing as a reverse Midas touch, he had it. Not one of my father's penny mining stocks ever went into orbit. He lost regularly at gin rummy. As younger, more intrepid brothers and cousins began to prosper, he assured my mother, "The bigger they come, the harder they fall."

My mother, her eyes charged with scorn, laughed in his face. "You're the eldest and what are you?"

Nothing.

After his marriage to my mother blew apart, he moved into a rented room. Stunned, humiliated. St. Urbain's cuckold. He bought a natty straw hat. A sports jacket. He began to use after-shave lotion. It was then I discovered that he had a bottle of rye whiskey stashed in the glove compartment of his Chevy. My father. Rye whiskey. "What's that for?" I asked, astonished.

"For the femmes," he replied, wiggling his eyebrows at me. "It makes them want it."

I remember him as a short man, squat, with a shiny bald head and big floppy ears. Richler ears. My ears. Seated at the kitchen table at night in his Penman's long winter underwear, wetting his finger before turning a page of the *New York Daily Mirror,* reading Walter Winchell first. Winchell, who knew what's what. He also devoured *Popular Mechanics, Doc Savage,* and *Black Mask.* And, for educational purposes, *Reader's Digest.* My mother, on the other hand, read Keats and Shelley. *King's Row. The Good Earth.* My father's pranks did not enchant her. A metal ink spot on her new chenille bedspread. A felt mouse to surprise her in the larder. A knish secretly filled with absorbent cotton. Neither did his jokes appeal to her. "Hey, do you know why we eat hard-boiled eggs dipped in salt water just before the Passover meal?"

"No, Daddy. Why?"

"To remind us that when the Jews crossed the Red Sea they certainly got their balls soaked."

Saturday mornings my brother and I accompanied him to the

Young Israel synagogue on Park Avenue near St. Viateur. As I was the youngest, under bar-mitzvah age, and therefore still allowed to carry on the Sabbath, I was the one who held the prayer shawls in a little purple velvet bag. My father, who couldn't stomach the rabbi's windy speeches, would slip into the back room to gossip with the other men before the rabbi set sail. "In Japan," my father once said, "there is a custom, time-honored, that before he begins, a speaker's hands are filled with ice cubes. He can shoot his mouth off for as long as he can hold the ice cubes in his hands. I wouldn't mind it if the rabbi had to do that."

He was stout, he was fleshy. But in the wedding photographs that I never saw until after his death the young man who was to become my father is as skinny as I once was, his startled brown eyes unsmiling behind horn-rimmed glasses. Harold Lloyd. Allowed a quick no-promises peek at the world and what it had to offer, but clearly not entitled to a place at the table.

My father never saw Paris. Never read Yeats. Never stayed out with the boys drinking too much. Never flew to New York on a whim. Nor turned over in bed and slept in, rather than report to work. Never knew a reckless love. What did he hope for? What did he want? Beyond peace and quiet, which he seldom achieved, I have no idea. So far as I know he never took a risk or was disobedient. At his angriest, I once heard him silence one of his cousins, a cousin bragging about his burgeoning real estate investments, saying, "You know how much land a man needs? Six feet. And one day that's all you'll have. Ha, ha!"

Anticipating Bunker Hunt, my father began to hoard American silver in his rented room. A blue steamer trunk filling with neatly stacked piles of silver dollars, quarters, dimes. But decades before their worth began to soar, he had to redeem them at face value. "I'm getting hitched again," he told me, blushing. He began to speculate in postage stamps. When he died at the age of sixty-five I also found out that he had bought a city backlot somewhere for $1,200 during the Forties. In 1967, however— riding a bloated market, every fool raking it in—the estimated value of my father's property had shrunk to $900. All things considered, that called for a real touch of class.

I was charged with appetite, my father had none. I dreamed of winning prizes, he never competed. But, like me, my father was a writer. A keeper of records. His diary, wherein he catalogued injuries and insults, betrayals, family quarrels, bad debts, was written in a code of his own invention. His brothers and sisters used to tease him about it. "Boy, are we ever afraid! Look, I'm shaking!" But as cancer began to consume him, they took notice, fluttering about, concerned. "What about Moishe's diary?"

I wanted it. Oh, how I wanted it. I felt the diary was my proper inheritance. I hoped it would tell me things about him that he had always been too reticent to reveal. But his widow, an obdurate lady, refused to let me into the locked room in their apartment where he kept his personal papers. All she would allow was, "I'm returning your mother's love letters to her. The ones he found that time. You know, from the refugee."

That would have been during the early Forties, when my mother began to rent to refugees, putting them up in our spare bedroom. The refugees, German and Austrian Jews, had been interned as enemy aliens in England shortly after war was declared in 1939. A year later they were transported to Canada on a ship along with the first German and Italian prisoners of war. On arrival at the dock in Quebec City, the army major who turned them over to their Canadian guards said, "You have some German officers here, very good fellows, and some Italians, they'll be no trouble. And over there," he added, indicating the refugees, "the scum of Europe."

The refugees were interned in camps, but in 1941 they began to be released one by one. My father, who had never had anybody to condescend to in his life, was expecting real *greeners* with sidecurls. Timorous innocents out of the *shtetl*, who would look to him as a master of magic. Canadian magic. Instead, they patronized him. A mere junk dealer, a dolt. The refugees turned out to speak better English than any of us did, as well as German and French. After all they had been through over there, they were still fond of quoting a German son of a bitch called Goethe. "Imagine that," my father said. They also sang opera arias in the bathtub. They didn't guffaw over the antics of Fibber McGee 'n' Molly on the radio; neither were they interested in the strippers who shook their nookies right at you from the stage of the Gayety Theatre, nor in learning how to play gin rummy for a quarter of a cent a point. My mother was enthralled.

My father was afraid of his father. He was afraid of my unhappy mother, who arranged to have their marriage annulled when I was thirteen and my brother eighteen. He was also afraid of his second wife. Alas, he was even afraid of me when I was a boy. I rode streetcars on the Sabbath. I ate bacon. But nobody was ever afraid of Moses Isaac Richler. He was far too gentle.

The Richler family was, and remains, resolutely Orthodox, followers of the Lubavitcher rabbi. So when my mother threatened divorce, an all but unheard-of scandal in those days, a flock of grim rabbis in flapping black gabardine coats descended on our cold-water flat on St. Urbain Street to plead with her. But my mother, dissatisfied for years with her arranged marriage, in love at last, was adamant. She had had enough. The rabbis sighed when my father, snapping his suspenders, rocking on his heels— *speaking out*—stated his most deeply felt marital grievance. When he awakened from his Saturday afternoon nap there was no tea. "Me, I like a cup of hot tea with lemon when I wake up."

In the end, there was no divorce. Instead, there was an annulment. I should explain that in the Province of Quebec at that time each divorce called for parliamentary approval. A long, costly process. A lawyer, a family friend, found a loophole. He pleaded for an annulment. My mother, he told the court, had married without her father's consent when she had still been a minor. He won. Technically speaking, as I used to brag at college, I'm a bastard.

Weekdays my father awakened every morning at six, put on his phylacteries, said his morning prayers, and drove his truck through the wintry dark to the family scrapyard near the waterfront. He worked there for my fierce, hot-tempered grandfather and a pompous younger brother. Uncle Solly, who had been to high school, had been made a partner in the yard, but not my father, the firstborn. He was a mere employee, working for a salary, which fed my mother's wrath. Younger brothers, determined to escape an overbearing father, had slipped free to form their own business, but my father was too timid to join them. "When times are bad they'll be back. I remember the Depression. Oh, boy!"

"Tell me about it," I pleaded.

But my father never talked to me about anything. Not his own boyhood. His feelings. Or his dreams. He never even mentioned sex to me until I was nineteen years old, bound for Paris to try to become a writer. Clutching my Royal portable, wearing my Sta. Wag. coat. "You know what safes are. If you have to do it—*and I know you*—use 'em. Don't get married over there. They'd do anything for a pair of nylon stockings or a Canadian passport."

Hot damn, I hoped he was right. But my father thought I was crazy to sail for Europe. A graveyard for the Jews. A continent where everything was broken or old. Even so, he lent me his blue steamer trunk and sent me $50 a month support. When I went broke two years later, he mailed me my boat fare without reproach. I told him that the novel I had written over there was called *The Acrobats* and he immediately suggested that I begin the title of my second novel with a B, the third with a C, and so on, which would make a nifty trademark for me. Writing, he felt, might not be such a nutty idea after all. He had read in *Life* that this guy Mickey Spillane, a mere *goy*, was making a fortune.

Insulted, I explained hotly that I wasn't that kind of writer. I was a serious man.

"So?"

"I only write out of my obsessions."

"Ah, ha," he said, sighing, warming to me for once, recognizing another generation of family failure.

Even when I was a boy his admonitions were few. "Don't embarrass me. Don't get into trouble."

I embarrassed him. I got into trouble.

In the early Forties, my father's father rented a house directly across the street from us on St. Urbain, ten of his fourteen children still single and rooted at home. The youngest, my Uncle Yankel, was only three years older than I was and at the time we were close friends. But no matter what after-school mischief we were up to, we were obliged to join my grandfather at sunset in the poky little Galliciander *shul* around the corner for the evening prayers, a ritual I didn't care for. One evening, absorbed in a chemistry experiment in our "lab" in my grandfather's basement, we failed to appear. On his return from *shul*, my grandfather descended on us, seething, his face bleeding red. One by one he smashed our test tubes and our retorts and even our cherished water distiller against the stone wall. Yankel begged forgiveness, but not me. A few days later I contrived to get into a scrap with Yankel, leaping at him, blackening his eye. Oh boy, did that ever feel good. But Yankel squealed on me. My grandfather summoned me into his study, pulled his belt free of his trousers, and thrashed me.

Vengeance was mine.

I caught my grandfather giving short weight on his scrapyard scales to a drunken Irish peddler. My grandfather, Jehovah's enforcer. Scornful, triumphant, I ran to my father and told him his father was no better than a cheat and a hypocrite.

"What do you know?" my father demanded.

"Nothing."

"They're anti-Semites, every one of them."

My grandfather moved to Jeanne Mance Street, only a few blocks away, and on Sunday afternoons he welcomed all the family there. Children, grandchildren. Come Hanukkah, the most intimidating of my aunts was posted in the hall, seated behind a bridge table piled high with Parcheesi games one year, Snakes and Ladders another. As each grandchild filed past the table he was issued a game. "Happy Hanukkah."

My grandfather was best with the babies, rubbing his spade beard into their cheeks until they squealed. Bouncing them on his lap. But I was twelve years old now and I had taken to strutting down St. Urbain without a hat, and riding streetcars on the Sabbath. The next time my father and I started out for the house on Jeanne Mance on a Sunday afternoon, he pleaded with me not to disgrace him yet again, to behave myself for once, and then he thrust a *yarmulke* at me. "You can't go in there bareheaded. Put it on."

"It's against my principles. I'm an atheist."

"What are you talking about?"

"Charles Darwin," I said, having just read a feature article on him in *Coronet*, "or haven't you ever heard of him?"

"You put on that *yarmulke*," he said, "or I cut your allowance right now."

"O.K., O.K."

"And Jewish children are not descended from monkeys, in case you think you know everything."

"When I have children of my own I'll be better to them."

I had said that, testing. Sneaking a sidelong glance at my father. The thing is I had been born with an undescended testicle and my brother, catching me naked in the bathroom, had burst out laughing and assured me that I would never be able to have children or even screw. "With only one ball," he said, "you'll never be able to shoot jism."

My father didn't rise to the bait. He had worries of his own.

My mother. The refugee in the spare bedroom. His father. "When you step in the door," he said, "the *zeyda* will ask you which portion of the Torah they read in *shul* yesterday." He told me the name of the chapter. "Got it?"

"I'm not afraid of him."

My grandfather, his eyes hot, was lying in wait for me in the living room. Before a court composed of just about the entire family, he denounced me as a violator of the Sabbath. A *shabus goy*. Yankel smirked. My grandfather grabbed me by the ear, beat me about the face, and literally threw me out of the house. I lingered across the street, waiting for my father to seek me out, but when he finally appeared, having endured a bruising lecture of his own, all he said was, "You deserved what you got."

"Some father you are."

Which was when I earned another belt on the cheek.

"I want you to go back in there like a man and apologize to the *zeyda*."

"Like hell."

I never spoke to my grandfather again.

But when he died, less than a year after the annulment of my parents' marriage, my mother insisted it was only proper that I attend his funeral. I arrived at the house on Jeanne Mance to find the coffin set out in the living room, uncles and aunts gathered round. My Uncle Solly drove me into a corner. "So here you are," he said.

"So?"

"You hastened his death; you never even spoke to him even though he was sick all those months."

"I didn't bring on his death."

"Well, smart guy, you're the one who is mentioned first in his will."

"Oh."

"You are not a good Jew and you are not to touch his coffin. It says that in his will. Don't you dare touch his coffin."

I turned to my father. Help me, help me. But he retreated, wiggling his eyebrows.

So many things about my father's nature still exasperate or mystify me.

All those years he was being crushed by his own father, nagged by my mother, teased (albeit affectionately) by his increasingly affluent brothers and cousins, was he seething inside, plotting a vengeance in his diary? Or was he really so sweet-natured as not to give a damn? Finally, there is a possibility I'd rather not ponder. Was he not sweet-natured at all, but a coward? Like me. Who would travel miles to avoid a quarrel. Who tends to remember slights—recording them in my mind's eye—transmogrifying them—finally publishing them in a code more accessible than my father's. Making them the stuff of fiction.

Riddles within riddles.

My father came to Montreal as an infant, his father fleeing Galicia. Pogroms. Rampaging Cossacks. But, striptease shows aside, the only theater my father relished, an annual outing for the two of us, was the appearance of the Don Cossack Choir at the St. Denis Theatre. My father would stamp his feet to their lusty marching and drinking songs; his eyes would light up to see those behemoths, his own father's tormentors, prance and tumble on stage. Moses Isaac Richler, who never marched, nor drank, nor pranced.

Obviously, he didn't enjoy his family. My mother, my brother, me. Sundays he would usually escape our cold-water flat early and alone and start out for the first-run downtown cinemas, beginning with the Princess, which opened earliest, continuing from there to the Capitol or the Palace, and maybe moving on to the Loew's, returning to us bleary-eyed, but satiated, after dark. Astonishingly, he kept a sharp eye out for little production errors. Discovering them filled him with joy. Once, for instance, he told us, "Listen to this, Clark Gable is sitting there in this newspaper office and he tells Claudette Colbert he will be finished typing his story in an hour. But when she comes back and we are supposed to believe an hour has passed, *the hands on the clock on the wall haven't moved. Not an inch."* Another time it was, "Franchot Tone is in this tank in the desert, you're not going to believe this, and he says 'O.K., men, let's go. Attack!' And they attack. But if you look closely inside the tank just before they push off, the fuel gauge is indicating EMPTY. No gas. Get it?"

The Best Years of Our Lives overwhelmed him.

"There's a scene in there where Fredric March burps. He's hung over, he drinks an Alka-Seltzer or something, and he lets out a good one. Right there on screen. Imagine."

My mother was fond of reminding me that the night I was born, my father had not waited at the hospital to find out how she was, or whether it was a boy or a girl, but had gone to the movies instead. What was playing, I wondered.

My father didn't dream of Italy, where the lemon trees bloomed. He never went for a walk in the country or read a novel, unless he had to, because it was one of mine and he might be blamed for it. Bliss for him was the Gayety Theatre on a Saturday night. My father and a couple of younger brothers, still bachelors, seated front row center. On stage, Peaches, Anne Curie, or the legendary Lili St. Cyr. My father rapt, his throat dry, watching the unattainable Lili simulating intercourse with a swan as the stage lights throbbed, then trudging home through the snow to sit alone at the kitchen table, drinking hot milk with matzohs before going to sleep.

We endured some rough passages together. Shortly after the marriage annulment, I fought with my father. Fists flew. We didn't speak for two years. Then, when we came together again, meeting once a week, it wasn't to talk, but to play gin rummy for a quarter of a cent a point. My father, I began to suspect, wasn't reticent. He didn't understand life. He had nothing to say to anybody.

In 1954, some time after my return to Europe, where I was to remain rooted for almost two decades, I married a *shiksa* in London. My father wrote me an indignant letter. Once more, we were estranged. But no sooner did the marriage end in divorce than he pounced: "You see, mixed marriages never work."

"But, Daddy, your first marriage didn't work either and Maw was a rabbi's daughter."

"What do you know?"

"Nothing," I replied, hugging him.

When I married again, this time for good, but to another *shiksa*, he was not overcome with delight, yet neither did he complain. For after all the wasting years, we had finally become friends. My father became my son. Once, he had sent money to me in Paris. Now, as the scrapyard foundered, I mailed monthly checks to him in Montreal. On visits home, I took him to restaurants. I bought him treats. If he took me to a gathering of the Richler clan on a Sunday afternoon, he would bring along a corked bottle of 7-Up for me, filled with scotch whisky. "There'll be nothing for you to drink there, and I know you."

"Hey, Daddy, that's really very thoughtful."

During the Sixties, on a flying trip to Montreal, my publishers put me up at the Ritz-Carlton Hotel, and I asked my father to meet me for a drink there.

"You know," he said, joining me at the table, "I'm sixty-two years old and I've never been here before. Inside, I mean. So this is the Ritz."

"It's just a bar," I said, embarrassed.

"What should I order?"

"Whatever you want, Daddy."

"A rye and ginger ale. Would that be all right here?"

"Certainly."

. . .

What I'm left with are unresolved mysteries. A sense of regret. Anecdotes for burnishing.

My wife, a proud lady, showing him our firstborn son, his week-old howling grandchild, saying, "Don't you think he looks like Mordecai?"

"Babies are babies," he responded, seemingly indifferent.

Some years later my father coming to our house, pressing chocolate bars on the kids. "Who do you like better," he asked them, "your father or your mother?"

In the mid-Sixties, I flew my father to London. He came with his wife. Instead of slipping away with him to the Windmill Theatre or Raymond's Revue Bar, another strip joint, like a fool I acquired theater tickets. We took the two of them to *Beyond the Fringe*. "What did you think?" I asked as we left the theater.

"There was no chorus line," he said.

Following his last operation for cancer, I flew to Montreal, promising to take him on a trip as soon as he was out of bed. The Catskills. Grossinger's. With a stopover in New York to take in some shows. Back in London, each time I phoned, his doctor advised me to wait a bit longer. I waited. He died. The next time I flew to Montreal it was to bury him.

Pages from
a Western Journal

MARCH 11, 1970.

On my last day in the West, I discover the 5,000 Magic Fingers of the Massaging Assembly, advertised on the unit bolted to my bed. "It quickly carries you into the land of tingling ease and relaxation, 25 cents for 15 minutes." Yielding to the magic fingers, which do not caress, alas, but instead grind away beneath me, adrift on a palpitating bed in the Highlander Motor Hotel, Calgary 42 ("A Place Ye Canna' Forget"), I try to splinter some sense out of the last, decidedly frenetic, eleven days. My western Grand Tour.

Swimming before me there is one triumphant image of prairie loneliness overcome by hubris. In Brandon, Manitoba, a teen-aged girl struggles toward me over towering snowbanks, defiantly wearing a maxicoat. Then I am on the spectacular Banff highway again, spinning toward Jasper through a blizzard, only the road ahead visible, when the snows suddenly recede and the menacing mountains emerge, closing in on me. In Edmonton, I am introduced to students as "a wandering tenderfoot." Yes, indeed. But to begin at the beginning.

FEBRUARY 28.

Like many Canadians of my generation, I have only a fragmented sense of country. Home, in my case, is Montreal; the rest, geography. I'm prepared to believe the fault is mine. I've never been to the North or to the Maritimes. To my shame, I have not even been west before. I have flown to Vancouver, that city by the sea with the soul of a remittance man, but never seen the prairies plain. Hitherto, I knew the West only by rumor of its most raucous ritual, the Calgary Stampede, and by its literary sensibilities, the books of Sinclair Ross, Margaret Laurence, and Adele Wiseman. And so, just before flying off to Toronto from England, I spend an evening skimming through these books again, seeking instruction. After a weekend in Toronto, I packed for the West.

Following Sir George Simpson and David Thompson, after the Selkirk Settlers, I, admittedly more carpetbagger than *voyageur*, was setting out without benefit of pemmican or bacon fat or even mukluks, but was armed instead with Rémy Martin, a plentiful supply of Havanas, and of course a return ticket. I was to speak at several universities, knocking an act into shape on the campus vaudeville circuit.

Above all, I was delighted to be invited to make a journey long overdue, perversely undertaken in March, our country's most grueling month, when everybody is justifiably fed up because the winter has lasted too long yet again. This year, like last, and next. The streets churn with slush, the cars are caked with filth, and one day's promise of spring is mocked by the next morning's blizzard.

MARCH 1.

Sunday. Flying off from Toronto on Air Canada flight 857, settling into my seat with yesterday's *Globe & Mail*, I was undone by the front-page headline: FARMERS OFFERED MILLIONS IF THEY DON'T PLANT WHEAT.

OTTAWA—Western wheat farmers were offered up to $140 million yesterday by the federal government in return for growing virtually no wheat or any other crop on their lands this year. . . .

Never underestimate Ottawa's subtlety. If, for instance, we accept that overpopulation is one of the worst problems of our time and that the ignorant peasants of third-world countries will not practice birth control no matter what, well then, by God, let's starve the bastards. Canada, for once, in the vanguard. After months of agonizing review, we *do* have a foreign policy independent of the United States. In a word, famine.

Reflecting further, I hope that next year the Canada Council will pay novelists not to write. After all, we have at least as deserving a case as the farmers. Too much is being written, there's almost no demand even for the best of it, and the silos of Macmillan, McClelland & Stewart, et al. are stacked as high with moldering, unwanted books as the West is with wheat.

My first evening in the West, I ate Winnipeg goldeye. Delicious. The king of kippers, certainly. After dinner, determined to explore, I sought out Portage and Main, deservedly reputed to be the chilliest corner in the country. "Hibernation is for bears—not for people," says the Winnipeg *Visitors' Guide.* "Anyway it's the attitude of Winnipeggers. When winter's withering winds sweep in from the north, the half million non-hibernating inhabitants of this cool metropolis . . . bundle up warmly and enjoy life."

Sunday night, below zero, the streets abandoned. Briefly, I consider taking a taxi to that club in the north end where, trailblazer Larry Zolf has assured me, Speedy Fogel and Montreal Moe prevail, but the cold shriveled my spirits. I returned to my hotel room and settled into bed with Murray Donnelly's biography, *Dafoe of the Free Press.* In 1865, a year before the editor was born, his parents, beguiled by colonization literature, went to settle on an Ontario farm.

The pamphlets they carried with them were full of enthusiastic and glowing descriptions of the new land between the Ottawa River and Georgian Bay, and predicted that the area would eventually have a population of eight million.

. . . They knew little of the true nature of the land their Protestant God had created in the highlands of Ontario. They did not know, although the evidence mounted as they traveled, that the seemingly fertile soil was strewn with stones and was actually little more than a shallow sprinkling of earth on the solid rock of the Precambrian Shield. They did note as they struggled up the Hastings Road that one in three homesteads had already been abandoned, but concluded that this was due to a lack of stamina on the part of the owner or to a false desire for the ease and sensual delight of the city.

Endure, endure, says Canadian experience. For tomorrow they will flock to the new and golden cities of the North as they now do to California. Tomorrow Winnipeg will bedazzle like Byzantium. Meanwhile, it's cold. We're getting older.

MARCH 2.

Bad start.

I'm supposed to drive to Brandon today, but the girl who brings my breakfast announces the winds outside are running to thirty-five miles per hour. Opening the curtains, I espy, through the swirling snow, a sign across the street. Barker's Funeral Parlor. Looming above, there is another sign, this one illuminated. The Investors Syndicate. In Winnipeg, something for most of your needs, but not all, as I shortly discover. For the Gateway to the Golden West has no morning newspaper. My breakfast cools as I desperately search for anything but the Gideon to read. Ah, the Hotel Sonesta has thoughtfully provided me with *Executive Digest:*

THRIFT-TIPS FOR TIME-SAVERS

Success or failure, every man has exactly the same number of minutes per day to spend. The successful man is usually the one who has learned how to spend his time as wisely as he spends his money. Here are some tips to help you likewise: (1) At the end of the day, sit down with a pencil and paper and plan your next day's activities. Or compile a list of the ways you've wasted time all day.

I send for the *Tribune,* Saturday's edition, and open it automatically to the want ads:

ARTIST WISHES TO MEET LADY (18–35) as helper in studio. Must be able to sell & MODEL occas. Send photo with letter to Box . . .

Big sky. Long winter. Hibernation is for bears.

8:30 A.M. Ensconced on the Greyhound bus to Brandon, sailing through a blizzard, I feel I've arrived on the prairies at last. Everywhere I turn, I'm greeted by a swirling white haze. No horizon defined, but here and there islands of black trees that could, for all I know, be floating on lakes or be rooted in snow-buried prairies. Both, as it turns out, for, as I should have remembered from sixth-grade geography, the prairie is the bed of an ancient lake, left flat as a snooker table by the retreating glaciers. And empty. My God, I have never seen such emptiness.

The good-natured bus driver, bound for Calgary, the Rockies, and Vancouver, serves as a latter-day pony express rider, heaving to at garages that emerge from the snow to hand over a bundle to the man in earflaps and fur-lined boots who comes barreling out of his office, bent into the wind.

As the snows let up, we bounce past drifting signs. PREPARE FOR ETERNITY . . . YOU WILL SOON BE THERE FOREVER. And churches. Russian Orthodox. Jehovah's Witnesses. Mennonite. At Portage la Prairie, we rock to a stop at a restaurant. "Ten minutes here, everybody."

There are two sets of bookracks. On one side, rows of Harlequin romances. On the other, paperbacks in cellophane wrappers, three bucks each. *New Meat, European Wife Swap Tour, Sex Bum, Modern Spanking.* And a complete row of Tarzans. I absorb my first prairie lesson. When they ask for Burroughs out here they want Edgar Rice, not William.

MARCH 3.

Shouldn't be so smart.

For I quickly learn the students at Brandon U. are bright, and well read. "What brings you," one of them demands, "to a hick university in a hick town?"

"I've never been to one before, that's what."

Instinctively, I like the students, but I am saddened by the university, the town, and its dilemma. Brandon, Manitoba (population 30,000 or so), is a place you come from, not somewhere you go to. The people here are kind, soft-spoken, and intelligent, but obviously they are educating their children to clear out of their environment. The young won't settle for life as an endurance contest, but will demand more, seeking it in Vancouver or Toronto. The university, to succeed, must drain the town of its most gifted progeny.

They are justifiably wary of strangers in Brandon, especially easterners, accustomed as they are to being conned. Traditionally, I discover, a speaker turns up here ill prepared and charged with condescension, talking off the cuff, for what does Brandon matter, it's Hicksville, and once back in Toronto, check in hand, the trip can be passed off as a joke in the Park Plaza Roof Bar. But the people of Brandon, on the other hand, seem to batten perversely on having the city slicker prove himself a phony. It seems to nourish them in the false assurance that, though they are camped in the middle of the sea of nowhere, they are not missing much.

Frequently, we bring out the worst in each other in this country.

It's a big sky, they say. Again and again I'm asked, have you ever seen such a big sky?

In North America's only socialist province, the sky belongs to the people. The rest, mostly to members of the Manitoba Club.

MARCH 4.

Winnipeg again.

On first sight, the city seems utterly without charm, built two stories high in most places, the streets snaggle-toothed, with little to delight the eye. Garages, loan companies, Canadian legion halls. Garish commercial streets. Slablike, functional houses. Except for the onion-head churches, no color, no fantasy.

The West has yet to develop a distinctive style of architecture, and suburban houses in Winnipeg, as well as in Edmonton and Calgary, seem to be anchored against the wind rather than built on foundations, as if the residents are not yet committed to settlement. The University of Manitoba, however lavish the appointments within, struck me as a particularly depressing opportunity missed. It resembles nothing so much as an industrial complex, a canning factory maybe, and pulling up to it in a car for the first time you expect the luncheon whistle to blow any minute.

Even so, after only a couple of days in town, Winnipeg was to have more appeal for me than any other city I visited in the West. The boom, promised so many times, by so many self-serving, lying politicians, will never come. Athens will always lie elsewhere. In tomorrow country, this is yesterday's city.

In the afternoon, I drove to Wellington Crescent, a willow

swamp and Indian encampment before the grain barons began to build there after the turn of the century, one grand house mock Tudor and the next a touching but misbegotten attempt to recreate Edinburgh on the steppes. Early in the Fifties the grandest homes began to go up for auction, the rich undone by heating bills and the cost of servants. The largest house on the Crescent, where the Prince of Wales was entertained in 1924, had thirty-seven rooms, nine fireplaces, and seven bathrooms, before it was split into apartments and then torn down. Another once-elegant private residence was for a time the home of the Canadian Mennonite Bible College, and a third enjoyed a brief life as the Convent of the Precious Blood before it too was demolished. Yet another is now the headquarters of the Masonic Order. On so-called Creed Corner, there stands a modern synagogue, a Bible college, a Lutheran church, and St. Mary's Roman Catholic Academy. But gone forever are the days when English governesses took the young master out for a turn on the Crescent, and, of course, there are no more horse-drawn traps. The worst news, however, is that socialism, creeping in with the frost, has come to a province with a hitherto unbroken history of right-wing government. With the largest, and probably most idle, railway yards in the country. And with a grain exchange that is now mainly of historical interest.

MARCH 5.

On entering the legislature, one is immediately confronted by two enormous buffalo, guardians of the central staircase, this pair surviving possibly because, being bronze, unlike the millions that once roamed the prairie, they would yield no fresh meat, grease, or hides.

Without ever having met Premier Schreyer, I was already on his side. He had, possibly to his own astonishment, ousted oafs from office. Only thirty-five years old, he has been an MLA or MP for twelve years. He speaks German, Ukrainian, and

French. In 1963, he asked the government to stop paying a minister's membership to the Manitoba Club, because it discriminated against Jews and Ukrainians. But the sad truth is Schreyer lacks presence; he seems to be without style or wit. Our dinner together at the Fort Garry foundered on stilted conversation and indifferent food. Schreyer, his eyes soft with appeal, revealed that he always flew economy-class. Of course, ten years later that would no longer be necessary. Schreyer, once considered the socialist for all seasons who might lead the NDP into office in Ottawa, had settled for becoming governor-general.

MARCH 6.

Soaring over Winnipeg in the morning, the prairie swiftly obscured by wads of cloud, I lowered into Edmonton before noon, where publisher Mel Hurtig awaited me. Instantly, we set out across the oppressive flatlands for the Shining Mountains of legend. Once the other side of Calgary, heading into rolling country with the mountains looming darkly ahead, I was hard put to contain my rising good spirits. The mountains are a spectacular sight and their initial effect is totally exhilarating.

The Rockies enjoy a rich tradition of plunderers and easy riders, for which information I am indebted to Esther Fraser's entertaining *The Canadian Rockies, Early Travels and Explorations*. Among my most cherished precursors there was the avaricious Sir George Simpson, the Hudson's Bay Company's Little Emperor, who was habitually preceded into the camps of the Cree, Blackfoot, Piegan, and Sarcee—where he had come to swindle—by a Scots piper in traditional attire, blowing on his bagpipes; and who, furthermore, was a self-proclaimed rake, acknowledging seven colonial bastards and many more bits of brown, as he put it, scattered over the mountain passes. Then there was the admirable young Earl of Southesk, who ventured into the Shining Mountains in 1859, in search of sport among the larger animals. He was accompanied by a valet and armed with Shakespeare to while away rainy afternoons. Snowbound on the prairies once, in a tent hung with icicles, the earl wrote in his journal: "Why am I enduring this? For pleasure—was the only answer, and the idea seemed so absurd that I laughed myself warm. Then as the circulation returned, I remembered that I was taking a lesson in that most valuable of human studies—the art of Endurance: an art the poor learn perforce, and the rich do well to teach themselves. . . ."

MARCH 7.

As one massive, towering peak yielded to another, emerging from the snow on the five-hour run to Jasper, I was unnerved by how primitive these mountains seemed. Certainly this wasn't the Alps, thoroughly domesticated, where almost every peak, closely looked at, reveals a village. "But one misses the voices of the dead," Rupert Brooke said when he visited.

MARCH 8.

In Edmonton, I ran into trouble in the Faculty Club, coming unstuck in an encounter with one of our lighter arms industries, Can. lit., its western sales force finding some virtue in the writing of Frederick Philip Grove.

If, as Edmund Wilson has written, Morley Callaghan is the most unjustly neglected novelist in the English language, then Grove, surely, is the man who fills the office of most justly neglected. His characters are so wooden they can be used for splintering. His prose is turgid. But in Edmonton, as elsewhere in the West, I was to hear him praised again and again, sometimes for nothing more than his accurate accounts of prairie blizzards and summer thunderstorms.

MARCH 11.

Riding the 5,000 Magic Fingers of the Massaging Assembly, rocking on my bed in the Highlander Motor Hotel, Calgary, I try to impose order on my last eleven days. I remember club sandwiches with curling french fries being proffered in hotels everywhere, by seemingly the same girl with the same false eyelashes, smile, and microskirt. Once more, I ride backward through dinner, tall in the saddle of the Château Lacombe restaurant in Edmonton, a turntable twenty-four stories high, watching airplanes lowering into an airport in the city center. Rolling into Portage la Prairie, I see again the enormous birthday cake of melting gray ice. 100 YEARS OLD. We survived.

From Roland Gladu, Through Kermit Kitman, to La Victoire Historique and After

PRONOUNCING ON MONTREAL, CASEY STENGEL ONCE SAID, "Well, you see they have those polar bears up there and lots of fellows trip over them trying to run the bases and they're never much good anymore except for hockey or hunting deer."

Unfortunately we have no polar bears up here, but kids can usually heave snowballs at the outfielders at the opening game of the season, and should the World Series ever dare venture this far north, it is conceivable that a game could be called because of a blizzard.

Montreal, it must be understood, is a city unlike any other in Canada. Or, more important, the National League. On the average, eight feet of snow is dumped on us each winter, and, whatever the weather, we can usually count on three bank robberies a day. This is the city of wonders that gave you Expo in 1967—the baseball Expos a couple of years later—and, in 1976, the Olympic Games, its legacy, among other amazing artifacts a stadium that can seat (or intern, as some have it), 55,000 baseball fans. The monstrous Big Owe, where the Expos have been disporting themselves in summer ever since they moved there from Jarry Park in 1977. For years the Expos' endearing idea of loading the bases was to have two of their runners on second. Hello, hello. Their notion of striking fear into the heart of the opposition was to confront them with muscle, namely one of their pinch-hitting behemoths coming off the bench: group average in 1978, .135.

Major-league baseball, like the Olympics and the Big Owe itself, was brought to this long-suffering city through the machinations of our very own Artful Dodger, Mayor Jean Drapeau. Bringing us the Games, the mayor assured Montrealers that it would be as difficult for the Olympics to cost us money as it would be for a man to have a baby. He estimated the total cost of all facilities at $62.2 million, but, what with inflation and unfavorable winds, his calculations fell somewhat short of the mark. Counting stationery and long-distance calls, the final tab was $1.2 billion. Never mind. To this day our ebullient mayor doesn't allow that the Games were run at a loss. Rather, as he has put it to the rest of us, there has been a gap between costs and revenue. Furthermore, considering the spiffy facilities we have been left with, it would be churlish of us to complain.

Ah, the Big Owe. The largest, coldest slab of poured concrete in Canada. In a city where we endure seven long months of winter, and spring comes and goes in an afternoon, it is Drapeau's triumph to have provided us with a partially roofed-over $650 million stadium, where the sun seldom shines on the fans. Tim Burke, one of the liveliest sportswriters in town, once said to me, "You know, there are lots of summer afternoons when I feel like taking in a ball game, but I think, hell, who wants to sit out there in the dark."

Shivering in the dark might have been more accurate, watching the boys lose line drives in the seams of the artificial turf.

"The outfield," another friend remarked, "looks like the kind of thing my aunt used to wear."

It's a shame, because the Expos, admittedly major-league in name only, at least until recently, came to a town rich in baseball history. To begin with, we were all charged with hope. On April

14, 1969, the 29,184 fans who turned up for the home opener at makeshift Jarry Park were electrified by an announcement over the public-address system. "When the Expos play a double-header," we were informed, "the second game will go the full nine innings, not seven."

Those of us old enough to remember baseball's glory days here, the Montreal Royals of the old International League, nodded our heads, impressed. This was the big time, baby. "Montreal," said Warren Giles, president of the National League, "is a growing and vibrant city." Yes yes. So we hollered and stamped our feet as our champions took to the field under the grim gaze of manager Gene Mauch, who had the look of a marine drill sergeant.

The morning after the season's home opener the big bold front-page headline in the *Montréal-Matin* exclaimed: *30,000 personnes acclament les Expos sous soleil radieux*: ECLATANTE PREMIÈRE. *La Presse* pronounced the occasion, in which our expansionist Expos humiliated the National League champion St. Louis Cards 8–7, a VICTOIRE HISTORIQUE.

If that wasn't sufficient glory to sustain us through the long losing streak to come, only four days later one William Hambly Stoneman, a pitcher hitherto noted for nothing so much as mediocrity, a youngster who had deservedly never started a major-league game in his life, strode to the mound, adjusted his potent red, white, and blue Expo cap for the nth time, fingered the rosin bag, loosened his shoulders, and, before you could utter SHAZAM, reared back and threw a no-hitter against the Philadelphia Phillies. Canada, only two years older than major-league baseball, had entered league history like a lion. Never mind that the *habitant* hero of the day, the suddenly incomparable Stoneman, was born in Oak Park, Illinois, and bred at Antonio Junior College in Walnut, California; his hobbies, like those of many a redblooded *canadien*, were golf and fishing. Something else. "Stoney" Stoneman's heart was in the right place. On his return from Philadelphia, he revealed to reporters, "I'm especially happy for the town . . . Montreal, I mean. Now they know we're not up there just to appear on the field. We're going to win ball games."

Jim Fanning, Expo GM at the time, responded munificently. "It is customary to give a no-hit pitcher a new contract or bonus, usually about a thousand dollars," he said. "But Montreal is an unusual city and this is an unusual team. We are giving him a two-thousand-dollar raise."

The team was also paying Maury Wills, who had been caught stealing base fifty-two times the year before, more than he ever earned in his halcyon years with Los Angeles or Pittsburgh. "Why," a reporter asked Sam Bronfman's then thirty-seven-year-old son Charles, "did you sink more than a million into the team in the first place?"

"I learned from my father," he replied, "that citizenship means more than paying taxes or writing checks for charity."

Let's face it, from owner to batboy, no-hit pitcher to bullpen bum, everybody connected with the Expos was . . . beautiful.

Canada, the prescient Bronfman told reporters in Florida, has a national inferiority complex and will gain status by being major-league in baseball. "Nothing is so big-league as major-league baseball. Mr. Average Citizen of Montreal can now feel just as good as Mr. Average Citizen elsewhere."

Happily for Montreal, the supreme importance of major-league baseball was also undoubted by big John McHale, club president and investor, who was formerly with Milwaukee and Detroit. Soon after joining the Expos, McHale was announced as a favored candidate for the office of commissioner of baseball. He turned down the post rather than abandon Montreal—our Montreal, his investment—but not without first informing the picayune natives that in the United States the job of baseball commissioner was second in importance only to that of the U.S. president. Of such conviction, surely, were future World Series winners made.

. . .

To come clean, when I first read that one of the most untiring and tiresome of our city councilors, hand-pumping Gerry Snyder, had cajoled a couple of second-generation multimillionaires, Bronfman and Lorne Webster, into staking a major-league ball club, enabling them to make their very own mark, I was exceedingly skeptical. After the grandeur that was Expo, Montreal was enduring the inevitable business slump as well as a sobering morning-after of whacking bills to be paid, with the upshot that escalating city property tax had become the highest in the country. Furthermore, French Canada was growing increasingly restive, separatists finally knit into one respectable political party by the formidable René Lévesque. English-speaking Montreal was beginning to feel the chill. While Ontario burgeoned, its investment plans calling for a 14 percent growth rate, all that went boom in the Montreal stock exchange was a separatist bomb, brokers sliding under the desks faster than Maury Wills ever broke for second base.

If this seemed a dubious climate for an expensive, risky new venture (the price of a National League franchise being $10 million), then cynics, myself *numero uno,* had not counted on the energy of Gerry Snyder and Mayor Drapeau's consummate hunger for glory. Or Charles Bronfman's boyish eagerness and matured money.

Among the supplicants for an NL franchise in 1968 there were Milwaukee, Dallas, San Diego, Buffalo, and Montreal. Milwaukee, with a lawsuit pending against the league, was immediately counted out. Dallas, deserving maybe, would have bitten into the Houston Astros' TV pie. The Buffalo ball park, league officials ordained, was unsuitably located, vulnerable to race riots. From the onset, Montreal was the most cherished of all the cities applying for entry into the NL. After all, the city had a proud (and profit-proven) baseball tradition. Until 1960, it was the home of the Montreal Royals, a Triple A club that used to be number-one farm team of the old Brooklyn Dodgers.

An article in the memorable opening-day program of the

Expos noted that while the province of Quebec had never been known as a hotbed of major-league talent, we had nevertheless produced a few ballplayers, among them pitchers Claude Raymond and Ron Piché, and that three native sons, Roland Gladu, Jean-Pierre Roy, and Stan Bréard, had once played for another ball club here, the Montreal Royals.

Oh, I remember the Royals—yes indeed—and if they played in a Montreal that was not yet growing and vibrant, *pace* Warren Giles, it was certainly a place to be cherished.

Betta Dodd, "the Girl in Cellophane," was stripping at the Gayety, supported by twenty-three Kuddling Kuties. Cantor Moishe Oysher, the Master Singer of His People, was appearing at His Majesty's Theatre. The Johnny Holmes Band, playing at Victoria Hall, featured Oscar Peterson; and a sign in the corner cigar & soda warned Ziggy Halprin, Yossel Hoffman, and me that

LOOSE TALK COSTS LIVES!
Keep It Under
Your
STETSON

I first became aware of the Royals in 1943.

MAY U BOAT SINKINGS
EXCEED REPLACEMENTS

KING DECORATES 625
CANADIANS ON BIRTHDAY

Many of our older brothers and cousins were serving overseas. Others on the street were delighted to discover they suffered from flat feet or, failing that, arranged to have an eardrum punctured by a specialist in such matters.

R.A.F. HITS HARD AT
COLOGNE AND HAMBURG
2,000 Tons of Bombs
Rain on Rhine City

On the home front, sacrifices were called for. Such was the shortage of ballplayers that a one-armed outfielder, Peter Grey, got to play for the Toronto Maple Leafs, and French Canadians, torn from the local sandlots, actually took to the field for our very own Royals: Bréard, Gladu, Roy.

Even in fabled Westmount, where the very rich were rooted, things weren't the same anymore. H.R., emporium to the privileged, enjoined Westmount to "take another step in further aid of the government's all-out effort to defeat aggression!"

HOLT RENFREW ANNOUNCE THAT BEGINNING JUNE FIRST
NO DELIVERIES OF MERCHANDISE WILL BE MADE ON
WEDNESDAYS

This forethought will help H.R. to save many gallons of gasoline . . . and many a tire . . . for use by the government. Moreover, will it not thrill you to think that the non-delivery of your dress on Wednesday will aid in the delivery of a "block-buster" over the Ruhr . . . Naples . . . Berlin . . . and many other places of enemy entrenchment?

Our parents feared Hitler and his Panzers, but Ziggy, Yossel, and I had enemies more immediate: Branch Rickey and his scouts.

1939, I should point out, was not only the date we had gone to war, it was also the year the management of the Royals signed a contract with Mr. Rickey, making them the number-one farm club of the Brooklyn Dodgers. This dealt us young players of tremendous promise, but again and again, come the Dodgers' late-summer pennant drive, the best of the bunch were harvested by the parent team. Before we had even reached the age of puberty, Ziggy, Yossel, and I had learned to love with caution. If after the first death there is no other, an arguable notion, I do remember that each time one of our heroes abandoned us for Ebbets Field, it stung us badly. We hated Mr. Rickey for his voracious appetite. "There has been no mention officially that the Dodgers will be taking Flowers," Lloyd MacGowan wrote in the *Star* on a typical day, "but Rickey was in Buffalo to watch the team yesterday. The Dodgers can't take Flowers without sending down a flinger, but chances are the replacement for the burly lefty will hardly be adequate."

The International League, as we knew it in the Forties, its vintage years, was Triple A and composed of eight teams: Montreal, Toronto, Syracuse, Jersey City, Newark, Rochester, Baltimore, and Buffalo. Newark was the number-one farm team of the Yankees, and Jersey City filled the same office for the Giants. But organized baseball had actually come to Montreal in 1898, the Royals then fielding a team in the old Eastern League, taking the pennant in their inaugural year. In those days the Royals played in Atwater Park, which could seat 12,000. From all accounts it was a fine and intimate stadium, much like Jarry Park, where the Expos first fielded their team. During the twenty-one years the Royals played in Atwater Park they offered Montreal, as sportswriter Marc Thibault once wrote, *"du baseball parfois excitant, plus souvent qu'autrement, assez détestable,"* the problem being the troubled management's need to sell off their most accomplished players for ready cash. Be that as it may, in 1914, long before major-league baseball came to Montreal, George Herman Ruth took to the mound in Atwater Park to pitch for the Baltimore Orioles. Two years later the Royals folded, a casualty of World War I, and another eleven years passed before the team was resuscitated.

1928 it was when George Tweedy "Miracle Man" Stallings bought the then defunct Syracuse franchise and built Delorimier Downs, a stadium with a 22,000 capacity, at the corner of Ontario and Delorimier streets. An overflow crowd of 22,500, among them Judge Kenesaw Mountain Landis, was at the opening game. The Royals won, defeating the fearsome Reading Keystones, 7–4. A year later Stallings died. In 1929, the Royals finished fourth. Two years later, Delorimier Downs, like just about everything, was in deep trouble. There were tax arrears and a heavy bank debt to be settled. The original sponsors resigned.

In the autumn of 1931 a new company was formed by a triumvirate which included a man who had made millions in gas stations, the rambunctious, poker-playing J. Charles-Emile Trudeau, father of the prime minister. Another associate of the newly formed club, Frank "Shag" Shaughnessy, cunningly introduced the playoff system in 1933, and two years later became the club's general manager. In 1935, fielding a team that included Fresco Thompson, Jimmy Ripple, and Del Bissonnette, the Royals won their first pennant since 1898. However, they finished poorly in '37 and '38, and the following year Mr. Rickey surfaced, sending in Burleigh Grimes to look after his interests.

Redemption was at hand.

Bruno Betzel came in to manage the team in 1944, the year the nefarious Branch Rickey bought the Royals outright, building it into the most profitable club in all of minor-league baseball, its fans loyal but understandably resentful of the head office's appetite, praying that this summer the Dodgers wouldn't falter in the stretch, reaching down for fresh bats and strong arms, just when we needed them most.

The Royals finished first in 1945, and in '46 and '48 they won both the pennant and the Little World Series. They were to win the pennant again in '51 and '52, under Clay Hopper, and the Little World Series in '53, when they were managed by Walter Alston. If memory serves, the Royals fielded their greatest team in 1948, the summer young Duke Snider played here, going to bat seventy-seven times before he was snatched by Mr. Rickey. Others on that memorable team included Don Newcombe, Al

Gionfriddo, Jimmy Bloodworth, Bobby Morgan, and Chuck Connors. Jackie Robinson and Roy Campanella had already come and gone.

Sammy Jethro was here in 1949, and two years later, Junior Gilliam was at third as George Shuba hit twenty home runs. In 1952, our star pitcher was southpaw Tommy Lasorda, the self-styled Bob Feller of the International League. Lasorda pitched his last game for the Royals on July 4, 1960, against Rochester, which seemed to be hitting him at will. Reminiscing recently, Lasorda recalled, "I knew I was in trouble when I saw our manager's foot on the top of the dugout step. If the next guy gets on base, I'm going to be out of there. I turned my back on the hitter and looked up toward the sky. Lord, I said, this is my last game. Get me out of this jam. I make the next pitch and the guy at the plate hits the damnedest line drive you ever saw. Our third baseman, George Risley, gets the tips of his fingers on it but can't hang on. The ball bloops over his hand and our shortstop, Gerry Snyder, grabs it. He fires it to Harry Shewman at second base, who relays it to Jimmy Korada at first. Triple play."

A year later the Royals were dissolved, and in 1971, Delorimier Downs was razed to make way for the Pierre Dupuy School.

On weekday afternoons kids were admitted free into the left-field bleachers, and by the third inning the more intrepid had worked their way down as far as the first-base line. Ziggy, Yossel, and I would sit out there in the sun, cracking peanuts, nudging each other if a ball struck the Miss Sweet Caporal sign hitting the young lady you know where. Another diversion was a porthole in the outfield wall. If a batter hit a ball through it, he was entitled to a two-year supply of Pal Blades.

Sunday afternoons the Royals usually attracted capacity crowds, but, come the Little World Series, fans also lined up on the roof of the adjoining Grover Knit-to-Fit Building, and temporary stands were set up and roped off in center field. Ziggy, who used to sit out there, liked to boast, "If I get hit on the head, it's a ground-rule home run."

In 1945, the Royals acquired one of ours, their first Jewish player, Kermit Kitman, a William and Mary scholarship boy. Our loyalty to the team redoubled. Kitman was a center fielder. On opening day, a story in *La Presse* declared, *"Trois des meilleurs porte-couleurs de Montréal depuis l'ouverture de la saison ont été ses joueurs de champ: Gladu, Kitman et Yeager. Kitman a exécuté un catch sensationnel encore hier après-midi sur le long coup de Torres à la 8e manche. On les verra tous trois à l'oeuvre cet après-midi contre le Jersey-City lors du programme double de la 'Victoire' au stade de la rue Delorimier."*

In his very first at bat in that opening game against the Skeeters, Kitman belted a homer, something he would not manage again until August. Alas, in the later innings he also got doubled off second. After the game, when he ventured into a barbershop at the corner of St. Catherine and St. Urbain, a man in another chair studied him intently. "Aren't you Kermit Kitman?" he asked.

"Yeah," he allowed, grinning, remembering his homer.

"You son of a bitch, you got doubled off second. It cost me five hundred bucks."

Leadoff hitter for the Royals, Kitman was entitled to a lower berth on all their road trips. Only twenty-two years old, but a college boy, rare in baseball in those days, he was paid somewhat better than most: $650 monthly for six months of the year. If the Royals went all the way, winning the Little World Series, he would earn another $1,800. On the road, his hotel bill was paid and he was allowed $3 a day meal money. Kitman, who married a Montreal girl and settled here, recently told me, "As a Jewish boy, I could eat on that money and maybe even save a little in those days. The gentile players had enough left over for beer and cigarettes."

The lineup for that 1945 team, which was to win the pennant, included Eddie Stevens, 1b; Salty Parker, 2b; Stan Bréard, ss; Stan Powalski, 3b; and Al Todd, c. Jean-Pierre Roy, Honest John Gabbard, and Jack Banta were the pitchers, and the others in the outfield were Red Durrett and Roland Gladu. "If I could hit pitchers like Gladu, I wouldn't be in the needle trade today," Kitman said.

He's an engaging man, a prospering partner in Leslie Fay Originals, Pretty Talk Fashions, and Fancy That. Fifty-four years old when I talked to him in 1978, somewhat chunky, he tried to take in at least one game in every Expo series and still can remember his own box scores as if it were yesterday. In 1946, he recalled, Dodgers with a certain seniority were released from the armed forces: Furillo, Olmo, Snider. Kitman didn't get to move up, as he had hoped, but was slated for the Royals again. And out there in Daytona, where they trained, a raw young man was seen to knock ball after ball into the wilderness.

"What can you do besides catch, son?" Leo Durocher asked him.

"I can play third base," Gil Hodges said

There was yet another change in the summer of 1946. After scouting the Negro leagues for more than a year, Mr. Rickey brought the first black player into organized baseball. So that spring the Royals could not train in the regular park in Daytona, which was segregated, but had to work out in Kelly Field instead.

Actually, Jackie Robinson had been signed on October 23, 1945, in the offices of the Royals at Delorimier Downs, club president Hector Racine saying, "Robinson is a good ballplayer and comes highly recommended by the Brooklyn Dodgers. We paid him a good bonus to sign with our club."

The bonus was $3,500 and Robinson's salary was $600 monthly.

"One afternoon in Daytona," Kitman told me, "I was leadoff hitter and quickly singled. Robinson came up next, laying down a sacrifice bunt and running to first. Stanky, covering the sack, tagged him hard and jock-high. Robinson went down, taking a fist in the balls. He was mad as hell, you could see that, but Rickey had warned him no fights. After the game, when he was resting, Stanky came over to apologize. He had been testing Robinson's temper, under orders from Rickey."

Kitman, a good glove man, was an inadequate hitter. Brooklyn-born, he never got to play there. Following the 1946 season, he was offered a place on the roster of another team in the Dodger farm system, but wisely elected to quit the game instead.

The 1946 season opened for the Royals on April 18, with a game in Jersey City. The AP dispatch for that day, printed in the *Montreal Gazette,* ran: "The first man of his race to play in modern organized baseball smashed a three-run homer that carried 333 feet and added three singles to the Royals' winning 14–1 margin over Jersey City. Just to make it a full day's work, Robinson stole two bases, scored four times and batted in three runs. He was also charged with an error."

Robinson's .349 average led International League hitters that year. He hit three home runs, batted in sixty-six runs, stole forty bases, scored 113 runs, and fielded .985 at second base. And, furthermore, Montreal adored him, as no other ballplayer who has been there before or since. No sooner did Robinson reach first base, on a hit or a walk, than the fans roared with joy and hope, our hearts going out to him as he danced up and down the base path, taunting the opposing pitcher with his astonishing speed.

We won the pennant that year and met the Louisville Colonels, another Dodger farm club, in the Little World Series. The series opened in Louisville, where Robinson endured a constant run of crude racial insults from the Colonels' dugout and was held to a mere single in two games. Montreal evened the series at home and returned to Delorimier Downs for the seventh and deciding game. "When they won it," Dick Bacon recently wrote, recalling that game in the 200th-anniversary issue of the *Gazette,* "Jackie was accorded an emotional sendoff unseen before or since in this city."

First they serenaded him in true French Canadien spirit with "il a gagné ses epaulettes," and then clamored for his reappearance on the field.

When he finally came out for a curtain call, the fans mobbed him. They hugged him, kissed him, cried, cheered and pulled and tore his uniform while parading him around the infield on their shoulders.

With tears streaming down his face, Robinson finally begged off in order to shower, dress and catch a plane to the States. But the riot of joy wasn't over yet.

When he emerged from the clubhouse, he had to bull his way through the waiting crowd outside the stadium. The thousands of fans chased him down Ontario Street for several blocks, before he was rescued by a passing motorist and driven to his hotel.

As one southern reporter from Louisville, Kentucky, was to write afterward: "It's probably the first time a white mob of rioters ever chased a Negro down the streets in love rather than hate."

That was a long time ago.

I don't know what ever became of Red Durrett. Roland Gladu, who got to start twenty-one games with the old Boston Braves, failed to sign the major-league skies with his ability. Robinson died in 1972, and six years later a plaque to his memory was installed in the Big Owe. Jean-Pierre Roy now does the French-language broadcasts for the Expos, and a graying, rotund Duke Snider is also back, doing the color commentary for the games on CBC-TV.

If major-league baseball finally did come to Montreal, then city councilor Gerry Snyder, it must be acknowledged, was the trigger. In December 1967 he put his case to NL President Warren Giles. Sure, Giles said, he would be happy to receive an expansion bid from Montreal, but it would have to be sweetened by a list of backers willing to plunk $10 million U.S. on the table and a guarantee of a domed stadium. Snyder hoped the Autostade, a prefabricated concrete stadium built for Expo, would do temporarily, if it was expanded to accommodate 37,500 fans. But the highly unpopular Autostade wasn't on the subway line, and the parking situation there was nightmarish. Furthermore, the Autostade was right next to an abattoir, which would not be so life-enhancing on a steamy summer afternoon. Nevertheless, the indefatigable Snyder began to pursue backers, all of whom were willing to listen, but not pledge. All except Charles Bronfman, whose father did so much to slake the thirst of Americans during Prohibition, the rock on which Mr. Sam founded one of the largest family fortunes in North America. Charles immediately promised he would come in for $1 million. Then Prime Minister Lester Pearson, who had once played semipro ball and remained an ardent fan, undertook to write his friend Philip Wrigley, owner of the Chicago Cubs, to solicit support.

There were, as I mentioned earlier, other contenders for the two expansion spots. But Walter O'Malley, one member of the three-man expansion committee, remembered with considerable warmth how much money he had made with the Montreal Royals. Another committee member, Judge Julius Hoffheinz of Houston, had enjoyed himself at Expo. The third member, John Galbraith of Pittsburgh, also liked Montreal's bid. So at a meeting in the Excelsior Hotel in Chicago in April 1968, it was ordained that San Diego would have one franchise and Montreal the other. Back in Snyder's hotel room, Dick Young of the *New York Daily News* suggested, "Call 'em the Expos."

Call 'em whatever you like, but where was the $10 million and where were they going to play ball?

Snyder had promised the National League a domed stadium for the club by 1971, but the city, looking at an estimated cost of between $35 and $45 million, said no. It also said no to tarting up the Autostade for an estimated $7 million. Everybody despaired but Mayor Drapeau. As potential investors faded, he got

Bronfman to come in for another $4 million, some say much more, and he drove NL President Giles out to Jarry Park, then a 3,000-seat junior baseball stadium. The public-address announcer let it out that Giles was in the park, and he was given a standing ovation. He left the park with tears in his eyes. "For years right until he died," Snyder has said, "he told me every time we met that this was the greatest thing that had ever happened to him in his life—total strangers giving him a standing ovation."

The federal government, though not moved to tears, came through with a huge tax write-off for multimillionaire Bronfman and the other investors, among them club president John McHale, and on August 14 a dry-eyed Giles returned to Montreal, endorsed the plans for a Jarry Park expanded to accommodate 30,000 fans, and accepted a $1.1 million down payment on the franchise.

The Expos were born. October 14, 1968, was declared Baseball Day, and the plebs, 10,000 strong, filled the Place des Nations to greet visiting NL dignitaries. Les Grands Ballets Canadiens offered a choreographed version of "Take Me out to the Ball Game." Warren Giles beamed. Mayor Drapeau, outspoken as always, came right out and declared Montreal to be the greatest city in the world. Later in the day, at the Windsor Hotel, the NL owners got down to the real business. The draft. The rendering, on consideration of $10 million, of thirty bodies to each expansion team, thirty players who, hereafter (unless traded before opening day), would be flesh-and-blood Expos. "It's only a day after [Canadian] Thanksgiving," a sportswriter said, "and we're being offered all the turkeys." Not so, another ventured, scrutinizing the list of command-generation players on offer from the league. "We could end up with the all-star team of 1954."

Come morning, Expos were more than a name. We had a team. At once fledgling Expos and senior citizens of baseball.

Among them, such reputable performers as Maury Wills, Manny Mota, Don Clendenon, Mack Jones, Larry Jaster, and Larry Jackson. "We've got to build for the day these guys retire," GM Jim Fanning said—prophetically, as it turned out, for the next day thirty-seven-year-old pitcher Larry Jackson, the team's only established starter, announced his retirement, and the Expos, yet to be rained out on a Sunday, were more than $300,000 out of pocket.

The other players procured at the NL-sponsored bazaar were either young and unknown quantities, or too-well-known nonentities. Considering they were largely fire-sale goods, the management was touchingly defensive. "The Expos hope," the official guide said, "Bob Bailey has matured enough to live up to the expectations the Pittsburgh Pirates had for him, when they outbid most of the other major-league clubs for his services in 1961." They did not emphasize unduly that for the last two years he had been punishing the ball, as sportswriters say, at a regular .227 clip. A highly esteemed baseball expert, the guide informed us, had said only three years ago of Don Bosch, another Expo acquisition, that "in the field, he can be favorably compared with none other than Willy Mays!" At the plate, alas, he could be compared but to you and me, his average being a far from lusty .171. We were also told that Jim "Mudcat" Grant, who was later to be traded to St. Louis, had won twenty-one games for Minnesota in 1965. However, another look at the record revealed he had won only five in 1967 and six in 1968. This, the guide suggested, is the year Don Shaw, who pitched all of twelve innings with the Mets the year before, might be coming into his own, and, who knew, "a change of scenery might be all the doctor ordered" for Bill Stoneman, who had won none and lost two in the minors in 1968.

Who knew, indeed? Stoneman went on to pitch two no-hitters for the Expos, and even before the season opened I had learned to respect John McHale's sagacity. At the Expos' training camp in Florida, a state where, surely, to be bilingual was to be fluent in English and Yiddish, the management saw to it that all announcements were made in English and French, thereby charming the locals. A month later, New York sportswriters were to delight in outfielders who were also *voltigeurs,* a shortstop introduced as an *arrêt-court,* and pitchers as *lanceurs.*

McHale & Co. also engineered a dazzling trade, surrendering one reputable and two fringe players to Houston for Rusty Staub, a twenty-four-year-old all-star outfielder. "The best ballplayer an expansion team ever had," wrote Larry Merchant in the *New York Post.*

Meanwhile, back in Montreal, we read of such springtime coups still deep in a severe and seemingly endless winter. Many doubted that Jarry Park—the stands still without seats, the field encrusted in ice and snow—would be ready or fit to play on come the April 14 opener. I, for one, anticipated disaster. Something to cherish, like the year Oxford sank in the boat race, or the autumn the Grey Cup Game had to be called because of fog, the players unable to find each other or the football.

The Expos trotted onto the field for their first major-league game out of town. They opened at Shea Stadium, in New York, on April 8, and before 45,000 outraged fans defeated the Mets with rare panache. The ubiquitous Mayor Drapeau threw out the opening ball, and amiable Charles Bronfman sat with his heart thumping as his team, well ahead going into the ninth, wobbled, finally squeaking by, 11–10. Rusty Staub, as advertised, hit a homer. So did rookie Coco Laboy. Larry Merchant wrote in the *New York Post:*

> Shed a tear for the Royal Canadian Mounties. Wear a black patch for the separatists of Quebec. A moment of silence please for the seal hunters on Hudson Bay. Send a word of condolence to the Indians. . . . Apologize to George Chuvalo. . . . The Montreal Expos are their team and never will they know the joys and agonies of the Amazin' Mets.

For the victors after the game, for team management and well-wishers, dinner in a private dining room at Toots Shor. Broadway. The Big Time. Mayor Drapeau shook any hand proffered and reached for many that weren't. Gerry Snyder scooted from table to table, grinning, never forgetting a name. Charles Bronfman sat quietly at his table. A rich young Montreal celebrant, the owner of a large laundry chain, turned to me, his face glowing, and said, "We will be able to tell our grandchildren we were here."

So, I imagine, did men good and true speak to each other at Agincourt, Waterloo, Normandy, and Iwo Jima. Anyway, the headline on the front page of the next morning's *Montreal Gazette* read:

Look who's in first place!
EXPOS TAKE OPENER

Ted Blackman's exuberant story began:

And 100 years later an upstart team from Canada showed the Americans how their game of baseball is really played.

Never mind that our upstart team from Canada was composed of Americans, too. Glory days are hard come by and chauvinism is ill-becoming. Blackman's story continued:

Well, not quite, but the Montreal Expos certainly avenged those Fenian Raids yesterday when they invaded the national pastime of the United States and swiped their centennial spotlight with an 11–10 victory over the Mets in the historic 1969 National League inaugural.

A week later, after the Expos had won one more and lost four on the road, the team came home, so to speak, heralded by a poem from pitcher Jim "Mudcat" Grant, which began,

Life is like a game of baseball,
and you play it every day.
It isn't just the breaks you get,
but the kind of game you play.

Workers toiled through the night at Jarry Park, hammering in seats and struggling with the soggy field, and, come morning, the sun shone brightly and the temperature soared, settling into a rare summer's day. EVERYONE BUT EVERYONE WAS OUT THERE, MY DEAR, a *Star* reporter wrote of the team brunch which preceded the game. "The Versailles Room at the Windsor Hotel," the reporter went on to say, "was simply filled to brimming with people who matter. . . ." Among them, the fellow who was in charge of Montreal's Public Water Works, the first dignitary to be introduced. We applauded. We also applauded Quebec Premier Jean Jacques Bertrand and, naturally, Mayor Drapeau. We ate an unspeakable chicken à la king without complaining and bolstered ourselves with Bloody Marys against the mighty St. Louis Cards, who even then awaited the sacrificial Expos at Jarry Park.

Then, in a park filled to capacity, we watched the Expos beat the Cards 8–7, Mack Jones driving in three runs with a homer and becoming an instant hero. Positioned in the choice seats on the first-base line, I recognized many of the plump faces there. Among them were some of the nervy kids who used to skip school with me on weekday afternoons to sit in the left-field bleachers of Delorimier Downs, cheering on the Royals and earning nickels fetching hot dogs for strangers. Gone were the AZA windbreakers, the bubble gum, the scuffed running shoes, the pale wintry faces. These men came bronzed to the ball park from their Florida condominiums. Now they wore foulards and navy-blue blazers with brass buttons, they carried Hudson's Bay blankets in plastic cases for their bejeweled wives and sucked on Monte Cristos, mindful not to spill ashes on their Gucci loafers.

Above all, they radiated pleasure in their own accomplishments and the occasion. And why not? This was an event and they were there, inside looking out at last, right on the first-base line. Look at me. "Give it some soul, Mack," one of them shouted.

I asked the portly man in front of me to remove his hat, a snappy little fedora. "I can't," he protested. "Sinus. Took pills this morning. The sun. I can't."

Jim "Mudcat" Grant's opening-day poem concluded:

> This game will not be easy,
>   there'll be struggle, there'll be strife,
> To make the winning runs,
>   for it's played on the field of life.
> So stand behind your team, son,
>   there'll be many who'll applaud.
> Remember you're the player,
>   and the umpire there is God.

Eleven years passed, managers had come and gone, the Expos abandoning delightful Jarry Park for the chilly Big Owe, before the team won more games than they lost, finishing 95–65; they also carried their divisional title dream into the final game of the season, before they succumbed to Steve Carlton and the Phillies. Over the years the Expos had been caught in some foolish, even demented, trades, but they also put together one of the best organizations in baseball. A farm system that produced Steve Rogers, Scott Sanderson, David Palmer, Bill Gullickson, Tim Wallach, Gary Carter, Tim Raines, Terry Francona, André Dawson, and Ellis Valentine. Ellis, alas, was adjudged *not a good citizen*. A boy playing a boy's game.

Going into the 1980 season, in the most curious addendum to

a contract this side of a third-grade report—Addendum No. 4—
Ellis, in the absence of a lollipop, was to be paid a $2,000
monthly bonus if he fulfilled the following conditions:

 a. general excellence of offensive and defensive play;
 b. general effort and practice effort;
 c. cooperation with management and field leadership;
 d. good physical condition;
 e. good citizenship.

In April, May, July, and August, Ellis was good hit, field, and
hygiene, winning untold brownies and the $2,000 per, but in
June the bad boy went and fractured his cheekbone and his bonus
was withheld until the last month of the season, when management decided not to award it, because he had been found wanting
in "practice effort" and "good citizenship." Seemingly, if Ellis so
much as sneezed or suffered a tummy tumble, he withdrew from
the field, saying he would not play unless he could give his best.
Furthermore, on September 22, he had to be threatened with
suspension unless he returned to Montreal pronto for the exami-
nation of a wrist he injured in St. Louis. "We didn't give a hoot
about the money," said Valentine's agent. "All Ellis wanted was
a 'thank you' from the club. Instead he had to sit through some
ninety-minute meetings about why he didn't deserve the bonus.
That hurt him."

Still grieving in October, Ellis asked to be traded, a demand
he was to repeat in spring training and after. Finally, in 1981,
even as Ellis was ailing again, he was sent to the Mets for reliever
Jeff Reardon, a minor-league outfielder, and a player to be
named later. "I love him," John McHale said, "and I hope he
does well."

Valentine was exuberant. "That's great," he said. "I hope
Shea Stadium will help my legs. Maybe McHale is trying to
make me happy by trading me to a place where there is natural
grass."

To which *Gazette* columnist Ted Blackman responded the following morning that he thought Ellis had been playing on grass all along.

When we acquired a franchise of our own in 1969, our cherished Montreal in the majors at last, we congratulated each other, because seemingly things had changed, we were in the biggies now. Increasingly, the engaging Expos brought us joy, a much-needed distraction, pulling in the town's largest and most good-natured crowds. Such was their appeal, in fact, that they attracted some 1,534,564 fans in 1981, the notorious split season when, with only the third-best divisional record overall, the Expos sneaked into the playoffs and damn near the World Series, finally undone by Fernando Valenzuela and a ninth-inning homer by Rick Monday, a hit that still resounds here as tragically as Bobby Thomson's historic blow against the old Brooklyn Dodgers.

Possibly, deep down in the adolescent Expo psyche, players too young to have seen the legendary Triple A Royals still consider themselves the Dodgers' number-one sons. Management may suffer from the same affliction. After all, it was only after the Expos let reliever Mike Marshall go that he went on to win 15, and save 21, games for the Dodgers, winning them a pennant and himself a Cy Young award. Manny Mota, the original Expo draft choice, and the first to be traded, went on to play ten very productive years with the same Dodgers. Ron Fairly, in all the years he played here, reportedly drove manager Gene Mauch wild telling him again and again what a grand organization he had sprung from. While Mauch himself, I'm told, always yearned to manage one team more than any other: yes, the Dodgers. After all this time, still Montreal baseball's Big Daddy. Obviously, the Expos' most urgent need is for a pitcher called Oedipus Rex.

Meanwhile, two other problems remain. The signing of free

agents. And holding on to players developed by the organization after their talent has matured.

John McHale insists that the Expos have no trouble competing for free agents, the players adore it in Montreal, but though he offered Reggie Jackson $1 million more than the Yankees, Reggie understandably opted for New York, where his chocolate bar would sell considerably better than 1981's Cro-bar named after outfielder–first baseman Warren Cromartie. Don Sutton also balked at playing for his good neighbor to the north.

"Do the players like it here?" I asked pitcher Bill Lee.

"I like it here and I want to stay, but most of the players dislike it intensely. There's the weather problem and the culture shock. The wives don't want to learn French. And then there's the tax situation."

At the gate, the Expos take in Canadian dollars, worth roughly eighty-one cents American, but they fork out U.S. funds at the pay window, and are also obliged to compensate players for any losses they suffer on double taxation. All the same, the players don't like the headache. Even more to the point, they feel neglected out on the tundra. Until they become contenders, they are seldom seen on the Game of the Week, and unless their relatives in Florida or California catch them on American TV, they have no idea how well their boys are doing in Canada.

The problem of holding on to draft choices who have been developed within the organization, becoming stars, could become prohibitively expensive. Take Gary Carter, for instance, an Orange County boy, long coveted by the Dodgers. Before he condescended to sign a new contract with the Expos for a rumored $15 million, spread over seven years, he told me, "When I play out there in California all the papers do interviews now. Even my old local paper—the one I used to deliver."

Other players, nourished by the Expos, but now on the threshold of stardom, say young Tim Wallach, may elect to shine under a larger media sun. To keep him, come contract-renewal time, the Expos would be required to pay more than any other team could offer, because of intangibles it is simply not within their power to provide. Danny Menendez, director of Expo scouting, told me, "A player, if he becomes a star here, can get maybe fifteen to twenty thousand dollars for an endorsement, but in the States he can earn from fifty to a hundred thousand for the same thing. It adds up."

So though we have ostensibly leaped from Triple A to the biggies, it could yet prove an illusion. Possibly we are doomed to be a farm club forever. Developing talent for California and New York. Meanwhile, there is hope. Hope of a kind. Next year, or maybe five years from now, the Big Owe will be completed. A retractable roof will be set in place. And in this city of endless winter and short hot summers, it will become possible to watch baseball played under a roof, on artificial turf, in an air-conditioned, maybe even centrally heated concrete tomb.

Progress.

St. Urbain Street
Then and Now

BAD NEWS. THEY'RE CLOSING BARON BYNG HIGH SCHOOL. Our Baron Byng. I speak of a legendary Montreal school, founded in 1921, that resembles nothing so much as a Victorian workhouse. Architecturally, the loss will be minimal (the building's a blight), but emotionally . . . ah, that's something else. If the Battle of Waterloo was won on the playing fields of Eton, then the character of Montreal's diminishing Jewish community was hammered into shape in the smelly classrooms of that big brown brick building.

> Themistocles, Thermopylae,
>   the Peloponnesian War,
> X^2, Y^2, H_2SO_4,
>   One, two, three, four,
> Who are we for?
>   Byng! Byng! Byng!

Today's Jewish community in Montreal is a group riddled with apprehension. Nobody is signing a long lease, every family has its own contingency plans. Once, however, many of us were at BBHS together. Everything possible. September 1944. Even as our elder brothers and cousins were thrusting into Holland, with the Canadian army battling on the Hitler Line, we stood in rows in the BBHS gym, raw and pimply, but shiny trousers freshly pressed. New boys we were. Rambunctious thirteen-year-olds, charged with hope. We were told, "I suppose most of you expect to go on to McGill University four years from now. Well, you will have to work hard. McGill entrance calls for a sixty-five percent average in the matriculations, but Jewish boys seeking admission will require seventy-five percent."

Baron Byng was being shut down because its student body, now largely Greek in origin, numbered only 405, but once those classrooms reverberated with the ambition of 1,000 strivers. Scrappy, driving boys and girls who led the province of Quebec in matriculation results year after year.

Baron Byng lies right out there on St. Urbain Street in what used to be the heart of Montreal's swirling Jewish quarter. In my day, St. Urbain Street was the lowest rung on a ladder we were all hot to climb. No, St. Urbain wasn't the lowest rung, for one street below came Clark, where they had no lane and had to plunk their garbage out on the street. Parked right before the front door. Immediately below Clark there came the fabled Main or, more properly, Boulevard St. Laurent. Levitt's delicatessen. Moishe's steak house. Richstone's bakery. The editorial offices of the *Canadian Jewish Eagle.* The Canada, where you could take in three movies for a quarter, but sometimes felt gray squishy things nibbling at your ankles. The Roxy and the Crystal Palace, where they showed only two movies, but offered a live show as well. A forlorn parade of pulpy strippers. "Put on your glasses, boys," the MC would say, "for here come the Hubba-Hubba Girls." It was to the Main we repaired for zoot trousers, ducktail haircuts, and free auto parts calendars that showed leggy girls, their skirts blown high by the wind. If the calendar was vintage, the real stuff, you could just make out the girl's nipples *straining against her blouse,* as they wrote in the best stories that appeared in *True Detective.*

Our world was largely composed of the five streets that ran between Park Avenue and the Main: Jeanne Mance, Esplanade, Waverly, St. Urbain, and Clark. Standing tippy-toe on St. Urbain's next-to-the-bottom rung, you could just peer over Park Avenue—Park Avenue, the dividing line—into blessed Outremont, with its tree-lined streets and parks and skating rinks and (oh my God) furnished basements. Outremont, where the girls didn't wear shiny discount dresses and gaudy shell necklaces, but frocks that had been bought retail and pearls, yes, strands of pearls that had not been pilfered from Kresge's grab-all counter, but paid for at Birks maybe. Outremont fathers, in their three-piece suits and natty fedoras, were in property or sweaters or insurance or (the coming thing) plastics. They were learning how to golf. They thought nothing of driving down to New York to "take in the shows" or of renting a summer cottage on the lakeside in Ste.-Agathe-des-Monts. For the children's sake, they bought sets of *The Book of Knowledge,* sheltering them in a prominently displayed glass-doored bookcase. *King's Row* or *Forever Amber,* on the other hand, was kept in the bottom desk drawer. Locked.

Outremont, our heart's desire, was amazing. Kids our own age there didn't hang out at the corner cigar store or poolroom, they had their very own quarters. *Basement playrooms, Ping-Pong tables.* There were heated towel racks in the bathrooms. In each kitchen, a Mixmaster. No icebox, but a refrigerator. I had a school friend up there whose mother wore a *pince-nez,* and had hired a maid to answer the door, and even the telephone.

We would ring the house again and again, crowding round the receiver, stifling giggles, if only to hear the maid chirp, "This is the Feigelbaum residence."

But on St. Urbain, our fathers worked as cutters or pressers or scrap dealers and drifted into cold-water flats, sitting down to supper in their freckled Penman's long winter underwear, clipping their nails at the table. Mothers organized bazaars, proceeds for the Jewish National Fund, and jockeyed for position on the ladies' auxiliary of the Talmud Torah or the Folkshule, both parochial schools. Visiting aunts charged into the parlor, armed with raffle books, ten cents a ticket. Win an RCA Victor radio.

Win a three-volume *History of the Jews,* slipcover case included. The ladies had a favorite record. It was Jan Peerce, one of ours, singing "The Bluebird of Happiness." "The poet with his pen/ The peasant with his plow/ It's all the same somehow."

We preferred Artie Shaw's "Stardust," which gave us a chance to dance close, or any boogie-woogie, an opportunity to strut. After supper, I had to sift the ashes before stoking the furnace for the night, emerging prematurely gray from the shed. I attended parochial school (studying English, modern Hebrew, and French), and after classes, three afternoons a week, I knuckled down to the Talmud with Mr. Yalofsky's class in the back room of the Young Israel Synagogue.

—If a man tumbles off the roof of an eight-story building and four stories down another man sticks a sword out of the window and stabs him, is that second man guilty of murder? Or not?

—Rabbi Menasha asks, did he fall or was he pushed off the roof?

—Rabbi Yedhua asks, was he already dead of heart failure before he was stabbed?

—Were the two men related?

—Enemies?

—Friends?

—Was the sword already sticking out of the window or was it thrust into the falling body?

—Would the man have died from the fall in any event?

Who cared? Concealed on our laps, below the table, at the risk of having our ears twisted by Mr. Yalofsky, was the *Herald,* opened at the sports pages. What concerned us, children of the new world, was would the Punch Line (Maurice "the Rocket" Richard, Elmer Lach, Toe Blake) finish one-two-three in the scoring race, and would the Canadiens thrash the dreaded Toronto Maple Leafs in the Stanley Cup Finals?

Our parents were counting on us—a scruffy lot, but, for all that, the first Canadian-born generation—to elbow our way into McGill, not so much Cardinal Newman's notion of a university

as the block and tackle that would hoist the family into blessed
Outremont. Many of us, but certainly not all, made it not only
into Outremont, which turned out to be no more than a way station, but into the once *judenfrei* Town of Mount Royal, and even
Westmount. *Above the Boulevard.*

Bliss, yes, but at a price.

En route, Schneider was anglicized to Taylor; Putterschnit
was born again Patterson; Krashinsky, Kane. Children were no
longer named Hershl or Muttel or Malke or Zippora, but, instead, Stuart, Byron, Melinda, and Vanessa. Rather than play
jacks under a winding outside staircase after school, the girls in
their trainer bras from New York, New York, were driven to the
nose-job doctor and ballet class and the orthodontist in Mommy's
Mercedes. The boys, instead of delivering for the drugstore after
classes, saving up for their very own CCM bike, took tennis lessons, which would help them to meet the right people.

And then (surprise, surprise) suddenly the old neighborhood,
the starting line, became modish and some of the children, the ungrateful ones, the know-it-alls, moved back into those yucky
moldering cold-water flats on St. Urbain, nudging out the new
tenants: Greeks, Italians, Portuguese. And there, on St. Urbain,
where it was whispered that they smoked pot and didn't even remove their Frye boots to screw on those filthy sheets, they filled
the front windows not with rubber plants of the old days, but
with protest posters. Those play-poor kids in designer jeans were
against nukes, acid rain, and herpes, and for organically grown,
good multiple orgasms and the Parti Québécois.

The Parti Québécois?

"You exploited the French," they lectured grandfathers who
used to eke out a living bent over a sewing machine, fathers who
remembered flying into street battles against the followers of
Adrian Arcand, armed with lengths of lead pipe.

"You've got to learn to identify with the real Québécois,"
they argued.

"What, at my age, I should acquire a taste for Mae Wests or sugar pie or french fries soaked in vinegar?"

"That's a racist remark."

"Listen, kid, they don't have to fast with me on Yom Kippur, I don't need to march in the St.-Jean Baptiste parade."

Red-letter days on St. Urbain.

Sent to Jack and Moe's barbershop, corner of Park Avenue and Laurier, for my monthly haircut, a quarter clutched in my hand, I had grown accustomed to the humiliation of waiting for Moe to slide the board over the barber chair's arms, which raised me high enough to be shorn. But this day of glory, Moe merely jerked his head at me and snarled, "Siddown." There was no board. I was now tall enough to sit in the actual chair. On the St. Urbain Street standard, my manhood had been certified. From this day forward anything was possible.

Another day, at Baron Byng High School, I came of political age.

Ramsay MacDonald's number-one son Malcolm, the British colonial secretary, came to address us in the gym, but those of us who were members of the Labour Zionist Movement absolutely refused to stand up to sing "God Save the King." We greeted MacDonald with hostile silence. Why, that bastard had cut off immigration to Palestine. Leaking tubs overflowing with emaciated concentration-camp survivors were being turned back or led to Cyprus.

On St. Urbain, we were either very observant Orthodox Jews, dedicated Labour Zionists, or red-hot communists. There were a few suspected homosexuals in the neighborhood, that is to say, young men who read poetry and smoked cork-tipped cigarettes; there was at least one professional hooker that I knew of; but nobody, certainly, who would admit to being a member of the Conservative Party.

Communist conundrums on St. Urbain were sometimes resolved in a peculiar fashion.

A cousin of mine, then a communist firebrand but now a
computer consultant, canvassed votes door-to-door for Labour–
Progressive Party MP Fred Rose. Standing on one supposedly
communist doorstep, expounding on Marx and Engels, the
worker's sorry plight in Montreal, he was cut short by the irate
housewife. "What you say may be true," she allowed, "but this
time I don't vote for him, you can count on it."

"Why?"

"When his niece got married last April, we were invited to the
ceremony but not to the dinner. The hell with him."

In my last year at Baron Byng High School, I worked nights
in a Park Avenue bowling alley, spotting pins. A year later, en-
rolled at Sir George Williams College, I found work reporting on
college events for the *Montreal Herald* on space rates. The bowling alley paid me three cents a line, the *Herald* only two, but I
chucked being a pin boy and stuck with the *Herald,* revealing, I
think, a precocious dedication to letters no matter what the cost.

St. Urbain.

Like many another old boy of my generation, I still wander
down there on occasion, tramping through the lanes where we
once played hockey—lanes still thick with garbage and abandoned mattresses bleeding stuffing. I make the obligatory stop at
the Bagel Factory on St. Viateur near Park Avenue. In deference
to the French Language Charter, Bill 101, it is now called La
Maison du Bagel, Boulangerie. The YMHA, on Mount Royal,
where we used to box, hoping to qualify for the Golden Gloves,
has become the Pavillon Mont-Royal of the Université de
Montréal. My old parochial school, the Talmud Torah, where
we once stumbled over Hebrew grammar, has happily maintained a connection of sorts with Zion. It is now École Primaire

Nazareth. Only a block away, on Laurier, the Stuart Biscuit Company, where we used to be able to buy a bag of broken biscuits for two cents, is still there. But immediately across the street, my father's favorite old cigar & soda, Schacter's, has become an overpriced antique shop, haunted—I like to think—by the ghosts of gin rummy games past. Laurier, above Park Avenue, is no longer a tacky street of bicycle and auto-parts shops. It has been transmogrified into a street of elegant restaurants, boutiques, fine-food shops, and bookstores. My God, my God, these days, only two blocks away from hot bagel heaven and Mehadrin's Marché de Viande Kosher, you can feast on hot croissants and espresso.

Jack and Moe's barbershop, where you could once also lay down two bucks on a horse, has been displaced by a more reliable investment house, a branch of the Banque Nationale de Grèce. The Young Israel synagogue is no longer on Park Avenue. The Regent Theatre—where I sat through at least four double features in the balcony before I dared slip my arm (slowly, slowly) around Riva Tannenbaum's bony shoulders, my heart thumping as I actually kissed her cheek in the dark—has, given such a start, slid into undreamed-of depravity. It has become le Beaver, where you can now catch HOT LEGS, "The Ups and Downs of the Stocking and Garter Industry Fully Exposed!" The Rialto, on the corner of Bernard, has also become a porn palace, this one showing the hot stuff in Greek. Indeed, this familiar chunk of Park Avenue, a street where our mothers used to comparison-shop for odd cups and saucers—an avenue where the nearest you could come to sin was to flip hastily through the latest *Esquire* at the corner newsstand, searching for the Vargas girl—is now totally disreputable. Where once it was a scandal for a neighborhood girl to be seen out for a stroll, wearing a tight sweater, acknowledging what she had there, you can now drop into SECRET SUPER SEXE, *danseuses nues,* as well as EXPO SEXE, both establishments serving hamburgers for lunch. To go with, as they say. But for all that, Park Avenue is still a street of Hasidic rabbis and their progeny. Immediately around the corner from Park Avenue, on Jeanne Mance, the two-fisted followers of the Satmar rabbi are rooted, and also in the neighborhood there are still many adherents of the Lubavitcher rabbi. Boys, wearing skullcaps and long sidecurls, who gather together to sing:

> "We only eat a kosher diet,
> Non-kosher food we'd never try it.
> To be healthy Jews is our main goal
> Non-kosher food is harmful for body and soul."

Nobody who was raised on St. Urbain ventures into the old neighborhood without stopping for a special at Wilensky's, corner of Clark and Fairmount. A special, I should point out, is made up of cuts of different kinds of salami, grilled in a delicious roll. Traditionally, it is washed down with a nonvintage cherry Coke, mixed at the fountain.

Wilensky's, which has been serving the neighborhood since 1931, is now presided over by Moe, son of the original proprietor. During World War II days, we gathered at the soda fountain for heated political disputes. Should the Allies OPEN UP A SECOND FRONT NOW, relieving pressure on the hard-pressed Russians but risking the life of many a St. Urbain urchin who had enlisted?

St. Urbain Street old boys, running into each other at Wilensky's forty years on, still talk politics, but now it isn't about the war over there, on the other side of the ocean, but about the trouble right here: the Parti Québécois. The boys I grew up with, parents themselves now, counting cholesterol rather than batting averages, drift off to whisper in the corners. "And what about you, are you staying on in Montreal?"

"What should I do? Take the chicken run to Toronto and make new friends at my age?"

In the quarrel between the English and French in Montreal, the Jews feel they are caught in the middle. "Look here," an old friend told me, "I don't think for a minute that the Parti Québécois is anti-Semitic. My God, you look at the faces on the front bench in the Assembly and they shine with intelligence. In a way, they're Zionists at home. I can understand everything they want. I can understand it in my head. But here," he continued, pounding his gut, "here, you know what I feel? If they don't get everything they want—we're the ones who are going to be blamed."

And now there are also the Italians, the Greeks, and the Portuguese, post–World War II immigrants for the most part, the inheritors of St. Urbain, Main, and Park Avenue, many of them with something like the old Jewish appetite.

Take feisty Jimmy Essaris, for instance. Forty-nine years old, dark, handsome, with flashing black eyes. Jimmy, sprung from a farming village near Athens, arrived here penniless in 1951, walking up and down the streets banging on doors before he finally surfaced with a job as a dishwasher in a Greek short-order restaurant in suburban Lachine. At the time, he spoke no English, no French, but within five months he was a counterman and had convinced the proprietor to stay open twenty-four hours a day, more than tripling his take. Jimmy stayed on there for three years, earning $100 weekly in 1954. "Don't mis-me-understand," he told me, "it was a lot of money at the time." But a year later, Jimmy had left to buy his own restaurant from an elderly Greek couple. They wanted $4,000; Jimmy offered them all the money he had saved, $3,000. " 'You will take it,' " he said to the couple, " 'because you are a Greek and I am a Greek and if not I will buy the place next door.' I laid the cash on the counter and the guy is shaking now. And you will pay the notary, too, I told him," Jimmy added.

"Soon I'm doing very good, I make maybe two hundred dollars a week net, but I don't like the place, it's too small for me, and I sell it for nine thousand dollars. It's 1955 now, and I have a little car, it cost me three hundred dollars. One night this girl phones me and she wants to go to a movie in Montreal. I still don't know what it means Montreal. But she wants Montreal, so we go. I can't park here, I can't park there. I have to go to a parking lot. The old man in the lot, he says to me one dollar. *One dollar parking.* I'm so polite I gave him the dollar and in the meantime I'm counting the cars. My head is pounding. I sit on the sidewalk and I think, hey, this is some fantastic business. One dollar parking, and you don't have to make club sandwiches or wash up. I can't concentrate on the movie. I tell the girl, hey, I will pay you twenty-five dollars a week, all I want is you find me a parking lot."

Early in 1956, Jimmy found one downtown, on Stanley Street, and rented it for $750 a month. But no sooner did he sign the papers in the landlord's office and stride down to the lot than the parking attendant said to him, welcome, sucker, you are the fifth man to rent this lot in two years. "The first night I made twenty dollars, the second, eighteen dollars. I multiply this by thirty and I see I can't even make the seven-hundred-fifty rent. Then one day I invite the cop on the street in for a coffee and I say to him, don't mis-me-understand, but now I will tell you a sad story. I am a poor Greek boy. I have nothing. I need help. Give tickets. Scare them. I can't do that, he says. But we become friendly, *very friendly,* and he says, I'm going to help you. First night, one hundred tickets. Now everybody gets the medicine. My third week, I'm full. I start to make money. I'm grossing seventeen hundred dollars a month."

Now Jimmy Essaris owns fifty parking lots in Montreal, Quebec City, and Toronto; he employs 300 people and grosses $12 million annually.

"I am against separatism," he said, "but I do not run. If I have to fight, I will fight. English is necessary. It is the language of business, and they have to accept that. But I would be disappointed if my kids did not speak French also. Poor Greek families on St. Urbain feel threatened. They work hard. They came here looking for stability, now there is a quarrel here, it is terrible. We went through enough from 1939 to 1951 in Greece. The way Lévesque is running the economy, everybody is going to go bankrupt and they will have to close the doors."

Making a Movie

My wife and I were in Yellowknife, in the Northwest Territories, when Michael Spencer, then the beleaguered head of the Canadian Film Development Corporation, telephoned from Montreal.

"Cold out there?" he asked.

"Forty-two below," I lied, not wanting to disappoint.

"Well, congratulations. You've been nominated for an Academy Award."

The nomination was for having written the screenplay based on my own novel *The Apprenticeship of Duddy Kravitz.* I didn't bother to call my editor, Bob Gottlieb, at Knopf, because I knew nothing would induce him to take out a full-page ad in *Variety,* saying, "CONGRATS, MORT. FROM ALL THE GUYS AND GALS AT KNOPF," but later in the afternoon I did have to telephone my old friend and former British editor, Tony Godwin, who was then working in New York. He wasn't impressed. "Wouldn't it be embarrassing," he suggested dryly, "if you won?"

Early the next morning, snug in a six-seater Navaho, locally known as the widow-maker, bouncing 10,000 feet over the Precambrian Shield, en route to Whitehorse, we celebrated with our good companions the Morrows. William Morrow, supreme court justice for the Territories, had been thoughtful enough to supplement his standard northern survival kit with two bottles of Veuve Clicquot, cracking the first one open as we slipped through cloud into the Yukon, looking down on the spectacular mountain pass called Nahanni Butte.

"It would be a big thing for Canada," Morrow said.

Back in Yellowknife, the following evening, old northern hand Ed Ogle, a fine raconteur and journalist, told us the story of the Eskimo who had been to the deep south—that is to say, Toronto—on a government junket. When he returned to his settlement on the Arctic shore, he was immediately surrounded. "What was it like?" he was asked.

Wonderful, he said. Very exciting. "They have tall, tall buildings there. Maybe thirty houses high."

Nobody believed him. "How would people get to the top?"

"You take an elevator."

"What's that?"

Glad to be asked, he explained. "You get into this small room, the doors shut, it shakes and shakes. The doors open. You get out. And it's a whole new world."

And so it was when, a week later, we descended from the top of the North American continent, stopping off to embrace our family of five in Montreal, right down into the Californian tail.

Beverly Hills.

Sealskin parkas and mukluks yielding to tailored denims and sneakers. Hardened drinkers of the midnight sun being displaced by early-to-bed health addicts of balmy California. Instead of overproof rum, Vitamin C tablets. Rather than snowmobiles, Rolls-Royces. In the absence of sidewalks encrusted with ice as unyielding as cement, soft green lawns, palms, and tree-sized rubber plants. More than 500,000 diaspora Canadians have settled in Southern California, where they endure smog, yet need no longer worry about the knifelike chill factor. Or Alberta's oil demands. Or the Parti Québécois.

Our taxi driver was from Sacramento. "I had thought," he said, "driving a taxi in Beverly Hills, I'd get to see the stars. But in two years, all I've seen is Morey Amsterdam, and oh yeah, Doris Day once, standing in her doorway, saying goodnight to her guests."

"Don't any of them take taxis?"

"Just the Portuguese maids. And they always want change for a twenty."

That the film of Duddy Kravitz has ever been made seems to me incredible. I still can't understand how we managed to muddle through. One day, a day absurd even by filmmaking standards, strikes me as typical of the whole demented venture. October 27, 1973. A day there was more than enough to ponder. Watergate, for instance. Israeli troubles. And in Quebec, Premier Robert Bourassa about to be tested in an election. But at 2:00 P.M., on that Saturday, there I stood on a Montreal street corner, ostensibly a mature man, waiting for a milkman's horse to shit. I wasn't alone. Counting bemused onlookers, extras, a cadets corps and commander, camera and production crew, director Ted Kotcheff, producer John Kemeny, and our principal backer, Gerry Schneider, we were almost two hundred. All eyes fastened on the horse's rump. A lady, oozing enthusiasm, drove me against a wall. "It must be very exciting for you," she bubbled, "to have your novel finally come to life."

"Yes."

The shots called for in my script seemed simple enough on paper.

EXT. DAY. ANOTHER STREET

CLOSE ON CADET COMMANDER JAMES

One arm raised to stop the FLETCHER'S FIELD HIGH SCHOOL CADET CORPS, *obliging them to mark time.*

JAMES: Hip! Hip! Hip!

ANOTHER ANGLE

Immediately before him, a MILKMAN'S HORSE *has stopped to defecate.*

ANOTHER ANGLE

CLOSE ON *sudden fall of steaming horse buns.*

ANOTHER ANGLE

RESUME COMMANDER JAMES, *a survivor of the mud of Flanders, as he marches unblinkingly through the steaming mess.*

ANOTHER ANGLE

The more fastidious CADETS behind contrive to pass on either side of the mess.

But our horse wouldn't deliver. A vet, with a plastic glove running elbow-high, administered a suppository to the recalcitrant animal, unavailingly. A half hour passed. The vet attended to the horse once more and, lo and behold, *the beast arched his rear legs. His tail rose. Cameras whirred into action. The cadet band began to play.* But then the unobliging horse farted resoundingly, no more.

Producer John Kemeny pulled me aside. "Ted can fake the shot. Why won't he fake it?"

"He won't fake it," I said.

"Do you know how much this is costing? Not that I'd say a word to him now."

"Forget it."

Gerry Schneider, the most solicitous of backers, disappeared briefly and returned with a bottle of Rémy Martin in a brown paper bag. Kotcheff drank, so did I. Finally, after a wait of an hour and five minutes, costing the production something like $2,000, the horse's bowels opened to release a deluge. A filmmaker's epiphany.

"Turn over."

"Speed."

"Action."

Two nights later, watching the rushes of the cadets' march in the screening room, Kotcheff turned to me, just as the camera eye closed in on the horse defecating, and said, "That's right where we superimpose 'From a novel by . . .' "

We're old friends.

Ted Kotcheff, who got his start directing television plays for the CBC, left Toronto a couple of years after I had put Montreal behind me. During the late Fifties, while I was waiting for a divorce from my first wife to come through, we shared a third-floor flat in a dilapidated house right near the Swiss Cottage tube station in London. The rotting floors were covered with tar paper—the stuff of roofing material. Broken slats showed through a large hole in the ceiling of Ted's bedroom. We heated the flat with a proliferating number of Aladdin paraffin heaters, whose charred wicks gave off a constant stink, because we were in the habit of eating dinner out in style, then tumbling into bed too drunk to remember to fill the tanks. Mice were also a problem.

Once, Ted's mother came over on a visit. She took one look at our flat, shook her head, and said, "To think you have to live like this."

We didn't, actually. But we happened to be perversely fond of 5 Winchester Road, and enjoyed nothing better than inviting people we considered snobbish over for drinks.

When I married again, Ted was my best man. Florence, my wife, was the first to read the Kravitz manuscript, and then I passed it on to Ted. That was a long time ago, the summer of 1958, in a villa in Roquebrune, on the Côte d'Azur, and I can still remember the three of us sitting on the floor, sipping cognac, Ted saying, "One day I'm going back to Canada to film this novel."

"Yeah," I said, "sure," and we all laughed and had another drink.

Ted and I had already done television plays together in

England, and in the Sixties we began to make films, among them *Life at the Top* with Jean Simmons and the late Laurence Harvey. But no British or American film company was willing to finance the filming of *The Apprenticeship of Duddy Kravitz*. They always wanted us to do something else, anything but the adventures of a teenage, working-class Jewish kid on the make in Montreal, circa 1949. There was, it's true, Canadian interest from time to time, but in those days any Canadian production company looked at closely turned out to be no more than a letterhead and a rented station wagon. Then along came the Canadian Film Development Corporation (CFDC), armed with a $10 million bankroll: a new dawn, making indigenous production a serious possibility. But in the early days of the CFDC, Ted and I were busy elsewhere. He was in Australia, making *Outback,* and I was immersed in another novel, *St. Urbain's Horseman.* We were seldom in England at the same time anymore. I had, to be truthful, given up on the project, but Ted persevered. He came up with a Canadian producer with a reputation for honesty, John Kemeny, and the promise, in principle, of the backing of the CFDC.

Which brings me to Cannes, May 1972. In theory a film festival, but in practice an international bazaar. John Kemeny was there; so was Michael Spencer, head of the CFDC. Ted drove down from London with his wife, and I was in Cannes writing a piece on the festival for *Life* magazine. My then twelve-year-old daughter, Emma, came down to stay with me for three days, and I took her to lunch with Groucho Marx.

"Will you marry me?" Groucho asked Emma immediately.

"I'm too young."

"All right, then, I'll ask you again in three weeks' time."

Anthony Burgess joined our table and told Groucho how much he had savored a little scene from *Love Happy,* recounting the episode in detail.

"Can you really remember that far back?" Groucho asked, astounded.

"Yes."

"Amazing," he said, shaking his head. "I've had three wives and I can't remember any of them."

Kotcheff, Kemeny, Spencer, and I assembled at the Carlton Hotel the next morning and talked about a production of *Duddy Kravitz,* one of a thousand dreams being floated on the terrace, only ten of which would ever be made, maybe one of them earning a profit. Nevertheless, it suddenly seemed real. Ted and I quit the terrace in a buoyant mood. In my case, it didn't last. For this, incidentally, happened to be the day of the official Canadian film opening and party, and that afternoon, standing at the bar with a Columbia executive, I asked, "Going to the Canadian gala tonight?"

"Aw," he said, "Canadian films have got no want-to-see," and popping a pill into his mouth, he gulped down his drink and was off in pursuit of somebody more important.

I was, at the time, already working on the script of *St. Urbain's Horseman* for director Alan Pakula, and once that was done I wanted to get on with a new novel. So I asked Ted to get somebody else to write the *Kravitz* screenplay.

Seed or development money was short. Kotcheff, back in London, had to settle for a writer with no previous screen credit. Then Kotcheff went off to make a western in Israel, of all places, and I returned with my family to take up residence in Canada again after a long absence.

The following spring it became uncomfortably clear that the screenplay Ted had commissioned simply wasn't good enough. The CFDC, once enthusiastic, refused to finance the project, and Kemeny couldn't realize any private investment on the basis of the existing script. Once more the film was shelved. Once more it was May.

After many delays, mostly caused by the upheaval of moving my family back to Montreal, I was even more eager to get on with my new novel, and Ted had been offered a fat fee to direct another film for United Artists. But on a trip to Hollywood, he stopped over in Montreal, and we sat and drank too much in my garden, recalling that evening in the south of France fifteen years ago, when we had both been young, unbeatable, and charged with appetite, and he had vowed to film *Kravitz* one day, however daunting the difficulties. Mellowing on cognac, tucking in our middle-aged spreads, we decided to drink less, exercise more, and give the project one more push—our best shot—and if we couldn't get it off the ground, to abandon it forever. I agreed to write a new screenplay for a token fee and Ted promised not to commit to the other film until I was finished. We had lunch with Michael Spencer, who assured us of $200,000, provided the CFDC liked the new script. Kemeny said he could raise $300,000 more, which left us $100,000 short, on an estimated budget of $600,000. So Ted got a shave and a haircut, put on his best suit, and flew off to Toronto to consult the CBC. We had reason to be hopeful. A year earlier, enthusiastic CBC executives had sought Ted out in New York to offer full financial support, if we ever got round to making *Kravitz.* It was, they assured him, just the sort of project they should get into, and to turn us down would be to shirk their mandate.

Ted asked the CBC for $100,000 for the rights to show the film three times, including a TV premiere eighteen months after its initial theatrical release. Or, put another way, we would supply seven and a half hours of prime-time drama, Canadian-made, for roughly $13,000 an hour. In return, Ted promised to deliver a professional film, with an international cast, based on a Canadian novel that was studied at many universities and high schools and, fourteen years after its original publication, still sold something like 30,000 paperback copies annually in Canada. Typically, the CBC didn't say yes, neither would they say no: instead, they procrastinated. We were told, on the one hand, that they could buy Canadian rights to run-of-the-mill American films for only $3,000, and on the other, that they were still without a head of drama production and did not wish to encumber any incoming director with a decision already made. They also smiled and wished us luck.

We went back to Michael Spencer, our most steadfast supporter, and told him we couldn't go into production unless the CFDC lent us $300,000. In return, we promised him an honest Canadian film, but not one, I hastily interjected, that would necessarily make money.

"That's refreshing, at least," Spencer said. "You're the first guys to come to me with a project and not swear up and down that it was going to bring in millions in profit."

Spencer, besieged by filmmakers across the country, had his problems. While French Canadian productions, funded by the CFDC, had often shown a profit, most English-language films backed by the corporation had ended badly. There had been two critical successes, *Goin' Down the Road* and *Wedding in White*, but on an investment of millions the CFDC had so far shown a return of only 10 percent on English-language films, and that included projects unfinished and others too embarrassing to be distributed. We were asking a good deal. Spencer, inclined to help, said if we needed $300,000 he would have to take the problem to his board, but not before July, when my new script would be ready.

Ted flew back to London, dejected, and I resumed work on the script without much hope. As the script called for three weeks of summer shooting in the Laurentians, we could not possibly begin filming any later than the first week of September. Assuming we would get a favorable answer from the CFDC early in July, that allowed us an unnervingly short time in which to find the right actor to play Duddy Kravitz, cast twenty other major speaking parts, put together camera and production units, and find locations, not to mention cars, costumes, and other props, circa 1948–49. Meanwhile, Ted had to take the chance of losing the other film (one that would pay him four times the fee he would get for making *Kravitz*) and ending up with neither. During his absence in England, I met with Spencer again. "Even if the CFDC comes through," I said, "I just want you to know we can't promise to go ahead unless we find the right actor to play Duddy. He's in every scene. And we'd have six weeks to find him."

"Why don't you delay until next spring?"

"We're not delaying. We make it now or forget it."

"I'm being pressured," Spencer said. "Everybody is pressuring me."

I finished a new script, salvaging some seven pages of original material from the first writer's draft as well as some useful editing done by Ted. Happily, the CFDC was pleased with the script. In July, Spencer, good as his word, telephoned immediately after his board meeting in Vancouver to say we could have the money we wanted. Five days later Ted flew back from London and we went out and got drunk together.

"Six hundred thousand dollars will never see us through," Ted said.

"Who knows," I said, "maybe they're not expecting a talkie."

Now we were no longer dejected; we were terrified. Hypothetical worries had overnight become real problems, and Ted started putting in twelve-hour days, hunting for locations, hiring crew, and casting. He was especially fortunate in surfacing early with Ann Pritchard, who took charge of design, and Tim Rouse, assistant director. Rouse was to prove invaluable.

The *Montreal Star* published a story saying we were looking for an unknown to play Duddy Kravitz, and the next morning the telephone began to ring. We were inundated with letters. From boys who had been born on St. Urbain. Or played a starring role in *The King and His Cabbages* in grade three. Or with an aunt who was on speaking terms with a cousin of mine.

My favorite letter began:

I've just finished reading *The Apprenticeship of Duddy Kravitz* and . . . I've decided I'll be quite willing to play the part for you. Of course the salary and contracts will have to be discussed with you personally. I imagine you want to know about my previous acting experience. I once played Max-

well Smart in a camp play. Besides that I've done other
parts in my earlier career, i.e., the Roman prince in a Sam-
son play in grade four. . . . I'm convinced I'm a natural for
the cinema. Movie acting is quite simple and the only real
difficult part is memorizing the lines. But I've just had a lot
of practice because I was in Nova Scotia selling encyclope-
dias and my entire sales presentation was word for word
verbatim. Believe me you have to be a good actor to sell 10
sets of books in two weeks. I made quite a bit of money.

Following a suggestion made by my wife, Ted screened *La
Vraie Nature de Bernadette* with Micheline Lanctôt, took the ac-
tress to lunch afterward, and engaged her to play the part of
Yvette. Searching for a likely Duddy, Ted interviewed actors in
Toronto; he also attended the Lennoxville Festival in Quebec's
Eastern Townships. As for me, off on a trip to the Maritimes
with my family, I covered the theaters in Fredericton, Charlotte-
town, and Halifax. In Ingonish, Nova Scotia, just as I was sitting
down to dinner with Florence and the children, Ted caught up
with me by telephone. He was in Los Angeles, and had already
read twenty-five actors for the part. "There's a boy out here
called Dreyfuss," he said, "Richard Dreyfuss. I screened his new
film, it's not out yet, *American Graffiti,* and I've read him twice. I
think he's terrific."

"Well, then?"

"He likes the script. That's no problem. But he does not phys-
ically resemble the boy you described in the novel. Would that
bother you?"

"Go with the best actor."

"He's also been offered a costarring role in a new George C.
Scott picture. I'm seeing him again today."

Dreyfuss signed and, in short order, Ted came up with a fistful
of first-rate actors for the other major roles: Jack Warden, Den-
holm Elliot, Joseph Wiseman, Joe Silver, and Randy Quaid.
Meanwhile, Tim Rouse and others were out hunting for loca-

tions. Among other things, we required an elegant Westmount home with paneled walls and a billiard room. Rouse was warmly received in one highly suitable mansion until the owner asked what, exactly, they would be filming there. "A novel by Mordecai Richler," Rouse replied.

"Richler," the owner said. "Filthy, disgusting fellow. Out!"

Ted had all but secured another location, this one in an old downtown office building, when he, too, revealed that the film was to be based on a novel of mine. "I knew him when he was a boy," the owner said. "He had a big mouth even then. No, thanks."

Which made for a devious but obligatory change in our location-hunting policy. From thereon in, asked what he was filming, Ted beamed and replied: "A lyrical, National Film Board–type story about the struggles of a poor Jewish boy."

One afternoon, I sat with Ted in his office as he interviewed performers. He was, at the time, looking for somebody to play a Main Street hooker. A bosomy stripper, some six feet tall, drifted in. "Did you bring any photographs?" Ted asked.

She showed us a set of color prints of herself taking a bath on stage, her specialty. Even as we ruminated over them, her manager, an ebullient French Canadian, burst through the door. Holding his cupped hands to his chest, simulating breasts, he exclaimed, "If you don't like her, don't worry, I've got them all sizes . . ."

"He's not looking for freaks," the stripper interjected snidely.

". . . fifty girls. Small, medium, large. You name it. I got it."

The stripper, her smile disdainful, said, "He's got one girl with watermelons so big they're going to seed."

Another day Ted was interviewing actors for the part of Cuckoo Caplan, a resort comic, when in walked a man who had actually filled that office at a hotel in the Laurentians in the Forties. Encouraged by Ted, he slipped into his old routines. "I walk onstage. 'Good evening, ladies and germs.' Then I turn to the band. 'Hey, any of you boys know "Clair de Lune"?' The drum-

mer nods. 'Give her my regards, then.' Then I introduce the
singer. 'This girl is very enjoyable. Mind you, she's been enjoyed
before.' I also do imitations. 'Want to see Fredric March?' " As
we sat there, the comic shot out of his chair and marched across
the office.

" 'Fredric March, ladies and germs. Fredric *March.* Get it?' "

We got it, yes, and we also got bad news. Costs, real and anticipated, were escalating wildly. The film had been ridiculously
underbudgeted. Producer and director, natural enemies on any
project, began to tear pieces out of each other. A dreadful sense
of unease, a project in jeopardy, percolated through the unit.
Suddenly, it seemed possible that we would never actually begin
to shoot. One night, even as extras were being signed in an outer
office, Ted, Kemeny, Schneider, and I met in a boardroom.
"Gerry," I said, "have a drink. You're going to need it."

Schneider drank without pleasure.

"We need another seventy-five thousand," I said, "or we
might as well wrap up right now and cut our losses."

Schneider and I had been at Baron Byng High School together, on St. Urbain, and though we had only been nodding ac-
quaintances in those days, we had no difficulty understanding
each other now. He looked from Ted to me and, without blink-
ing, said, "I'm in."

So Ted, Dreyfuss, Micheline Lanctôt, and the camera unit
moved out to Ste.-Agathe to prepare for the first three weeks of
a ten-week shooting schedule. Troubles, troubles. We had taken
over a kosher hotel in the Laurentians, the glory of the Forties,
but now sadly dilapidated. Fences were mended and painted.
Flower beds laid. The tennis courts restored. As carpenters and a
hundred extras milled about, the owner, now eighty years old,
wandered in a daze through his world reclaimed. "Boy, are you
ever in trouble," he warned me.

"What's wrong now?"

Lowering his voice to a whisper, he confided, "Last night in
the dining hall, they served chopped liver *and then borscht with*

sour cream. It's not kosher. Wait till your film comes out. Oi."

Back in Montreal, Ted had found the one cemetery that suited him for a scene in which Duddy attends his uncle's funeral and then asks to see his mother's grave. A tombstone with the name MOLLY was found and the production manager fixed a thick tape underneath, superimposing the name KRAVITZ. He forgot to remove the tape when the unit left, however, and the next day was the very one Molly's son chose to pay respects to his late mother. He was, understandably, shaken to discover that she was now called Kravitz. Seething, he collared the caretaker.

"Me," the caretaker said, "I didn't see a thing. I don't know what happened here."

But Molly's son soon figured it out, and the next morning he threatened to sue. Kotcheff exploded. This was, he insisted, the best shot in the film, and if it was cut he was walking off the production.

The shot was cut, and Ted and the unit moved on to shoot in a synagogue that was procured with tremendous difficulty for the film's bar-mitzvah sequence. The rabbi, anxiety-ridden, lingered in the background, watching as Ted lined up a shot, leading the synagogue's cantor and three actors to their places before the holy ark, a Torah opened before them.

"I would like you to sing in this sequence," Ted said to the cantor.

"It's against my principles," the cantor said.

Ted, his manner ingratiating, shot the cantor a pompous line about the importance of the film and its part in Canadian cultural history.

"It's against my principles to sing," the cantor said.

Perplexed, Ted, who is not Jewish himself, huddled with the rabbi. "What principle is involved?" he asked.

"To tell you the truth," the rabbi said, "I have no idea."

Suddenly inspired, Ted approached the cantor again. "I'll pay you another two hundred dollars to sing," he said.

"O.K.," the cantor said, "I'll sing."

. . .

Shooting was completed in November, in eleven weeks, something like ten days behind schedule, and the film, which ultimately cost just slightly short of $1 million to make, was edited in time for its April opening in Montreal. A charity affair, black tie, $100 a couple, sponsored by ORT at the Place des Arts. The Canadian reviews were all but uniformly splendid, and *The Apprenticeship of Duddy Kravitz* went on to become the first Canadian film to win the major prize at an important international film festival: the Golden Bear Award in Berlin. Later, we also earned the ultimate Canadian accolade, a bit player in the film being the subject of an ad in the *Ottawa Journal* for Pandora's Box, "Canada's biggest and best live nude show."

This week only!
Featuring
the co-star of the movie
The Apprenticeship of Duddy Kravitz
in person
NATACHA

And the next thing we knew there we were in Beverly Hills for Academy Awards night.

Hollywood.

The biggies.

Florence and I were to stay at my agent's house on the Beverly Hills "flats"—an embarrassment—but at least in the 600 block, which, I was relieved to discover, was a three-star-rated neighborhood after all. "Diana Ross lives right around the corner," our driver assured us.

The next morning, I joined Ted, who was now living in Beverly Hills, and another old friend from London for breakfast in

the Polo Lounge of the Beverly Hills Hotel. Clearly, the most affluent of hiring halls. Middle-aged men, bronzed but drawn,
dressed like teenagers, conspired together at tables, Gucci attaché cases thrust between them. Nobody was so involved at his
own table that he didn't scrutinize all the others, checking out
who was complaining to the wrong agent, and which untanned
New York director, bulging out of his safari suit, the hanger
folds still evident, was popping Valium and freshly squeezed orange juice with what producer. To be paged was desirable. To
have the telephone actually brought to your table, heaven. "It's
Sue Mengers on the line. Excuse me a minute, will you?"

At the next table, somebody pleaded that his picture, which
could go through the roof, *I mean really go through the roof,*
would only cost north of $4 million. There was some tax-shelter
money he could sweeten the pot with. "I've got access," he said.

His companion pondered; he fiddled with his book of matches.
"You'd have to bring us one of the *shtarkers.*" A strong man:
Paul Newman, Steve McQueen, or Robert Redford.

Ted motioned me closer. "Take a good look at that man. His
luckiest day was when his last picture dropped two million."

"Why?"

"Because he had already sold more than one hundred and
twenty percent of the profits."

Last year, Ted explained to me, a picture had to be "rele-
vant," but in 1975 the seal of approval was "viable." A studio
never "turned down" a film—it "passed." It was not sufficient
for a film to be "do-able"; it also had to be "go." In quest of further illuminations, I turned to one of the trades, the *Hollywood
Reporter,* where I learned that "Jim Miller, a small-town Montana sheriff who got both paws shot off fighting in Vietnam, is
drawing production-booth raves for his reprising of Harold Rus-
sell's 'Look, ma, no hands!' act in 'The Best Years of Our Lives.'
Jim hooks on to a film career with his hooks into 'Returning
Home,' Lorimar M.O.W. pilot of 'Best Years' spin-off of the
great Goldwyn flick. . . ."

Noon. Lunch with Josh Greenfield, author of the screenplay *Harry and Tonto.* Josh was an old friend. Like me, he had been nominated for an award by the Writers Guild of America, and would be attending their annual banquet that night.

Passing our table, a man paused to ask Josh how his project was going. "You know what a project is?" Josh asked me. "In the old days, in Brooklyn, it was a housing development. Harry, you'd say, has moved into a project. Here it's a film that hasn't got off the ground yet."

Mario Puzo, I learned elsewhere, was getting $300,000 for the first draft of *Superman,* and fifty more big ones for the polish. He was, as they say, bankable. Josh wasn't; neither was I.

I am indebted to Art Buchwald for the following story: A fastidious eastern novelist, suspicious of Hollywood, refused to sell his book to the studios, though it was much in demand. Frantic, his agent invited him out to the Coast, all expenses paid, so that he might judge for himself that film types were not necessarily crass. Alas, nothing worked, and so the agent slyly turned to sex and subterfuge. He invited the novelist to meet him for dinner at the Polo Lounge, but when the novelist arrived he found his agent already seated there with a glamorous young lady. Her date, the agent explained, had stood her up, and so, if the novelist didn't mind, she would join them for dinner. No sooner had the novelist acquiesced than the agent, as prearranged, was summoned to the telephone. He returned, ostensibly dismayed, to say there was a crisis. He had to run. So why didn't the two of them have dinner together? At his expense, of course. Again, the novelist agreed, unaware that the lady was actually a call girl the agent had hired for the occasion.

The next morning, the gleeful agent asked the novelist, "Well, have fun last night?"

"I have been married for twenty years," he replied. "I'm a faithful husband. I love my wife, I adore my children . . ."

"Yes, yes . . ."

". . . but the young lady is one of the most exciting I've ever met. And please don't think badly of me, but I'm taking her out again tonight."

"Oh, no."

"And this time," he added, his voice suddenly charged with bravado, "I wouldn't be surprised if I went to bed with her."

To be fair, Paramount, the studio that distributed *Duddy* in the United States, offered me no such arrangement, but, like the novelist in Buchwald's story, apocryphal or not, I was incredibly naive about the generosity extended to me.

Arriving in New York for the opening of *Duddy* in July 1974, I was met at the airport by a big black limo, had an interview schedule thrust into my hands, and was transported to an immense suite in the Sherry-Netherland. There were red roses for my wife, who couldn't come, and a bottle of champagne riding in an ice bucket, with the compliments of Frank Yablans, then the president of Paramount Pictures. But the publicist who was with me looked around the suite and obviously found it wanting. "They haven't set up your bar."

A quick learner, I exclaimed, "Good grief, yes, where's my bar?"

He scooped up the telephone immediately and within minutes a rattling, fully laden bar was wheeled into my suite. Reviews had not yet appeared, and the film, playing at the Coronet, was doing poorly, but the next morning the Paramount diagnosticians in the swaying Gulf & Western building were all smiles and solicitude. "Everything was soft in New York last night."

When reviews finally did appear, most of them generous, and crowds actually began to materialize, nothing, so far as Paramount was concerned, was good enough for me. Even as I sat in one office, an executive beaming at me, his telephone rang. It was somebody connected with another Paramount film, one that had opened the previous night to singularly dreadful reviews, asking a favor for the film's director. "Tell that cocksucker," the executive shouted, "that there are no more fucking limos for that fucking film," and then, hanging up, he turned back to me, smiling again. "Have you got everything you need?"

One publicist or another chaperoned me to all my interviews. I did badly. Again and again, a reporter, scanning Paramount's release, would say, "I see your novel, published in 1959, was a best-seller."

"It sold twelve hundred copies here."

"In Canada, then?"

"It wasn't a best-seller anywhere."

The film of *Duddy* did well enough in New York and other large cities. And, ignoring the *New Statesman,* the London *Observer,* and the *New York Review of Books,* old intellectual loyalties all, I turned to the altogether headier delights of *Variety,* and became an expert on where we were "hotsy," "boffo," "hefty," or, God help us, "tepid." If we did reasonable business in most first-run cinemas, we were, I'm afraid, largely "tame" or—whisper it—even "limp" in the multiples. Duddy, to enter into the trade idiom, while not exactly a basket case, "lacked legs"— which is to say, we earned money, but not enough, obviously.

And so, come Academy Awards week, my Hollywood epiphany, there was no limo, not even a taxi, waiting at the airport, and it was only by accident I discovered that I had also been nominated for a Writers Guild Award. My agent, Bob Shapiro, managed, with difficulty, to get us four tickets for the banquet. As an afterthought, we were placed next to the door at a table with four Paramount second-floor maids, flacks, each one of whom leaped up, as if stung, when director Francis Ford Coppola or screenwriter Robert Towne entered the ballroom. Paramount production chief Robert Evans, looking like a startled male model, somebody who leaned on sports cars in the back pages of *Gentleman's Quarterly,* sailed past, showering blessings.

I queued up at the bar to buy drinks for our party, returning just in time to catch one of the Paramount flacks signing huge bar bills, one for *The Godfather, Part II* table, another for the *Chinatown* set. Nice, very nice. Then, all at once, it was prize-giving time. Somebody in a western outfit won something for a *Gunsmoke* episode. The award for the best variety special went to *Alan King's Energy Crisis, Rising Prices and Assorted Vices Comedy Hour,* and a mob of writers shot out of their chairs to claim their plaques. The award for the best variety program was won by *The Carol Burnett Show,* and another battalion of writers mounted the dais. There was also something for the best daytime serial, *Search for Tomorrow,* and yet another group of writers rose. Finally, to my surprise, I won a plaque for the screenplay of *Duddy Kravitz.* Mind you, it was for the "Best American [sic] Comedy Adapted from Another Medium," which would take a lot of explaining to the nationalists back home, but let it pass, let it pass. It was a prize, after all.

I returned to my table, a long walk, just in time to see the Paramount flacks sending more drinks to their other winners, Francis Ford Coppola and Robert Towne, but not offering me so much as a soda water. I summoned a waiter and asked him to take a drink, with my compliments, to Mr. Evans. Evans declined, with thanks. Too late, I grasped that what would have been understood as a gesture of contempt in civilized Yellow-knife was mistaken for an act of ingratiation in picayune Hollywood.

O God! O Hollywood!

There were more adjustments to make. Ted Kotcheff, who was driving a Peugeot in those days, was warned, just before he set off to meet a producer in Palm Springs: "What! Are you crazy? You can't pull up in front of the Racquets Club in a little Peugeot. *With a Quebec license plate!* They'll think you're no-body." I also discovered that women, unless they were *impor-tant*—that is to say, stars or agents—were ignored at parties, the men drifting off to their own side of the room, hustling. "If you're going to make it here," a knowledgeable insider told me, "you've got to know how to play the room."

Furthermore, in a company town, nobody was interested in anything but product. Track records. Grosses. Development deals. To mention the Arctic, where I had just come from, was to watch eyes glaze over with boredom, until I finally learned to say not that I had just come down from Yellowknife, but rather that I had returned from location in Yellowknife.

"Oh, really? What are they shooting there?"

Caribou.

A studio executive I met told me that, having left his office for the afternoon, he returned to discover there were twenty-two telephone calls for him to answer. Another executive, whose office I visited, excused himself at one point to go to the toilet. On his return, I told him that his telephone had rung twice. "Took it in the can," he shot back, and then he called for a studio car to take me to Beverly Hills.

"Where you from?" the driver asked.

"Montreal. You?"

Glowing, he replied, "I've been in the film business for ten years." In all that time, he had driven lots of biggies about. And they were, he assured me, mostly very human beings.

Maybe. But I found that conversation with a studio biggie, even at a party, was all but impossible. They were immediately restless, defensive, it being clearly understood you couldn't be without motives, that you must have a proposition, some property you want to move. And it wouldn't do to tell them, yes, certainly, there were things you wanted, but happily it was not within their power to grant them. They wouldn't understand. And so, at parties, increasingly, I found myself retreating to the ladies' corner.

One night, a woman whose husband was a film writer I had known in London pressed my arm and whispered that Harry was working on a new script. I nodded, unimpressed.

"You don't understand," she said. "He's writing it alone. Without a collaborator."

"Yes, indeed."

"Every morning he goes into this room, sits there all alone, *with nobody to bounce things off* and . . ."

". . . writes?"

"Yes," she exclaimed, delighted. "And then he comes out for lunch, a quick sandwich, and do you know what? He goes back into that room, *all alone.*"

"With nobody to bounce things off?"

"Yes!"

"Amazing."

In the morning, I could no longer delay my visit to the House of Uniforms to rent a tuxedo for Academy Awards night. On entering, I was immediately disheartened to espy rack upon rack of outrageous evening wear. Purple velvet, ruffles, suede. I asked, in my most proper Canadian voice, if I might just possibly have a conventional black tuxedo.

"Yes, certainly," the tailor said, bringing something out of the back room. "And now, tell me, sir, will you be wearing high heels or short?"

As we prepared for *the* night, I was given to understand the importance of writers, even the intrepid ones, those who labored alone, in balmy California. Film critic Charles Champlin, making book in the *Los Angeles Times,* speculated on the award chances of actors, actresses, directors, supporting actors and actresses, of cinematography, original score, best song, best sound, best art direction, best costumes, and best editing, but made no mention of writers whatsoever. On the other hand, the *Times* did include some mention of home. California, I read, was enduring the coldest April on record. The mercury had slid into the fifties. The cold front, declared the *Times* unequivocally, came from Canada.

Good, I thought, as my wife and I arrived at the Dorothy Chandler Pavilion in a lashing rain, mobs of fans squealing in the bleachers. The ceremony itself, watched, according to the *Hollywood Reporter,* by no fewer than 65 million Americans, does not bear much comment here. Suffice it to say that once more Bob Hope read one-liners off the TelePrompTer and a hefty Frank Sinatra traded more inane rat-pack jokes with that most singularly unattractive of entertainers, a man whose appeal remains a mystery to me, Sammy Davis, Jr.

Mario Puzo won the award for the best screenplay (*The Godfather, Part II*) adapted from another medium. Josh Greenfield and I, losers both, obviously still unbankable, emerged with our wives into the chaos and storm outside the theater, as men with bullhorns shouted, "Playboy 38, your limousine is here. Mr. Carney, your limousine is waiting. The Governor of New Mexico, your limousine. Art Carney, your limo . . ."

An hour later, we arrived for the banquet at the Beverly Hilton to be greeted by even more frantic fans, autograph books in hand. My wife and I elected not to eat, but to stand at the bar, where we were soon joined by a studio executive, somebody else we knew from our London years.

"The first thing you've got to realize," he said, swaying, "is that nobody, but nobody, has friends here. This isn't London. Forget it." Then, having made his point, he asked me about another novel of mine, *St. Urbain's Horseman.*

"It's very difficult to set up," I confessed.

"O.K., O.K. What would it cost?"

"North of three million."

"Listen," he said, "I'm going to help you. It's action-adventure now. Nobody makes 'interesting' pictures today."

"Look here," I said, sailing on scotch. "*Duddy Kravitz* has made money. It's in the black."

"How much?" he asked.

Trapped, I had to tell him.

"Aw, we're not interested in singles-hitters. At our studio, we only back potential home runs. You've got to give us something that has a chance of going through the roof."

Footnote: My nomination did serve some useful purpose—at least until April 8, the night of the Academy Awards. Leaving a party in the opulent wilds of Bel Air a couple of nights earlier, I asked our hostess if she would be kind enough to call us a taxi.

"A taxi?" she asked.

Fortunately, a young lawyer and his wife, obviously a princess, were standing in the hall. "Where are you going?" he asked.

"Beverly Hills."

"I'll take you as far as the Beverly Wiltshire," he offered, "and you can get a taxi there."

"It's three blocks out of our way," his wife interjected.

Nevertheless, we got into their car.

"Where are you from?" the lawyer's wife asked, her manner sour.

"Montreal."

Displeased, she added, "And what are you doing here?"

"Visiting."

We were, I thought, going to be dropped at the next block. We would have to hitchhike the rest of the way. But, fortunately, the lawyer came to our rescue. Leaning close to his wife, his smile imploring, he whispered, "He's been nominated."

"Oh," she said, smiling, and we were driven all the way home.

The October Crisis,
or
Issue-Envy in Canada

ELSEWHERE—THAT'S THE OPERATIVE WORD. THE BUILT-IN insult. Canadians my generation, sprung to adolescence during World War II, were conditioned to believe the world happened elsewhere. You apprenticed for it in Canada, on the farm with a view, and then you packed your bags and lit out for the golden cities: New York, London, Paris. Home was a good neighborhood, but suburban, even bush, unless you happened to be a hockey player. Of all our boyhood heroes, from Joe DiMaggio to Humphrey Bogart, only hockey players were Canadian *and* undoubtedly the best. Well, *once* undoubtedly the best. While we did have other indigenous heroes, they were badly flawed by being pint-sized versions of an altogether larger American or British presence. They were world-famous—in Canada. Put plainly, any candidate for excellence was bound to be suspect, unless he proved himself under alien skies. The Canadian kid who wanted to be prime minister wasn't thinking big, he was setting a limit to his ambitions rather early.

History, for us, was a spectator sport. Revolution, earthquakes, civil war, racial strife, famine—all were other people's miseries. We had never withstood a Spanish Armada. Or overthrown a tyrant. Why, we even lacked an Alamo. In 1970, after more than a hundred years of confederation, we remained a fragmentary country, yet to be bound by nationhood, a mythology of our own. Mind you, beginning in 1963, we were starting to get a little action.

Terrorists of the Front de Libération du Québec (FLQ) began to plant bombs in Montreal mailboxes and addressed a NO-TICE TO THE POPULATION OF THE STATE [sic] OF QUEBEC calling for INDEPENDENCE OR DEATH. The FLQ manifesto concluded: STUDENTS, WORKERS, PEASANTS, FORM YOUR CLANDESTINE GROUPS AGAINST ANGLO-AMERICAN COLONIALISM.

From 1963 to 1970, every ten days, on the average, a bomb was planted in Quebec Province. But nothing, absolutely nothing, prepared me for the turbulent October of 1970. Watching TV, wide-eyed, in the safety of my study in Kingston Hill, Surrey, I was both flattered and astounded to see my hometown coming up as the first item on the BBC news, intrepid, world-weary reporters broadcasting solemnly from the front line, the very street corners where I used to girl-watch. And then, even as I was preparing a Guy Fawkes bonfire in the backyard for our children, there was a long-distance call from New York. It was *Life* magazine. Could I leave for Montreal immediately?

I didn't get to Montreal until two weeks after the funeral of Quebec Labour Minister Pierre Laporte, who had been kidnapped and murdered by the FLQ. But the FLQ was still holding British Trade Commissioner James Cross. Immediately, enthusiastic friends drove me past consulates, public buildings, and certain rich private mansions, where battle-ready soldiers stood guard. "There are a lot of people who are insulted," I was told, "because they aren't considered important enough to have troops posted outside their door."

Strolling through Westmount, it was impossible not to note the plethora of mountain mansions for sale, seemingly unmovable at bargain prices. Everybody knowledgeable, according to the gossip, was going liquid. A French Canadian novelist I had known for years invited me to lunch at his house, a framed portrait of General Charles de Gaulle glaring down at our table. "It is no longer a question," he assured me, "of if we separate, but when. How soon. Our children no longer call themselves Canadian, but Québécois."

Moving on to Ottawa, I discovered Lester B. Pearson, the amiable seventy-three-year-old former prime minister, in a philosophical mood. "We have never fought for our freedom," he said, "and we have no independent political history." He recalled that when he was a young man, "We were Canadians, yes, but in a British sense; our foreign policy made on Downing Street. We emerged from World War I with newfound pride and confidence, but just at a time when we could have built up something especially our own, we fell under U.S. economic imperialism. Once more we failed to stand on our own feet."

In Toronto, where doom-watching was the style, I found the French Fact was compounded by yet another volatile mixture, resurgent English Canadian nationalism. I tangled with one of the new nationalist zealots, a novelist-cum-publisher. He would not, he told me heatedly, read any American novels, because they were all contaminating.

"Not even Saul Bellow?" I asked.

Not even Bellow.

Bellow, he argued, had a publisher which was owned by a multinational corporation, and this corporation also manufactured electronic equipment that was being used in Vietnam, ergo, old Saul was no better than any other imperialist fascist dog.

But I could have replied, equally perversely, that his publishing firm, albeit radical, was financed by Maclean Hunter. Their flagship, *Maclean's* magazine, welcomed advertisements from Kotex, ergo, he was riding to revolution on a menstrual floodtide of exploited Canadian women and, therefore, was just another male chauvinist pig.

In Ottawa, that same year, nationalism's murky underside,

anti-Americanism, surfaced in a fashion that was embarrassingly coarse. An incensed professor protested against Pierre Elliott Trudeau's right to escort Barbra Streisand to the Manitoba Centennial Party at the National Arts Centre. "Since it is a Canadian birthday," he wrote in the *Citizen,* "one might at least have expected him to appear with a Canadian. But Pierre-baby is a realist. He knows where it's at . . . when you're prime minister of a colony, you appear with one of the princesses of the empire. It's called pragmatism, baby."

Which philosophy, admittedly yet another dirty foreign influence, possibly explained why Trudeau, venturing north later in the year in the hope of establishing our jurisdiction over the Arctic, shlepped Elizabeth II with him, not Barbra. Looked at another way, you can sweet-talk a nice Jewish princess into a weekend in Ottawa, but you can't lead her into the blackfly country. With the Queen, however, it's duty above all.

The spirit of rampaging nationalism was evident in bookshops everywhere. Windows bristled with militant new titles. *Partner to a Behemoth, The Military Policy of a Satellite Canada, The U.S. and Us.*

Suddenly, the land I had always disdainfully thought of as tomorrow country was steaming into sufficiently treacherous waters—the French Canadian lake within and its relationship with the U.S. without—to try its soul. The root issue of many of our troubles, such as they were, remained our linkage (many would say humiliating economic dependency) with the U.S., and its changing nature.

For years, our country was annually depleted by the departure of some of its brightest young men; in 1963 alone over 35,000 Canadians emigrated to the U.S., swelling the numbers of Americans of Canadian origin to over a million, a high proportion of whom were doctors, professors, and businessmen. Since then, we had increasingly come to regard our traditional good neighbors to the south with distaste, even scorn. Symptomatic of the fresh political winds were such books as the best-selling anthology *The New Romans,* wherein Robert Fulford, editor of *Saturday Night* magazine, wrote, "For anyone who loves the U.S., the years since 1964 have been torture. . . . I've always been profoundly grateful that Canada shares this continent with the American people . . . [but] now doubts swarm around me. . . . Vietnam is a terrible disaster for everyone involved; the Vietnamese suffer horribly, but what may finally be even worse is that the American spirit, on which so much of the future of mankind depends, is buckling under the strain. . . ."

Canada, if not exactly buckling, had suffered some fallout, not only from the war in Vietnam, but also from student unrest and black uprisings in the ghettos. This country, remember, isn't where the action is, it's where it reverberates.

In 1968, I returned to Montreal for a year with my family to become a writer-in-residence at Sir George Williams College, now called Concordia University, and there I was to witness yet another variation on the theme of our American dependence. 1968, for anyone even remotely connected with Sir George, will always be remembered as the wasteful season of the Great Computer Fire. To recap briefly. In the winter of '68 a handful of West Indian students, doing badly in biology, charged they were the victims of racial discrimination. Investigations fumbled on, then faltered, activists rallied, and the upshot was occupation and ultimately destruction by ax and fire of the Sir George Williams computer, the damage being estimated at more than $2 million.

It was an ugly business, disheartening too.

I happened to be in Ottawa the night of the conflagration, and only found out about it when I read the morning newspapers. An hour or so later, ruminating in the gallery of the House of Commons, I watched the doyen of our politicians, former Prime Minister John Diefenbaker, rise to deliver one of his vintage one-liners. He wanted to know, in view of the fact that many of the Sir George students had been found with copies of *Quotations from Chairman Mao* on them, if the government should reconsider its policy of recognizing Communist China. Well now, I suspected that many of the student radicals, bunked down in the computer room for days and nights, also had copies of *The Story of O* on them, yet Dief hadn't come out for a ban on sex. Which was a plus, as they say. I also felt that Dief's statement couldn't help but flatter, not to say inflate, the students, some of whom were in the slammer at the time.

Two things struck me most forcibly about the incident. Where there had been no black problem whatsoever, the students had superimposed one out of issue-envy of the country to the south of us. And then, a few days later, there was the student radical who brandished a copy of *Time* at me, gleefully pointing out a full-page article. "Look," he exclaimed, "we made the Education section. Now, when I go down to New York, nobody will ask me again where and what is Sir George Williams."

Come 1970, however, the traffic was in the other direction for the most part. The emigrant tide had been reversed. We were being flooded with U.S. doctors and engineers, university professors in overabundance, and, especially, young draft dodgers— as many as 70,000 between 1967 and 1970. Not everybody in Canada was pleased.

Going back to my student days, the U.S. has always been something we both loved and resented. Loved, because the novels we consumed with appetite, the intellectual as well as the pop cultural ideas that shaped us, were largely American-made. Resented, because to visit New York, brimming with goodwill, and to proffer a Canadian $10 bill was to be told, "What's that, kid, Monopoly money?" To introduce the subject of Canadian politics to socially concerned American friends, fascinated by all things African, was to witness their eyes glaze over with boredom.

Of all the client states in the school of American economic dominance, we were not so much the rank-one boy as teacher's pet; no nose-picker or truant, like Fidel, or irretrievable delinquent, like Ché, but the freckled fink who volunteers to wipe blackboards clean and never omits to practice the Ten Rules of Hygiene as set down by the Junior Red Cross. So we never had to stay in after school to endure a Bay of Pigs. Or be punished with a Santo Domingo. Instead we were blessed with branch plants by General Motors, Ford, and the rest. Flattered, we did not come to school merely with apples. Instead we laid everything on the table. You need oil? Come and get it. Iron ore you want? Take. Pulp and paper? Enjoy, enjoy. Natural gas? Uranium? Nickel? Help yourself. With the disheartening and potentially explosive result that in 1970, the U.S. owned more than 50 percent of our basic industries.

We had not only given the U.S. our iron and oil, whiskey during prohibition, eight-year-old Saul Bellow (from Lachine, Quebec), Deanna Durbin, Bobby Orr, Harlequin paperbacks, pitcher Ferguson Jenkins and catcher George Chuvalo, Walter Pidgeon, Norma Shearer, Lillian Gish, onetime Public Enemy No. 1 Alvin Karpis, John Kenneth Galbraith, Donald Sutherland, the RCAF exercise book, Jack Kent Cooke, Louis B. Mayer, and the musical score for *Hair,* but, above all, Superman. He was created by Toronto-born cartoonist Joe Shuster, which made Superman's assumed identity of bland Clark Kent not merely understandable, but artistically inevitable. Come 1970, however, Canada, traditionally seen as mild Clark Kent, had done a quick change in the political telephone booth. We emerged from World War II into a fleshpot of prosperity, but this big payday had been bought by mortgaging the land to America, and now young politically conscious Canadians were indignant at having been left with the debt. Indignant and unforgiving.

To be fair, there was only a modest pool of development capital in Canada to begin with; it is also true to say that Canadians are notoriously cautious, and for years the custodians of the big money secured it in stormproof trust companies, rather than risk it as venture capital. Simultaneously, our timorous capitalists appeared in public as indefatigable tub-thumpers, assuring us, as late as the '50s, that Canada was on the very brink of greatness.

The prime minister of my boyhood, William Lyon Mackenzie King, was in office twenty-two years and, possibly to my credit and his advantage, I cannot recall any of his pronouncements. But I do remember him standing awfully close to Roosevelt and Churchill in wartime photographs, a beaver badly in need of a bear's hug. Arguably he was an Aquarian before his time, deeply committed to his own (very peculiar) thing. In Laurier House, King's residence that is now maintained as a museum, you are proudly shown, among other curiosa, the former prime minister's crystal ball. He was, of course, a spiritualist, a bachelor fervently devoted to his mother's memory, and nightly for twenty-two years he sat by his crystal ball, beneath an illuminated portrait of his mum, and rapped with her spirit, seeking guidance on how much to tax, when to call an election, and where to send the troops.

Our next memorable prime minister, old Johnny Diefenbaker, made an enormous fuss over his red NORAD emergency telephone, the hot line that connected his Ottawa outpost directly to the head office, the president of the U.S. Diefenbaker habitually kept his hot line in full view, hoping to bedazzle visitors. "I can get Ike anytime," he would say.

Lester Pearson—Peter Newman wrote in *The Distemper of Our Times*—not only removed the offending telephone from his desk, but concealed it so carelessly that when it rang one winter's morning in 1964, he couldn't find it. Paul Martin, then the minister of external affairs, was with the PM at the time.

"My God," Martin exclaimed, "do you realize this could mean war?"

"No," Pearson said. "They can't start a war if we don't answer it."

Finally the telephone was discovered behind a curtain, and the caller, who wanted to speak to "Charlie," turned out to have the wrong number; incidentally, the most top-secret number in Ottawa.

In 1961, Mort Sahl, come to Toronto to entertain, was confronted by a nationalist zealot. "Do you realize," he charged, "that this country hasn't even got a flag?"

"That's a start," Sahl replied.

In 1965 we acquired a flag of our own, in 1967 we got Expo, and in 1968 Prime Minister Pierre Elliott Trudeau. It was on an extended visit to Ottawa in 1968 that I first met Trudeau, then Minister of Justice. Certainly he was the most intellectually resourceful and charming politician I encountered in the capital, but if anyone had suggested that within months, he would succeed Pearson as Liberal leader and, furthermore, ride into power with a majority government, I would have thought him demented. Obviously, this bachelor, brave enough to venture that the state had no business in the nation's bedrooms, legalizing homosexuality between consenting adults, was too chic, too French, for western Canada. And as far as Quebec's smoldering intellectuals were concerned, he was "Lord Elliott." Ride into power he did, however, wafted thereto on waves of Trudeaumania, as it was called. For a country without a mythology, here was the promise of a hero. For the first time within my experience, sophisticated Canadians argued heatedly, without cover of the usual self-deprecating jokes, about our political affairs. Gifted and ambitious young men, traditionally scornful of Ottawa, were suddenly eager to serve.

When I next met Trudeau, in the spring of 1969, disenchantment had set in, beginning to harden. Hustle wheat, not women, the West enjoined him. And to the dismay of once-smitten editors, academics, and TV brokers, who had helped shoulder Trudeau to power, our country had not, overnight, quit NATO or redeemed our resources from the U.S. Trudeau's "Just Society" was still a catch phrase. But, above all, the public image had begun to pall. To those who had labored through the night to elect a man they took for a complete Gene McCarthy, it seemed, on wakening, that they had thrust Fred Astaire into office. Sliding down banisters and doing the boogaloo while Canada began to fracture. Ever with a delicious young thing, a *Candy* rather than an attaché case to hand. But, tiresome swinger's image notwithstanding, the truth was that in private he was working assiduously all along. To see him in 1969 looking oddly fragile, even monkish, in his own sitting room was to be totally disarmed. Trudeau was certainly arrogant, even boyishly vain. But once more I was struck by his candor, his self-evident pleasure in people and places, and the feeling that, come a crisis, he had plenty to draw on.

We weren't to meet again until several weeks after the FLQ terrorists had brutally murdered Pierre Laporte. James Cross was still missing, possibly "executed" as well. Trudeau had already invoked a World War I security act, sending troops streaming into Montreal, claiming there had been a "state of insurrection, real or apprehended" in the province. At lunch, he adamantly insisted that given the climate in Montreal following the kidnappings—abandoned streets, deserted restaurants— there had been nothing else for it. Possibly. But once recovered from the initial shock, early intellectual boosters of Trudeau, especially in Toronto, were horrified and turned against him. George Bain, of the *Globe & Mail*, made a particularly telling point. If, Bain ventured, "because of some terrorist act in, say, the South, the president of the United States had proclaimed orders under which persons could be picked up on suspicion, denied bail, and held for up to 90 days without a trial, the thicket of protesters outside the U.S. Consulate on University Avenue in Toronto would have been impenetrable. It is a peculiar Canadian trait to be able to spot an inequity better at a distance, especially if facing south, than close up."

Speaking off the cuff to Ontario students in 1968, Trudeau had observed, "If in the next half-dozen years we see great riots and the beginnings of civil war in the U.S., there is no doubt it will overflow the borders and link up with underprivileged Mexicans and Canadians. We are not threatened by communism or fascism or even by atomic bombs as much as we are by the fact that very large sections of our society do not find fulfilment in our society."

In Ottawa, during the October Crisis, he was disposed to chat with me about Sartre, Fanon, and Marcuse, rather than the daily political grind. "Traditionally," he said, "French Canadian intellectuals lack vigor. They tend to build castles in the sky."

Trudeau was totally committed to a federal, bilingual Canada. In the long run, if he earned one, I felt he was right. Still only a loosely connected union of convenience, its regional needs exasperatingly contradictory, Canada had now either to knit together as a country or fragment, wasting like Ireland, Montreal filling Belfast's depressing office. Separatism for Quebec would be the undoing of English Canada, possibly reducing it to an inchoate jigsaw of Balkanlike states, and it would serve French Canada even worse. As Lester Pearson told me, "Independent, they would become even more dependent."

But in the short run, I felt, at the time, that Trudeau could be undone by his autocratic manner, his inability to suffer fools, admirable in private life, self-indulgent in a politician.

There were other dangers. Trudeau, by inclination, pursued a privileged life, festooned with glitter. The people he cultivated were uncommonly bright or beautiful or accomplished, whether they were writers or academics or architects or filmmakers. He mingled with the stars, not the studio chars. Mean lives, the condition, after all, of much of the electorate, were not in his idiom.

This is not to say that he didn't care, but that, on his part, it had to be an effort of will.

But the leader of the Parti Québécois, René Lévesque, whom I met in an East End Montreal restaurant, seemed effortlessly in touch with the bookkeeper with sour breath, the wasting clerk with dandruff, the abandoned mother of five, the truck driver on welfare, in fact with all the discontented lives. The chain-smoking Lévesque seemed obviously, even dangerously, weary, high-strung and romantically wrong politically. But, at that first meeting, I took him for an authentic people's tribune. The lean man of stature who had to be answered, if we were to survive as a nation.

Trudeau was obviously right when he pointed out that it had been the acquiescence of French Canadians, as well as the avarice of the English Canadians, that had allowed the Québécois to drift as second-class citizens for too long; they have never been without a vote. And yet—and yet—Lévesque was also right when he insisted that Quebec—35 percent of Canada's population, 6.5 million people with their own language and culture—was simply not a province like the others. They had bona fide grievances and in 1970 were still suffering unnecessary insults.

Item: In Montreal, I went to see David Molson, who then ran the Canadiens hockey team for the brewery family, one of the richest in Canada.

"Of all the old WASP families in the province," he said, "ours has always been closest to the natives."

Were his children, I asked, bilingual?

"We have a French maid in the house," he said, "and the children are taking advantage of it. They're learning."

Item: A Montreal friend of mine, thoroughly bilingual, and speaking French, attempted to book a flight at Toronto airport. But absolutely nobody at the Air Canada desk could understand him. The help of a Dutch immigrant porter was enlisted and my friend was led onto the airplane grasping a form with the following disabilities listed: FIRST FLIGHT, BASSINET AUTH., SPECIAL

MEAL, WHEELCHAIR. X'd off in his idiot's case was SPEAKS FRENCH ONLY.

Finally, what impressed me most as I skittered between Montreal, Toronto, and Ottawa, several weeks after the War Measures Act had been introduced, was that while some people were gravely concerned, many more burned with a rosy glow of inner satisfaction. If we had not yet earned an earthquake or a famine, defeated a Spanish Armada or died in an Alamo, then tribal strife and civil war were rumored, maybe even possible. The world, so long elsewhere, might at last pay Canada a visit.

Hello, hello.

The streets of Montreal, Trudeau had said at lunch, were abandoned, and that was why he had been driven to bring in the War Measures Act. But the streets, I felt, had been abandoned not because Montrealers were afraid, but because they were all gathered gleefully round their TV sets, waiting for Walter Cronkite to pronounce. Look, look, there we are. Real at last. On CBS, NBC, ABC. Montreal, our Montreal, making prime time. How about that?

In Ottawa, a small group of terrorists, scanned through a magnifying glass, was pronounced a state of real or apprehended insurrection. In Toronto, outraged liberals responded by comparing Trudeau's government to that of the Greek colonels. Fascism, we were warned, was just around the corner. In Quebec, separatists, identifying with exploited black Africans, and finding their own condition worse, compared mild English-speaking Quebecers to rampaging white Rhodesians. Those who had not been rounded up by the cops, and briefly imprisoned, sulked, while those who had been in the slammer walked tall about Crescent and St. Denis streets, everybody standing them to drinks. But at the day's end, at the risk of appearing callous, I must say damn little actually did happen in 1970. In an American year in which there were 13,649 homicides, eighty cops were killed, and Weathermen blew up banks and university buildings, in Canada a politician was murdered and a diplomat kidnapped, later to be freed. Everybody in the house, not only Trudeau, overreacted. To some extent, I think, out of issue-envy.

On the Road

IN THE SPRING OF 1975, I FOUND MYSELF SEATED IN THE STU-
dio of a rather tacky radio station in midtown New York, a guest
on *The Joey Adams Show*. I was there, at my publisher's request,
to plug shamelessly a children's book I had written. Joey had yet
to arrive. But, anticipating his appearance, the man responsible
for the commercials squeezed my arm, his manner urgent, and
warned me, "Joey likes jokes. Think of some jokes. Quick! Here
he comes!"

Joey sat down, nodded abruptly, and announced to the waiting
public, "We have another brilliant, talented author with us this
morning, um," and, consulting his script, he added, "Mordecai
Rikkler."

"Richler," I interrupted compulsively.

"Author of *Jacob Tooty and the Hooded Fang*."

"Excuse me, no, it's *Jacob Two-Two Meets the Hooded Fang*."

Even as Joey sat there, glaring at me, the announcer inter-
vened, "And I'm sure Mr. Rikkler's book is mighty fine. Just
like Mi-T-Fine kosher puddings, which come in eight different
flavors . . ."

"Why'd you write it?" Joey demanded.

"For our children, in the first place. We have five."

"You mean," Joey ventured, grinning, "you didn't want anybody else to read it?"

"Ho, ho, ho."

"What's wrong with it?"

Stung, I was driven to pointing out that the book had gone
into a second printing. But I was up against a real pro.

"What was wrong with the first one?" Joey asked, heaving with laughter. "Was it smudged?"

In a more decent age, before writers were flattered into becoming radio and TV fodder, if we ran into one another at all it was in bars, where we could knock each other's books, or at the publisher's rare cocktail party, where the drinks were free, and you could usually sneak off into an empty office to make a long-distance call. But nothing delights a publisher more these days than punishing a writer who may never earn his advance by sending him out on the road, if only because the publisher can announce to the sales conference that this or that author will be getting "national exposure." Barbara Walters will bless, Johnny Carson will be at home.

I don't really think this kind of exposure helps with the sales of most respectable books. There are about 650 TV and radio talk shows across the United States that use authors. My guess is that these shows appeal mostly to nonreaders, but publishers seem to like them because they give writers the idea that somebody is doing something to help along with their books.

And so authors keep colliding in airports and hotel elevators at dawn, this one returning from a late show in Boston, that one bound for an early-morning shot in San Francisco, where between the inevitable cooking demonstration and local sports roundup, he will demand that the folks out there read more fiction, beginning with his own, preferably. Unless he has written this season's eat-fat-grow-slim diet book or a new, graphically illustrated sex manual . . .

"I'm sorry I can't hold up the book and show any of the illustrations to your audience, but, ah, there might be children watching."

"Or even adults who might find it obscene."

"*Obscene?* Eight people making love together in a gym is not obscene. It's sharing. An act of discovery. Watergate, *that's* obscene."

Though I enjoy traveling at somebody else's expense, I fail to understand how anyone out there could be interested in the most frequently asked questions. How many hours a day do you work, and do you write in longhand, using a quill, wearing your feather boa and silk dressing gown from Cardin, or do you tap it right out on a typewriter, while picking your nose? But I think I now understand why writers, many of whom tend to be shy, even incoherent, in public, are in such demand on radio and TV talk shows. We usually come free of charge, provided by publishers, just as the garages of my boyhood used to offer free blotters.

In impoverished England, with its richer cultural history, there is a clearer understanding of what most inspires a novelist between books—which is to say, no writer is asked to appear on radio or TV without a fee. The BBC, in my experience, also unfailingly sends a taxi to pick you up, and before being thrust into a studio, you are led into a hospitality suite, the booze flowing freely. This, it's true, adds a certain element of risk to proceedings that are otherwise predictable. On one memorable occasion Brendan Behan burst into song in mid-interview. Another time, a friend of mine never made it out of the hospitality suite, sliding to the floor and passing out just before "national exposure" time.

But in New York, Detroit, and Chicago, there are no perks. The best you can hope for on arrival at the studio is something brown, reminiscent of coffee, poured into a Styrofoam cup that, in most cases, you are advised to hold on to as it must also serve as your on-camera ashtray.

Once, asked to promote a book of my short stories, I grudgingly embarked on just such a tour, waving, in passing, at other benumbed writers, appropriately embarrassed but, all the same, out there, like me, peddling. Whether it was Washington, Baltimore, or Boston, each morning began with a 6:30 A.M. wake-up call, before breakfast was available in any hotel; and a dash to a studio on the outskirts, where I was greeted by what seemed to be the same zippy host, his smile menacingly cheerful even at that hour, armed with the same fact sheet, asking the same questions. Again and again in my case, on the evidence of the film of my novel *The Apprenticeship of Duddy Kravitz:* "Are you—well, you know, an anti-Semite?" The tenth time around I was tempted, emulating William Faulkner, to smile sweetly and reply yes, yes indeed, but I didn't like gentiles either. However, good sense—or, more likely, cowardice—prevailed, and for the tenth time I fumbled through my rehearsed response. "The writer's, ah, function, well, um, is primarily critical and, um . . ."

No sooner did I fly home, boorishly refusing to answer my family's questions about the tour, feeling that to have lived through it once was sufficient, than I was off again, this time to speak at the *Detroit News* Book and Author Luncheon as well as handle the usual batch of TV and radio interviews. Upon arrival in a seemingly abandoned city at 7:30 on a Sunday evening, I checked into the Hotel Pontchartrain. The desk man, noting my Canadian address, cautioned me, "You're in Detroit now. You're not to go out for a walk. Right?"

At 6:45 the next morning, I turned up as scheduled at TV-2 News, and there I encountered another scheduled speaker at the lunch, Irving Stone. After lighting up a Schimmelpenninck, a Dutch cigarillo, I offered him my hand. Stone, glowering, snapped, "You're not going to blow that stuff in my face on camera, are you?"

At lunch, Stone began by telling the audience of 1,200 ladies that they were wonderful, absolutely wonderful; obviously not a walker, he added how pleased he was to be in Detroit. "Why," he asked in a booming voice, "do people read my books? I don't deal in sex or violence."

The ladies applauded.

"They read my books because I tell great human stories!"

More applause.

"And what are the great human stories?" he asked. *"Tom Jones, The Brothers Karamazov, War and Peace, Madame Bovary."*

Stone, a fine performer, speaking without notes, told the ladies that he did not want them to read his books, *no,* he wanted the ladies to *live* them, just as he had not merely written his historical novels, but had actually *become* Van Gogh and Michelangelo.

Well now, I've never been to Stone's house in Beverly Hills, and so I don't know what magic he's done to his ceilings, but I'm willing to swear he wasn't missing an ear. Anyway, I was grateful for the sake of all the ladies present that he hadn't also written *The Carpetbaggers.*

I appeared with Stone again on a radio show later in the afternoon; there was a live audience.

"Today," our ebullient host declared, "we have with us the great American novelist Irving Stone; one of the world's ten best-dressed men, actor George Hamilton; and a writer from Canada."

Soon Stone was saying, "Why do people read my books? I don't deal in sex or violence. They read my books because I tell great human stories. . . ."

"And exactly how many books have you written, Mr. Stone?"

"Twenty-five."

"Twenty-five. That's amazing. And how many years did each one take?"

"Four."

George Hamilton was wearing a gold bracelet and gold ring; the first two buttons of his shirt were undone. As Irving Stone lived his books, so George Hamilton said he lived the characters he played. Then, turning to me, he added how much he had disliked the film of *Duddy Kravitz.* You start out by liking the character, he said, finding him funny, and then you discover he's nasty. With John Wayne, he pointed out, you always knew where you stood.

Now it was my turn to shine. Our host, glancing at the studio clock, said, "Sorry we never got a chance to mention your book."

"Pourquoi Pas?" —
a Letter from Ottawa

SAY WHAT YOU LIKE ABOUT CANADIANS, WE ARE, HISTORI-
cally, big givers. But what (*if anything,* the nationalists would say)
was left to present the U.S.A. for its 1976 Bicentennial? Bobby
Orr was already there. So was Ottawa's very own Paul Anka.
Prince Edward Island was too expensive to wrap; Baffin Island,
even bigger, was bound to melt en route. And so in 1975 a committee of Ottawa mandarins, backs to the wall, pondered and
pondered, finally surfacing with a grabber. *A picture book.* Our
government allocated $1.5 million to produce a book, compiled
by our leading photographers, of Canadian-American border
scenes (not, one hoped, including draft dodgers sneaking home
through the tall grass), and elegantly wrapped freebies were to be
presented to senators, congressmen, and small-town mayors—in
fact, to most American elected officials, as well as President
Ford.

Happy birthday, U.S.A., happy birthday to you! In 1976, they
got not so much a gift book as a Canadian *Whole Earth Catalog,*
showing what was left on the shelves, prices available from Ottawa on request.

It was not only a singularly unimaginative gift, but a grudging
one. Which is to say, there was trouble out here on the tundra.
The natives, reduced to tenant farmers on their own estate, were
growing restless. *And creative.* As witness a recent issue of *The*

Independencer, a bimonthly published by a hard-line nationalist faction known as the Committee for an Independent Canada. The paper displayed a stirring two-page-long poem, the group inspiration of the Lorna Mayfield Chapter. Called "The Canadian Children's Plea," it began:

> Please, Mr. Prime Minister,
>   don't sell us out to the USA!
> Please, Mr. Prime Minister,
>   don't give our heritage away!
> When we are grown and take
>   our place as men and women
>   of our race,
> We want to be FREE—to control
>   —to decide; not to the will
>   of a giant tied!

No less talented is another writer prized by the independencers. Reserve Air Force General Richard Rohmer, *our* Steve Canyon, whose most recent novel, *Exxoneration,* was a Canadian best-seller. *Exxoneration* begins where Rohmer's earlier political dream, *Ultimatum,* ended, with the American president, at 6:30 P.M., October 7, 1980, announcing the annexation of Canada, and our governor general seeing no alternative but to "follow the instructions of the president," even as U.S. Air Force planes are landing at all Canadian air bases to begin occupation of the country. But wait, wait, the imperialists' fascist bullies hadn't counted on *Exxoneration*'s hero, the incomparable Pierre Thomas de Gaspé, of whom our prime minister says, "There is something I didn't know about, that is that de Gaspé, as well as being president of the Canada Energy Corporation, is also your Toronto district commander and is running Operation Reception Party at Toronto International Airport. God, how versatile can a man be!"

Even the Texan president of the U.S.A. respects us, thanks to de Gaspé. "Sure the United States owns most of the country. But those people have a fighting record in the First World War and the Second World War like you wouldn't believe."

De Gaspé's Operation Reception Party totally defeats the superior American invading force, and the crushed U.S. Air Force general, just possibly a southerner, is moved to comment: "Ah gotta hand it to you all, you sure gave it to us good. Ah didn't know you Canadians had that much gumption, but ah sure know it now and ah take my hat off to you."

Rohmer is also a master of the British idiom. The American invasion defeated, de Gaspé moved to take over Exxon, his machinations taking him to an exclusive Mayfair hotel, where the valet porter awaits him. "Mr. Reimer and another gentleman are waiting for you in the sitting room, Mr. de Gaspé! Cor, you ought to see the chap with 'im. Cor blimey!"

Ultimately, the Texan president is defeated in an election by none other than David Dennis, the first Jewish president of the U.S.A., who says of his trip to Israel: "Such a welcome. For a Jewish boy from Detroit, a boy who's come up the hard way . . ."

Rohmer's novel put me in mind of my deprived World War II boyhood in Montreal, where, with American comic books unavailable for the duration, we had to make do with our own inferior black-and-white inventions, but I should add that the sales of *Exxoneration* were prodigious for Canada, something like 18,000. Even so, nationalists protested, with some justice, that the Canadian publishing industry was being swamped by the American—also with some justice, alas. For we are only some 15 million (English-speaking, that is) and they are more than 200 million, and we are dependent on American publishers not only for their own books but also for almost all British and European and Asian books we receive in translation. So, naturally enough, American publishers provide most of the books for those of us who still read for pleasure, rather than as a patriotic duty.

· · ·

Item: After my return to Canada, in 1972, it was my good luck to hear from the Committee for an Independent Canada directly. Their letter, which actually sprang from the committee's cultural think tank, began: "Dear Author, You have been chosen along with seventy-nine other major contemporary authors to present your views. . . ."

Seemingly, if on my departure for England twenty years earlier the flower of Canadian letters, like the British Liberal Party, could fit snugly into a taxi, now a veritable charabanc was called for. Since then, the nationalists had made it clear that they were determined to win through legislation, for the second-rate but homegrown writer, what talent alone had hitherto denied him: an audience, applause. In 1973, they argued, of the $291 million spent on English-language books in Canada, only $15 million was for books written and published by Canadians. Furthermore, only 2 percent of the paperback books sold on the Canadian mass market were in fact written and published by Canadians, which made things hot for Ottawa in general, Hugh Faulkner in particular. A representation was made to Faulkner, then our secretary of state, the minister responsible for cultural affairs, by the militant Independent Publishers' Association. He was asked to consider, among other enormities, Canadian content quotas that would oblige bookshops and those who maintain paperback racks, as well as the foreign book clubs operating in Canada (Book-of-the-Month Club, Literary Guild), to display or offer as much as 20 percent Canadian content.

Following the narcotics squad, after the antisubversive division, enter the RCMP paperback detail—plainclothes, of course— each constable only five-foot-four, bespectacled, checking out your corner drugstore and newsie against his Canadian-content pocket calculator. And if, perchance, it only registered 19 percent indigenous shlock, he would run them in, charged with displaying too many Wallaces, Robbinses, and Susanns, while concealing their slower-moving Canadian imitators under the counter, like condoms. Fortunately, Faulkner wouldn't buy, telling our own variation of the Red Guard, "The right to read is basic. The Canadian public will want to read foreign books, to have access to them, and to have them reviewed in the Canadian media. Publishing is an international activity judged by international standards. Canadian publishing is necessarily judged against the output of foreign publishing, and often by the best of foreign publishing. That is as it should be." But Faulkner did come up with a suggestion of dubious value, a program that would make book display racks of Canadiana available in post offices. Now if, as one Ottawa wag put it, the post office handled books no better than they did mail . . .

Meanwhile, Jack Stoddart, then our only publisher of mass-market paperbacks (Paperjacks), complained that he couldn't compete with American reprint houses who were poaching here, seeking only well-known and established authors. "If they get the top authors," he said, "none of us will be able to afford to develop new authors." Consequently, with the surprising support of the newly formed Writers Union of Canada, he called for a six-month moratorium on the sale of rights to U.S. paperback houses. Hugh Kane, then vice-chairman of Macmillan, refused to subscribe. "We have," he said, "an obligation to serve our authors to the best of our ability." And what's more, said the plain-spoken Kane, the moratorium would simply protect Paperjacks, the only real Canadian presence in the field, from any competition.

Even so, I had a grudging sympathy for Stoddart's dilemma until I happened to espy one of his model contracts. It appeared that his concern for developing Canadian authors was so deeply felt that in paying for the Canadian rights he also acquired an exclusive license to print, publish, and sell, in the U.S.A. and British Commonwealth, and, fully grasping that too much bread was bad medicine for scribblers, paid them only 50 percent for these aforementioned rights. Some, admittedly, might have protested that Stoddart was brandishing nationalism as a shield for sharp practice, but that would only have revealed woeful ignorance of the nationalist idiom. Look here, for an American publisher to seek Canadian rights was cultural imperialism, but for a Canadian to demand U.S. and Commonwealth rights, creaming 50 percent off the top, was to protect innocent colonials from foreign exploitation.

Content quotas, already imposed on Canadian television, made for some decidedly Talmudic conundrums. If, for instance, our hired southern crackers play the American crackers, that is to say, the Montreal Expos take to the field against the Dodgers in L.A., and this is broadcast on CBC-TV, is it 100 percent Canadian content? Fifty percent? Or does it depend on the final score? Similarly if a bona fide Canadian publisher were to bring out a book on the Philadelphia Flyers, Canadian roughnecks to the man, would this be Canadian or American content?

Who knows, and who cares, was the subject of an outraged article (*Toronto Globe & Mail*, March 22, 1975) by a frequent visitor to Ottawa, one of our more impassioned Canada-firsters, the publisher Mel Hurtig. "One year ago," Hurtig wrote, "the Surrey-Langley chapter of the Committee for an Independent Canada conducted a 'Canadian Awareness Survey' of students in their last year of high school in six schools in and around Vancouver. When I read the results I was in turn stunned, dismayed and skeptical."

For example:

Fewer than 30% could identify the B.N.A. Act as Canada's constitution. The Magna Carta, Declaration of Independence and Bill of Rights were frequent answers.

71% could not name the capital of New Brunswick.

Asked to name any three Canadian authors, 61% were unable to do so. Pierre Berton was named by only 20%, Farley Mowat by 19%. All of the following were named by

fewer than 5%: Eric Nicol, Leonard Cohen, Stephen Leacock, Emily Carr, Mordecai Richler and Morley Callaghan.

Me, I'm not stunned or dismayed. I'm flattered. For I take it
that less than 5 percent of high school students in and around,
say, Santa Barbara would know if Philip Roth was a delicatessen,
Bernard Malamud a furrier, or Saul Bellow an orthodontist.

Something else.

One student, embarrassed to have flunked his Canadian
awareness test, a student whom Hurtig quoted with something
like despair, I, on the other hand, applaud for redeeming himself
with a quality distinctly Canadian—a self-deprecating sense of
humor. His comment: "Margaret Atwood, Margaret Laurence
—never heard of them, so they must be Canadian."

I had my own experience of Canadian students in Ottawa, at
Carleton University, where I was a visiting professor for two
years.

One morning, early in September 1972, newly if uneasily ensconced in my professorial office, I set out to interview applicants
for the dubious course I was offering: English 298, a writing
seminar. Outside my window there stretched the Rideau Canal.
In the seemingly endless winter months ahead, it would be transformed into the longest and, probably, most delightful man-made
skating rink in the world, threading through the capital and its
environs for four and a quarter miles, providing noon-hour play
not only for children, but also for civil servants and MPs. Come
December, many a colleague, and even more students, would
skate three miles to classes.

The students who drifted into my office that morning were
engaging, and touchingly vulnerable, but I was shocked, even
appalled, by how little most of them had managed to read. One
young man in particular permanently endeared himself to me. I
asked him, as I had all the others, "What's the last novel you

read?" But this groovy Aquarian wasn't going to be conned by a loaded question from an aging writer. He searched the ceiling; he contemplated the floor. Finally, his eyes lit with triumph, he asked, "Fiction or nonfiction?"

Our capital, for years no better than a cow town, without so much as one decent restaurant, is still the subject of Main Street–like scandals. On a recent visit, for instance, I was confronted by an announcement on the front page of the *Citizen* proclaiming that it had suspended body-rub shops and services from its ad columns until such time as the newspaper was satisfied that such spas as Pandora's Health Studio, with its beautiful nude hostesses, the Bodee-shop, and the Tempest ("Everything in a Man's Dream") *were not fronts for bawdy houses.* The next day a street-smart reporter repaired incognito (and, I hope, freshly showered) to test the health services available and discovered, "A massage it ain't." One solicitous hostess suggested, "For another five dollars I can stay in the room and watch you masturbate."

To be fair, Ottawa had now been much enhanced not only by its marvelous skating rink, but also by the building of the National Arts Centre, which opened in 1969 on a splendid six-acre site in the heart of the city, bounded by Confederation Square and the Rideau Canal. Admittedly, the concrete slablike exterior is forbidding, suggesting culture is a sentence, not a pleasure, but the facilities are magnificent, and the orchestra first-rate. There are three halls, including a 2,300-seat opera house, a semicircular 900-seat theater, and a smaller, more experimental studio. The NAC complex also boasts one of the few decent restaurants in town, l'Opéra.

L'Opéra has displaced the more traditional Canadian Grill of the Château Laurier, its food unbelievably bad, as the favored lunchtime watering spot of cabinet ministers, civil servant mandarins, and general staff officers of our fairly new unified military command. The latter, clustered around the bar, in their uncommonly drab olive-green uniforms, looked more like Bavarian bus conductors or commissionaires than soldiers, sailors, or airmen. I was not so much tempted to salute as to offer them my coat, rubbers, and fifty cents.

On a visit to l'Opéra, I dined with Marc Lalonde, one of the most astute politicians in town. Lalonde, like Trudeau a former Montreal law professor, was for some years the prime minister's principal secretary and adviser, but had since been elected to Parliament himself. At the time, he was our highly successful minister of national health and welfare, his future prospects marred by a tendency to slip on banana peels. On an official visit to Israel a year earlier, for instance, he had been sufficiently naïve to fly on a Bronfman private jet, Air Seagram, which had led to some embarrassing questions in the house. Even more recently, when it was revealed that the hamburger meat on sale in Canada was often laden with impure ballast—that is to say, animal dung—Lalonde declared that proper cooking would eliminate any danger, which was as close as the Liberals, notably arrogant, had ever come to saying, "Let them eat shit."

Lalonde, who was also the minister for women's rights, sailed into l'Opéra, his smile radiant and, 1975 being International Women's Year, a committed badge riding his jacket lapel. The badge, which was being offered to Canadian women everywhere, was rather more ambiguous than militant. Clearly not recommended for wear in singles bars. It read: *"Pourquoi Pas?"*

Lalonde professed not to be worried about Quebec and separatism. A recent Gallup Poll had revealed that only 40 percent of Quebecers felt that separatism was coming, whereas five years earlier 51 percent had believed it all but inevitable. Even so, that was 40 percent, and the Liberal government still in office in Quebec at the time, led by an ineffectual Robert Bourassa, was sinking in an all too familiar sea of corruption, one damning investigation following another. Lalonde responded rather weakly, "At least the government is investigating itself." Lalonde also felt that obviously our traditional state of dependency on the U.S.A. was no longer what it was. "We've got more options," he said, "for now it's the producers of energy who can be more choosy. The continentalist energy policy," he added, "is a trap, when we are only 20 million and they are 200 million." But he did admit to feeling genuinely uneasy about some aspects of the new legislation aimed at ending the special advertising privileges of *Time* and *Reader's Digest* in Canada.

The legislation, proposed by Hugh Faulkner, would finally do away with the provision that allowed Canadian companies to deduct expenses from their income tax when they advertised in the American-owned *Time* or *Reader's Digest*. This was a ruling that Canadian-owned magazines had been ardently seeking for years, arguing that only this had prevented the development of a genuinely indigenous national magazine. In presenting the proposed amendment to the income tax act, Faulkner said, "We in the government are not so much concerned with certain of the nation's industries as we are deeply committed to the nation's integrity. What happens in the area of Canadian books, magazines, and broadcasting, as in other areas of Canadian cultural expression, is not a matter of marginal interest and importance. The strength, originality, and vision we find therein is the true measure of what constitutes our national life." He also ventured, "I am confident that the enterprise and skill of the Canadian magazine industry will seize this opportunity. It is my hope and expectation that this decision will result in the creation of a Canadian newsmagazine."

As not only Hugh Faulkner but just about everybody else expected, Maclean Hunter, already approaching something like a Canadian magazine monopoly, leaped hungrily into the breach, promising rather more than they were likely to deliver, the transformation of their flagship publication, the monthly *Maclean's*, into a weekly newsmagazine with bureaus worldwide. This prompted one observer, the Ottawa columnist Geoffrey Stevens, to write, "The danger is that the Canadian newsmagazine industry will be transformed from a profitable U.S. monopoly to an unprofitable Canadian monopoly."

The expectation was that if *Time/Canada* (circulation 554,-000), with editorial offices in Montreal, and some six weekly pages of Canadian content, was to disappear, then undoubtedly some, if certainly not all, of its advertising income would accrue to the new *Maclean's*. As things stood, the Canadian magazine issue was already fraught with embarrassments and ambiguities. Months before *Time* was directly threatened, this country's oldest and best magazine, *Saturday Night*—its content sometimes self-consciously nationalist—seemed to be folding. Then a savior—a savior most embarrassing—emerged with the offer of a $100,000 loan. It was (whisper it) none other than Imperial Oil, that is to say, Exxon, and accepting its money was equivalent, in the old days, to a right-wing periodical's taking Moscow gold. But *Saturday Night*, with no other options, took the money and happily survives unto this day.

In 1975, almost everybody would have supported a measure that obliged "our" edition of *Time* to become more than 51 percent Canadian-owned and belatedly extend the range of its Canadian news coverage. But the ambiguity that worried Marc Lalonde, and frightened a good many others, was the rider that also said our *Time*'s content had to be "substantially different" from the American. Ron Basford, then minister of national revenue, under whose jurisdiction the income tax amendment fell, explained "substantially different" as meaning 80 percent Canadian content, which was not only a ridiculous proposal, but also an act of censorship. Outraged, the editorial writer in the *Toronto Globe & Mail* clearly saw foreign ownership and editorial content as two distinctly separate issues. Legislating against the content of a magazine, he wrote, would "be a direct interference with the right of all Canadians to freedom in choosing. . . . Government would be defining what can be published."

The legislation, introduced by Hugh Faulkner, had some unexpected, even surprising, results, not the least of which later involved Faulkner himself in a political somersault.

In the end, *Reader's Digest*, all but forgotten in the heated struggle over *Time,* was rescued by a convenient loophole in the law which allowed it to continue to publish a Canadian edition without any real content restrictions. The *Digest,* printed in Montreal, providing some three hundred jobs there, was saved by the Quebec caucus of the Liberal Party, which simply wouldn't stand for its extinction. *Time/Canada,* its proposals for a 51 percent Canadian-owned magazine with enlarged Canadian content turned down again and again, folded its headquarters in Montreal and closed its bureaus in Ottawa, Toronto, and the West. But Canadian companies, even without benefit of income tax deductions, continued to advertise in *Time.* *Time's* circulation increased here, and so did its revenue, because, among other things, it was no longer required to sustain a $2 million Canadian editorial budget. *Maclean's* did become a weekly newsmagazine, its "originality and vision" modeled on *Time* and *Newsweek.* The magazine's national coverage is both intelligent and extensive, but its international sections, as might be expected, are very thin indeed. Though its masthead lists, as promised, bureaus world-wide, with correspondents as far-flung as Accra, Bangkok, and Nicosia, they are not in fact *Maclean's* staffers but stringers, that is to say, employees of other journals who file the occasional piece for *Maclean's* on space rates. *Maclean's,* given Canada's population base, can simply not be expected to match the editorial budget of a *Time* or a *Newsweek.*

Hugh Faulkner is another matter.

An ardent nationalist, passionately opposed to Canada's branch-plant economy, he lost his seat in the 1979 election and did not run again in 1980. Instead, he moved to Montreal and joined a Canadian multinational, Alcan, as a vice-president. In 1983, he was dispatched to Calcutta, appointed to administer Alcan's Indian branch plant. In his new role as latter-day raj, he will, I expect, make his decisions based on the needs of the head office.

. . .

For all that, the pity is that our economic nationalists, if only they would stay clear of cultural matters, obviously beyond them, do have a case. We are too much subject to the whims of multinational corporations, largely American-owned. Our problem, unique in the western world, perhaps, was not an indigenous buccaneering capitalist class, indifferent to those they exploited, yet intrepid and imaginative nation-builders. Our problem was the Scots, the most inept and timorous capitalists in the West. Not builders, but vendors, or, at best, circumspect investors in insurance and trust companies.

If the pre–World War I American boy, at the age of sixteen, was dreaming of how to conquer and market the rest of the globe, his Canadian equivalent, at the same age, was already seeking a position with an unrivaled pension scheme.

And so, Canadian branch plants proliferate, there's an imbalance, corrections are called for. But mindless, impassioned objection to all things American is a fool's solution. It's no answer. After all, we could eschew all things American, even the Salk vaccine, making our children "FREE—to control—to decide; not to the will of a giant tied!" But plainly, cripples for Canada.

"I'm the Kind of a Guy Who Likes to See All the Legs Kick at the Same Time and at the Same Height"

In this country, in 1976, there was no hinge more celebrated than Bobby Orr's knee, no myth more overriding than that evolved around the construction of a railroad, and the most sought-after masters of magic were plumbers or the managers of tax-shelter funds. All the same, it was also the year the National Ballet of Canada observed its twenty-fifth anniversary. From the beginning, ballet couldn't be reckoned an integral part of our national tradition. It was a cultural implant. Like garlic in an Orangeman's salad. Or the introduction of knives and forks in Tuktoyaktuk. Which is to say, we were raised on radio's Hockey Night in Canada. "He shoots! He scores!" Not on *demi-plié, pirouette en dehors, arabesque.*

Ballet, if it ever slipped into the idiom, was something the humpty-dumpty daughters of Rosedale, Westmount, or Rockcliffe fitted in between visits to the orthodontist. They endured these lessons not in the hope of growing up to enchant us, but rather to bolster their postpubescent sales value, just as, in the absence of Dostoevsky on the glass-enclosed family bookshelves, a tenure in the Brownies was calculated to instill in them a sense of right or wrong. Ballet was Mr. Vaughn Monroe belting out "Dance, Ballerina, Dance," and oh yes, Barbara Ann Scott on ice. It was also, like poetry, for the sort of guy you wouldn't want to share a bar of soap with in the shower room.

Celia Franca, the founder of the National Ballet of Canada, recalls that when she first came here in 1950, trying to stitch a company together, "Everybody thought I was crazy. Who wanted to see a bunch of sissy boys running around in long underwear or girls floating on stage tiptoe?"

Mind you, it could be argued that things were not much better in England a few years earlier. In *The Age of Uncertainty,* John Kenneth Galbraith writes that when John Maynard Keynes took a wife, Lydia Lopokova, a star of Diaghilev's ballet company, old family friends asked, "Has Maynard married a chorus girl?"

I pass this on only to take the edge off another bit of Canadian tittle-tattle.

In 1972, when Team Canada journeyed to Moscow for the final games in that fabled hockey series, the perfidious Soviets robbed our heroes of an early night to bed, obliging them to endure instead an evening at the Bolshoi, *Swan Lake.* After the first act, a despairing Frank Mahovlich, too impatient even to wait for the Zamboni to roll out, started out of his seat, asking his neighbor, "Is it O.K. to go now?"

Courage, as we understand it in this country, is Toronto Maple Leaf Bobby Baun, his ankle broken, taking a shot of novocaine and leaping over the boards to resume play. It's climbing the Chilkoot Pass. The Dieppe Raid. Speaking French in Calgary. Courage, as we grasp it, is certainly not Frank Augustyn, a Hamilton steelworker's son, coming in out of the snow to tell his old man that he has won a scholarship to the National Ballet School. "Betty Oliphant wants me." Neither is it Celia Franca, *née* Franks, a bona fide Cockney, coming to Canada in 1950 at the invitation of the Toronto rich, sweet-talking them out of some small change, and starting a national ballet company the following year.

Consider, if you will, the Canadian cultural wind-chill factor of 1950. We were, in those days, still reading Beverly Baxter's schmaltzy "London Letter" in *Maclean's*. There were fewer than fifty bookshops in Canada, coast-to-coast, and many of them, I'm sure, moved envelopes faster than Hugh MacLennan and took Hallmark cards to be a hotter item than Morley Callaghan. Louis St. Laurent was our charismatic prime minister and one S. Morgan Powell, the book critic of the *Montreal Star*, had already stumbled on *The Naked and the Dead*, pronouncing it obscene, as he later would another novel, *The Catcher in the Rye*. There was no Canada Council, no Film Development Corporation, no National Arts Centre, no Stratford. To say you wanted to write, as some of us did at the time, was to invite the immediate rejoinder, "What name are you going to use?" as if the act, like housebreaking, were anti-social. So I can only conclude that saying you wanted to dance, if you were a man, was even more suspect.

I was, if I may introduce a brief personal note, working on the now-defunct *Montreal Herald* in 1950, lowest man on the assignment pole, likely to be sent on the most trivial errands. For example, one afternoon a reporter stopped at my desk. "You like music?"

"Yes."

"Classical?"

"Sure."

"Arthur Rubinstein's playing here tonight. Here are two tickets. You're covering."

Another unlikely young man laboring in the same city room was Brian Macdonald, who would shortly quit, surrendering an honest job, to dance with the newly formed National Ballet. He was one of ten boys and eighteen girls, equally money-crazed, who joined Miss Franca on the promise of $35 a week and an opportunity to rehearse in the then derelict and rat-filled St. Lawrence Hall, on King St. E., which the generous city of Toronto provided rent-free.

More good news.

When Miss Franca, seconded by Betty Oliphant, a fellow and examiner of the Imperial Society for Teachers of Dancers in London, let it out that they also required a summer school, Toronto high society rode to the rescue. Mrs. George Hees came up with a $500 founding loan. It came with a covering letter from the National Ballet Guild that stated, in effect, that if the money was lost the young ladies would be held personally responsible for the loan, but if the school turned a profit, such monies would accrue to the Guild.

On November 12, 1951, an early freeze-up trapped twenty-six hunters in northern Ontario. Princess Elizabeth, leaving Canada after a five-week tour, said, if she was happy to be going home, she was also leaving a country that had become a second home in every sense. Judy Garland suffered a collapse backstage at the Palace Theatre in New York. The University of Toronto Blues defeated the McGill Redmen, 11–7, taking the college football title. And that night, at 8:30, in the Eaton Auditorium, the National Ballet of Canada presented the premiere performance of *The Dance of Salome,* choreographed and performed by Miss Celia Franca, former leading dramatic dancer at Sadler's Wells. Others in the cast included Jury Gotshalks as Herod and Grant Strate as John the Baptist.

Fortunately for us and the ages, Frank Tumpane of the *Globe & Mail* was there. "Well, fellows," he wrote, "I've been hearing about it all my life, but the other night I finally got to see the Dance of the Seven Veils." The horny Mr. Tumpane endorsed what he saw. "You can just sink back if you want to and look at those pretty girls who look as graceful as all get-out in those white ballet skirts."

Betty Oliphant, principal of the National Ballet School, told me, "In those days, the first thing we had to do was educate an audience."

An audience, dancers, dance teachers, and possibly, just possibly, a board of directors as well.

Lyman Henderson, of Davis & Henderson, printers, didn't join the board until 1961. "How did I come to ballet? My wife had always been keen and she used to drag me there. To begin with, I was a firm believer that it was really for fairies, not for men. But it got to me."

Though it got to him, Mr. Henderson, by his own account, has never become a knowledgeable balletomane. He remains, as he puts it, an enthusiast. "I'm the kind of a guy who likes to see all the legs kick at the same time and at the same height."

Celia, Mr. Henderson ventured, was sometimes insufficiently appreciated by certain members of the board. The feeling, it would appear, is reciprocated. Speaking of the company's twenty-fifth anniversary, Celia said to me, "Why should I go out and dance there in front of all my enemies?"

Celia, Celia.

"Celia's strength," Betty Oliphant says, "was that she was determined to make the National a major company. She was totally uncompromising about standards and absolutely right about that. Celia was also a magnificent coach, somebody who came into her own in the rehearsal room."

Toronto lawyer Eddie Goodman also believed in Celia. "In my experience of artists in this country, I have never met anybody with as much artistic genius as she had."

Goodman was on the board of directors in the adventuring days, when the dancers often had no choice but to eschew their $35 a week; and the company, on tour, had to be bailed out of more than one out-of-town hotel, Goodman raising the ransom on the telephone. "We were determined to get to New York," Goodman recalls; and so, in 1954, he pressured a prospering group of real estate clients into forking out the necessary, some

$5,000. "Taking your tax benefits into consideration," he pointed out, "it will only cost you $1,250 anyway."

Even so, the company continued to teeter just this side of bankruptcy. The old Toronto rich, whose creature it was, did not exactly shake out booming postwar investment portfolios, empty shoeboxes hidden in the attics of Lakes Simcoe or Muskoka, or dip into dollars taking the sun in Bermuda to furnish the wherewithal. Instead, come a crisis, they would clap hands and lovingly organize *an occasion. A fund-raising ball.* Bringing in Count Basie, perhaps, and yielding an opportunity for simply everybody who counted to turn out in their finery. Heaven. And, in the absence of Marcel Proust, a bedazzled Zena Cherry would be there to list the names for the next morning's *Globe & Mail,* our paper of record. But, alas, at the end of the day, Betty Oliphant recalls, "We would be lucky to end up with maybe $5,000 in proceeds. I'd tell them that if instead of a ball each one had put up $100, we could have had $25,000, but . . ."

Those, those were the days when Celia still ruled supreme, but already there was dissension. Actually, to pay tribute where it is properly due, the wonder is that the old Toronto rich (their clubs restricted, their playgrounds *judenfrei*), having sent to Ninette de Valois of the Sadler's Wells Ballet for a lady of quality, a compliant nymph out of South Kensington, perhaps, and being lumbered with a gutsy East End Jewish girl instead, could have tolerated her for so many years. "And what, my dear, if she has a husband and I invite them to the York for lunch? Will he wear a yarmulke? Or will she order bagels and lox if we take her to the Badminton & Racquet Club?" Indeed, the long association, however turbulent, speaks well for both the old Toronto rich and Celia.

Celia, on her side, still given to amusing yet scathing remarks about former colleagues, was obviously a difficult as well as resourceful lady. Celia, even her advocates allow, was uncommonly severe with young dancers, and some of the bruised dancers themselves protest that she was also so abrupt with visiting choreographers that soon none would accept invitations from the company.

What has happened, it seems to me, was inevitable, and it is a pity that so many people connected with the National Ballet Company remain defensive about it. Celia Franca, having miraculously founded a ballet company and hammered it into a thing to be judged by international standards, where before there was only money and yearning, has made herself redundant. This is, in fact, the measure of her own success.

Where once the company had to be bailed out of a Vancouver hotel, it now travels with élan to London, Tokyo, and New York.

In London, in 1975, Oleg Kerensky praised the company, in the *New Statesman,* for its sound classical style and tradition, but criticized it for failing to produce dancers of strong personality or a sufficiently distinctive repertoire. The *Guardian* pronounced Karen Kain and Nadia Potts proficient and delectable and, among the men, Stefanschi and Schramek outstanding. Alexander Bland, writing in the *Observer,* thought Karen Kain made a striking Giselle and Frank Augustyn, her lover, a fluent, stylish dancer and convincing actor.

Augustyn, the Hamilton steelworker's boy, first came to the National Ballet School as a visiting gymnast. After one look at him, Betty Oliphant proclaimed, "I want that boy," and get him she did, though his parents required a good deal of convincing. Six years later, when Augustyn was eighteen, Nureyev lifted him out of the corps de ballet to make him his understudy in *The Sleeping Beauty,* and in 1973, with Karen Kain, he was unanimously voted the prize in the *pas de deux* category of the Moscow International Ballet Competition. Two years later, Clive Barnes, writing in the *New York Times,* adjudged the National Ballet "one of the more interesting companies in the international market—not a great company, but a company with honest aspirations to greatness."

Where once there were but thirty-five dancers, there were

now sixty-five. Where once the dancers had to make do on canned sardines and $35 weekly, and Celia Franca herself struggled for years on no more than an annual salary of $7,000, now the principal dancers were paid a decent wage. Rather less, come to think of it, than your neighborhood television repairman, and with a much shorter career. On the other hand, principal dancers do not make housecalls, though invitations abound. "Older men, you know, in their forties, are waiting at the dressing-room door. In New York there's always this little guy standing there when you come out. 'Can I wash your tights for you, please?' "

The Fall of the
Montreal Canadiens

1980, CERTAINLY, WAS THE WINTER OF MONTREAL'S DIS-
content.

During the last week of February, our sidewalks were still
bare of snow. Unheard of here, bizarre beyond belief. In fact,
only a piddling thirty-odd centimeters of snow (in other years,
one blizzard's good blow) had fallen on our stricken city by February 24, the least amount since 1875, when the McGill Obser-
vatory first began to monitor the weather here. Knowledgeable
Montrealers were shaking their heads. Incredulous, apprehensive. Something was wrong somewhere.

That freaky winter our city had endured good news and bad
news—all of it mind-boggling.

The unpredictable Montrealer we leased to the country as
prime minister for eleven bumpy years, Pierre Elliott Trudeau,
had risen again like Lazarus, having announced his retirement
the previous November only to reconsider and lead the Liberal
Party back into power in Ottawa in February. Meanwhile, in
Quebec City, where the separatist Parti Québécois was rooted in
provincial office, another Montrealer, that party's cultural aya-
tollah, Dr. Camille Laurin, had pronounced again, urging
French-only announcements at the Forum, hockey's undisputed
shrine. Moved to outrage, *Montreal Gazette* sports columnist
Tim Burke wrote, "Only minds filled with mischief and vindic-
tiveness could lean on the Forum to strike the language of 25

percent of its fans from its program. It is the kind of mentality dedicated to converting Montreal from a once-great metropolis into a sickly, swollen Trois-Rivières."

Within a couple of days another columnist, Jerry Trudel, countered with equal heat in the pages of *Dimanche-Matin:* "*Aujourd'hui, Tim Burke me fait rire: il demeure, lui, l'un des nombreux bastions du bigotisme anglo-saxon dans cette mosaïque balkanisée qu'on appelle le Canada.*" Furthermore, a seething Trudel pointed out that when *"ces bons Canadiens"* were playing in Vancouver, and a stanza of the national anthem was sung in French, the team was greeted by a *"crescendo des poumons."* Resounding boos from the yahoos in the stands.

"Politics and sports don't mix," a slippery Guy Lafleur has insisted more than once, but that embarrassing night many of *ces bons Canadiens* were deeply offended. "Some of the players were so angry," Serge Savard said, "they didn't even want to go out on the ice."

Other nights, other yahoos. At a game in Toronto a separatist-inclined columnist who travels with the team remained resolutely seated in the press gallery when "O Canada" was sung, this time *en anglais.* A security guard, fulminating behind him, promptly jerked him upright by the scruff of the neck. "In *this* city," he advised him, "we stand up for *that* song."

But it was not the eerie absence of snow, Trudeau's second coming, or the continued squabbling between English and French Canadians that profoundly perplexed Montrealers that season, making it a winter of infamy. It was something far more incredible, infinitely more unsettling. In the longest November we could recall, the Montreal Canadiens, our fabled Canadiens, actually managed to lose six games in a row, something that hadn't happened for forty years, not since the season of 1939–40, a year uninformed out-of-towners may remember for other reasons.

A few days after the fall, I ran into Tim Burke in a favored downtown bar. "The Canadiens," he said, fuming, "are now on a two-game win streak." And then, contemplating his rum and Coke, he added, "Can you imagine even thinking such a thing? A two-game win streak! The *Canadiens!*"

Soon, floating on too many drinks, we were reminiscing about what was by common consent the greatest Canadiens team ever, the club that in the season of 1959–60 won its fifth Stanley Cup in a row, Toe Blake on the boil behind the bench. My, my. There was the incomparable Jacques Plante in the nets, Doug Harvey and Tom Johnson and Jean-Guy Talbot minding the blue line, and up front, big Jean Beliveau, Dickie Moore, Boom Boom Geoffrion, Henri Richard, Claude Provost, Ralph Backstrom, Phil Goyette serving as the *fourth* center. And still to come were Yvan Cournoyer, Jacques Lemaire, and a college kid called Ken Dryden.

In those days, Tim recalled, glowing, we would quit the Forum after a game as emotionally drained as any of the players were. Such, such was once the quality of the action.

In Montreal, easily the most prescient of hockey towns, everybody you meet these days is down on the game. "There was a time, not so long ago," a sportswriter told me, "when if I walked into the Press Club with two tickets for a game, I was immediately surrounded, I was going to make enemies, everybody wanted them. Now I walk in with two tickets and I can't even find a taker."

The players, they say, are fat, indolent, and overpaid. Frenetic expansion, obviously fed by avarice rather than regard for tradition, has all but ruined a fine institution. The season is horrendously long and the present playoff system an unacceptable joke. Come mid-May the Stanley Cup finals have usually yet to begin. And yet—and yet—Saturday night is still "Hockey Night in Canada." Diminished or not, *les Canadiens sont là.* And so am I, my eyes fixed on the television set.

The legendary Canadiens.

For as long as I can remember, *le Club de Hockey Canadiens* has always been something unique. Never just another hockey club. To appreciate that properly, what's called for, first of all, is some grasp of my Canadian generation's dilemma.

An earlier generation, not mine, was raised to manhood on a British standard. *The Boy's Own Annual.* "Fear God, Honour the Crown, Shoot Straight, and Keep Clean." But those of us who were kids during World War II (flipping the diddle as the battles raged elsewhere) and went on to become teenagers in the late Forties were a thoroughly American bunch. We endured Montreal and blackheads, but New York, New York, was our heart's desire. The real world, the big time. We tolerated our own CBC but couldn't wait for Monday night when Cecil B. De Mille presented Hollywood on Lux Radio Theater. We accepted Montreal welterweight Johnny Greco because he actually got to fight Beau Jack and others in Madison Square Garden. He was rated in *Ring*. Later, we also took Morley Callaghan seriously, because we found out he had been to Montparnasse with Hemingway and Fitzgerald, real writers, who hadn't spit on him. We rooted for Deanna Durbin because, after all, she was a Canadian like us, a born flunk; but the star we yearned for and wanted to go the limit with was Lana Turner.

Taking sports as a metaphor for the country, our predicament was best illuminated by the plight of the Montreal Royals, a Triple A ball club that was once the class of the old International League. Come the crunch, the ball club, like our country, was no more than number-one farm club.

Not only a farm club, but an obsequious one at that. Why, as late as the Fifties, Pierre Berton reveals in *Hollywood's Canada,* there was a government-sponsored film group in Ottawa, the Canadian Co-operation Project, composed of grown men who actually compiled an annual list of film mentions of Canada which they had pried out of obdurate Hollywood. Such dialogue gems as, from *Red Skies of Montana,* "We tie in with the authorities north of the border in Canada," or, from *The Tanks Are Coming,*

"The Canadians were on our left and although taking a terrific pounding were holding magnificently." In fact, the CCP was so effective it was even responsible for the occasional dialogue change. Originally a line in *New York Confidential* read: "They caught Louis Engelday in Detroit." But a rare combination of Canadian imagination and muscle altered it to read: "They caught Louis Engelday on his way to Canada."

If, in larger terms, our indigenous culture had always been suspect, most of it not for export, our ball clubs traditionally minor-league, and even our Prime Minister a what's-his-name, then we were at least armed with one certitude, and it was that when it came to playing the magnificent game of ice hockey we were, indeed, a people unsurpassed. At least until the nefarious Russians moseyed into town in 1972.

I can remember exactly where I was on VE-Day, on the day John F. Kennedy was shot, and when the first man landed on the moon. If I can't recall what I was doing on the day Stalin died, I do remember that a journalist I know was in the elevator of the *Montreal Star* building the morning after. Ascending, she turned to a neighbor and said, "Stalin died."

The elevator operator overheard. "Oh my God, that's terrible," he said. "Which floor did he work on?"

The point I'm trying to make is that on days that shook the world, or my world at any rate, I was never on the spot until the night of September 2, 1972, when Team Canada tested our belief in God, the free-enterprise system, and the virility of the Canadian male, by taking on the Russians at the Montreal Forum in the first of an eight-game series. A series, Tim Burke wrote in the *Gazette*, that the Canadian public viewed as something of a political Armageddon. Going into the contest we were more than overconfident—with pity our hearts were laden. The pathetic Russian players had to lug their own equipment. Their skates were shoddy. The players themselves had names appropriate to a plumbing firm working out of Winnipeg's North End, but otherwise unpronounceable: Vasiliev, Liapkin, Maltsev, Mikhailov, Kharmalov, Yakushev, and, oh yes, Tretiak. Everybody but John Robertson, then with the *Montreal Star,* predicted that our champions would win all the games handily or, at worst, might drop a game in Russia. A matter of *noblesse oblige.* Robertson called for the USSR to win the series six games to two. On the other hand, Alan Eagleson, one of the organizers of the series, ventured, "Anything less than an unblemished sweep of the Russians would bring shame down on the heads of the players and the national pride."

After Ypres, following Dieppe, Team Canada and our very own belated St. Crispin's Day. Brad, Rod, Guy, Yvan, Frank, and Serge, once more unto the breach, once more for Canada and the NHL.

> From this day to the ending of the world,
> But we in it shall be remember'd;
> We few, we happy few, we band of brothers . . .

We were only thirty seconds into the fray at the Forum when Phil Esposito scored. Some six minutes later, Paul Henderson, taking a pass from Bobby Clarke, scored again. But the final count, as we all know, was Communism 7, Free Enterprise 3. And our players were booed more than once in the Forum, ostensibly for taking cheap shots at the Russians as they flew past, but actually for depriving us of one of our most cherished illusions. We already knew that our politicians lied, and that our bodies would be betrayed by age, but we had not suspected that our hockey players were anything but the very best. If Team Canada finally won the series, Paul Henderson scoring one of hockey's most dramatic goals at 19:26 of the third period in the last game in Moscow, the moral victory clearly belonged to Russia. After the series, nothing was ever the same again in Canada. Beer didn't taste as good. The Rockies seemed smaller, the northern lights dimmer. Our last-minute win came more in the nature of a relief than a triumph.

After the storm, a drizzle. Which is to say, the endless NHL season that followed was tainted, revealed as a parochial affair, and the Stanley Cup itself, once our Holy Grail, seemed suddenly a chalice of questionable distinction. So, alas, it remains. For the Russians continue to be the dominant force in real hockey, international hockey, with the Czechs and Swedes not far behind.

But when I was a boy, and the Russians were still learning how to skate, the major league was right here. And furthermore, the most dashing and aesthetically pleasing team to watch, in the old vintage six-team league, was our own unrivaled Montreal Canadiens.

Les Canadiens sont là!

The legend began before my time, on the night of November 29, 1924, with Aurel Joliat, Howie Morenz, and Billy Boucher, the first of many fabled lines. On that night, their first night in the Montreal Forum, the line scored six goals, defeating Toronto St. Pats, 7–1. "Of course," wrote sports columnist Andy O'Brien, "the line had a lot of ice time because the Canadiens only carried three subs, while Georges Vezina (the Chicoutimi Cucumber) in the goal left back-checking superfluous."

Actually *le Club de Hockey Canadiens* even predates the NHL; it was founded in 1909, eight years before the NHL came along, and won its first Stanley Cup in 1915–16, with Vezina and Newsy Lalonde in the lineup. But the team didn't enter into legend until 1923–24 when Howie Morenz arrived and the Canadiens won the Stanley Cup yet again.

Morenz was our Babe Ruth. Alas, I never saw him play; neither was I present in what must be accounted the most tragic night in hockey, January 28, 1937, when Morenz, in a rush against the Chicago Black Hawks, crashed into the boards and suffered a quadruple leg fracture. He was still in the hospital early in March, complications set in, and the Stratford Streak was no more. His fans, French Canadian factory workers and railroaders, had once filled the Forum's cheap seats to the overflow, and to this day that part of the Forum is known as the "millionaires' section." "His body," wrote Andy O'Brien, "was laid out at center ice and the greats of hockey took turns as guards of honor around the bier day and night. Then a sportswriter with the old *Standard*, I arrived at the Forum to find the front doors jammed. I entered by the furnace room and, as I walked toward the Closse Street entry, the stillness made me wonder—was nobody else in the building? But there were, fifteen thousand fans, quiet and motionless in a tribute to a man—and hockey—that has never been matched."

Morenz played on three Canadiens Stanley Cup winning teams, but with his passing a drought set in. The Flying Frenchmen, or the Habitants, as they came to be known, a team that has won the Stanley Cup twenty-one times, more often than any other club, did not claim it again until 1943–44, with the lineup that became a golden part of my childhood: Toe Blake, Elmer Lach, Ray Getliffe, Murph Chamberlain, Phil Watson, Emile "Butch" Bouchard, Glen Harmon, Buddy O'Connor, Gerry Heffernan, Mike McMahon, Leo Lamoureux, Fernand Majeau, Bob Fillion, Bill Durnan, and, above all, Maurice "the Rocket" Richard.

To come clean, this was not the greatest of Canadiens teams—that came later—but it remains the one to which I owe the most allegiance.

1943–44. Cousins and older brothers were overseas, battling through Normandy or Italy, and each day's *Star* brought a casualty list. Others, blessed with a nice little heart murmur, stayed home, making more money than they had ever dreamed of, moving into Outremont. But most of us still lingered on St. Urbain Street, and we seldom got to see a hockey game. Our parents were not disposed to treat us, for the very understandable reason that it wouldn't help us to become doctors. Besides, looked at closely, come playoff time it was always our pea-soups, which is what we used to call French Canadians in those days, against their—that is to say, Toronto's—English-speaking roughnecks. What did it have to do with us? Plenty, plenty. For, much to our parents' dismay, we talked hockey incessantly and played whenever we could. Not on skates, which we also couldn't afford, but out on the streets with proper sticks and a puck or, failing that, a piece of coal. Saturday nights we huddled around the radio, playing blackjack for dimes and nickels, our eyes on the cards, our ears on the score. And the man who scored most often was Maurice Richard, once, memorably, with an opposing defenseman riding his back, and another time, in a playoff game against Toronto, putting the puck in the net five times. Then, in 1944–45, Richard accomplished what no other player had done before, scoring fifty goals in a fifty-game season.

I only got to see the great Richard twice. Saving money earned collecting bills for a neighborhood butcher on Sunday mornings, my friends and I bought standing-room tickets for the millionaires' section. And then, flinging our winter caps ahead of us, we vaulted barriers, eventually working our way down to ice level. Each time we jumped a barrier, hearts thumping, we tossed our caps ahead of us, because if an officious usher grabbed us by the scruff of the neck, as often happened, we could plead, teary-eyed, that some oaf had tossed our cap down and we were only descending to retrieve it.

Among the younger players on ice with the Rocket during his last years was the consummate artist who would succeed him as the leader of *les Canadiens:* Jean Beliveau.

I was, by this time, rooted in London, and used to make a daily noontime excursion to a Hampstead newspaper shop especially to pick up the *International Herald Tribune,* turning to the sports pages first, seeking news of big Jean and his illustrious team-mates, easily the best *Club de Hockey Canadiens* ever to take to the Forum ice. They won the Stanley Cup five years running, and such was their prowess on the power play that they were responsible for a major change in the NHL rule book. With Beliveau at center, Dickie Moore on one wing, an aging Richard on the other, Geoffrion at one point, and Doug Harvey on the other, the Canadiens, with the man advantage, could score as many as three goals in their allotted two penalty minutes. Consequently a new rule was introduced. It allowed the penalized team to return to full strength once a goal had been scored.

I didn't get to see Beliveau play until 1956 and was immediately enthralled. He was not only an elegant, seemingly effortless skater, but an uncommonly intelligent playmaker, one of the last to actually carry the disk over the blue line rather than unload before crossing, dumping it mindlessly into a corner for the others to scramble after, leading with their elbows. "I not only worry about him when he's carrying the puck," said Punch Imlach, then coach of the Toronto Maple Leafs, "but about where the fuck he's going once he's given it up." Where he was going was usually the slot, and trying to budge him, as Toronto's Bill Ezaniski once observed, "was like running into the side of an oak tree."

Ah, Beliveau. Soon, whenever I was to fly home from England, I would first contact that most literate of Montreal sportswriters, my friend Dink Carroll, so that my visit might coincide with a Canadiens game, affording me another opportunity to watch big Jean wheel on ice. I was not alone. Far from it. In those halcyon days knowledgeable Montrealers would flock to the Forum to see Beliveau on a Saturday night as others might anticipate the visit of a superb ballet company. Big, handsome Jean was a commanding presence, and as long as he was on ice, the game couldn't degenerate into Ping-Pong: it was hockey as it was meant to be played.

Beliveau was truly great, and a bargain, even if you take into account that *le Club de Hockey Canadiens* had to buy an entire team to acquire him. In 1951, Beliveau, already a hockey legend, was playing for the "amateur" Quebec Aces, his salary a then stupendous $20,000 a year. The cunning Canadiens bought the Aces, thereby acquiring the negotiating rights to Beliveau. He received a $20,000 bonus and signed a five-year, $105,000 contract, which was unheard-of in those days for a twenty-three-year-old rookie. Beliveau went on to score 507 goals for *les Canadiens.* He made the All-Star team nine times, won the Hart Trophy for the most valuable player twice, and led his team to ten Stanley Cups in his eighteen years with the club as a player.

If Beliveau was the leader of the best Canadiens team ever, it's also necessary to say that decadence, as well as grievous loss, characterized those memorable years. Decadence came in the unlikely shape of one of the team's most engaging and effective forwards, Bernie "Boom Boom" Geoffrion, who introduced the slap shot, wherein a player winds up like a golfer to blast the puck in the general direction of the net, sometimes scoring, more often watching the puck ricochet meaninglessly off the glass. Loss, irredeemable loss, came with a change in the draft rules of 1969. Until then, *les Canadiens* had call on Quebec's first two draft choices, but come '69 and expansion, that was no more. In practical terms this meant that Marcel Dionne and Gil Perreault, among others, were lost to Montreal. Sadly, if either of them had a childhood dream it was certainly to play with *le Club de Hockey Canadiens,* but when they skate out on the Forum ice these days, it is as dreaded opponents.

A tradition was compromised in the dubious name of parity for expansion teams. For years, years and years, *les Canadiens* were a team unlike any other in sports. Not only because they were the class of the league—for many years, so were the New York Yankees—but also because they were not made up of hired outsiders but largely of Québécois, boys who had grown up in Montreal or the outlying towns of the province. We could lend them our loyalty without qualification, because they had not merely been hired to represent us on ice—it was their birthright. As boys, Beliveau and I had endured the same blizzards. Like me, Doug Harvey had played softball in an NDG park. Downtown had always meant the same thing to Henri Richard as it had to me. So the change in the draft rules meant that *les Canadiens* were bound to lose a quality that was unique in sport. Happily, however, the time was not yet. Not quite yet.

For one player promising true greatness did slip through the revised draft net. After Morenz, following Richard and Beliveau—Guy Lafleur. Lafleur, born in Thurso, Quebec, in 1951, was, like Beliveau before him, a hockey legend even before he came to *les Canadiens.* In 1970–71, still playing with the Quebec Remparts, a junior team, he scored a record-making 130 goals and graduated to *les Canadiens* under tremendous pressure. Universally acclaimed Beliveau's heir, he was even offered Beliveau's number 4 sweater. "He asked me what he should do," said Beliveau. "I told him if you want number four, take it. But, in your shoes, I would take another number and make *it* famous."

Lafleur chose number 10, and for his first three years in the league, helmeted years, he was a disappointment. His manner on ice was tentative, uneasy. Seated on the bench between shifts, he seemed a solitary, almost melancholy figure. Even now, having acquired some of Beliveau's natural grace by osmosis, perhaps, he is far from being a holler man, but then in the winter of 1974 he suddenly bloomed. Not only did Guy score fifty-three goals, but, eschewing his helmet, he was undoubtedly the most dazzling player on ice anywhere that year, leading old-style end-to-end rushes, splitting the defense, carrying the puck as if it were fastened to his stick with elastic, unleashing swift and astonishingly accurate wrist shots, dekeing one goalie after another and coming back with the play, going into the corners. Once again the Montreal Forum was a place to be, the Saturday-night hockey game an occasion.

Even so, *les Canadiens* failed to win the Stanley Cup in 1974, ignominiously eliminated by Buffalo, an expansion team, in the semifinals. Little Henri Richard, then thirty-nine years old, silvery-haired, the last player who had skated with the vintage

Canadiens, kept his stick after the final defeat, a clue that he would be retiring. The end of one era and, it was to be hoped, the beginning of another. Though the *Gazette*'s Tim Burke was far from convinced. After *les Canadiens* went out, seemingly with more golf than hockey on their minds, he sourly observed that the league, and *les Canadiens* in particular, was not what it used to be.

"Most fans apparently feel the same way. They no longer concern themselves about the Canadiens the way they once did."

Before brooding at length on reasons and rationalizations for the fall, I should emphasize once more that the Canadiens are a team unlike any other. From Howie Morenz through Richard and Beliveau to Lafleur, they have been a family. This team was not built on haphazard trades, though there have been some, or on the opening of the vaults for upwardly mobile free agents, but largely on the development of local boys who had dreamed of nothing more than wearing that red sweater ever since they first began to play Pee Wee hockey at the age of eight. Morenz, it's true, came from Ontario, but the Richard brothers were both Montreal boys; Beliveau sprang from Trois-Rivières and Lafleur from Thurso. They are the progeny of dairy farmers and miners and railway shop workers and welders. There is a tradition, there is continuity. Eighty-seven-year-old Frank Selke, who built the original dynasty, still sits brooding in the stands at every game. If the late Dick Irvin, a westerner, was the coach who fine-tuned the team for Mr. Selke, it is now his son, also called Dick, who still travels with the team, working on the television and radio broadcasts. Gilles Tremblay, a star with the team until asthma laid him low in 1969, handles the French-language telecasts. Scotty Bowman was a player in the organization until he fractured his skull, as was Claude Ruel until he lost an eye. Beliveau is still with the team, a vice-president in charge of public relations, a job Guy Lafleur would like to fill one day. Another former player, Floyd "Busher" Curry, acts as road secretary. Former GM Sammy Pollack comes from one end of Montreal, and his successor, the embattled Irving Grundman, from another. Traditionally, following the Stanley Cup parade, the team repairs to Henri Richard's brasserie. "Every year," Richard told me, "I think they will forget, they won't come this time. But win or lose, the boys are here."

However, the man who most personifies continuity on the team today is Toe Blake. Originally a winger on the high-scoring Punch Line in the Forties, then the team's most successful coach, at the age of sixty-eight he was still padding up and down hotel lobbies on the road, remembering never to throw his fedora on the bed, which could only bring bad luck; a once fierce but now mellowing Toe, available to all the players, a consulting vice-president with the team. "But vice-president of what," he says, "they never told me."

Try to understand that in this diminishing city we have survived for years confident that any May the magnificent Canadiens did not bring home the Stanley Cup was an aberration. An affront to the fans. Or just possibly an act of charity. *Pour encourager les autres.*

Yes, yes. But in 1980, in the very Forum where the rafters were festooned end to end with Stanley Cup pennants, our champions, who came back—even after Tim Burke pronounced them dead in 1975—to win the Stanley Cup for four years running, had been humbled by the sadly inept Colorado Rockies and the St. Louis Blues. On the road, they had come up shockingly short against the kind of pickup teams they were expected to toy with: the Edmonton Oilers, the Winnipeg Jets, and the Quebec Nordiques.

Bob Gainey maintained that the rot, such as it was, had set in in 1979. "Looking back, people remember we won the Stanley Cup again, so they think we whistled through another year. But we didn't whistle. We dropped fourteen points on the previous season and twenty goals against. We snuck out with the Cup. We were lucky enough to have the momentum of the previous year to carry us, and that, with the talent and experience, got us by. We ran the tank empty last year and now it's showing up."

Actually, fissures in the dynasty began to appear as early as the summer of 1978, when Molson's Brewery bought the Canadiens from Peter and Edward Bronfman for $20 million. A month later, Sam Pollack, the unequaled dealer and hoarder of draft choices—with the organization for thirty-one years, the last thirteen as GM—took his leave with the Bronfman brothers. Pollack, who built the present dynasty, anointed Irving Grundman as his heir. Grundman had come to hockey and the Forum with the Bronfmans in 1972: he was now appointed executive vice-president and managing director of the Canadiens, that is to say, GM. Coach Scotty Bowman, who believed he was going to get the job, exploded. "World War III could have broken out in the Forum and I wouldn't have known a thing about it." An embittered Bowman, who had agreed to a two-year contract with the club a couple of months earlier, let it be known that he had been conned. He never would have signed, he said, had he realized that Pollack was leaving. "I've got my own future to think about," he said. "I don't want to spend the rest of my life behind the bench."

And later on, he would hint darkly that in making Grundman GM, Pollack had ensured his own continuing career with the Bronfman brothers' investment company.

Along came the 1978–79 season. Bowman, a hot-tempered disciplinarian, seemed to let up some, and acute observers of the team noted that once-safe leads now tended to evaporate. Teams lacking the Canadiens' talent made games much closer than they ought to have been. All too often games that should have produced a cozy two points became a tough one point, that is to say, ended in a tie.

Steve Shutt told me, "For the first couple of years here, Scotty was a yeller and a screamer. But it was his team, he built it. Besides, I think everybody needs a good kick in the ass once in a while. Last year, however, when it became obvious Scotty wasn't going to get the GM's job, he didn't want to do anything. He was really, really upset."

In the summer of 1980 the inevitable happened. Bowman, arguably the best coach in hockey, however personally unpopular—Scotty, ferocious leader of the team since 1971, a street-wise Montreal boy himself—walked out of the Forum to become general manager and director of hockey operations for the Buffalo Sabres.

Something else happened that summer. Ken Dryden, five-time winner of the Vezina Trophy, announced that he was retiring from the game to practice law. More bad news. Jacques Lemaire, just possibly the most complete center in hockey, surprised even his best friends on the team by saying that he had had quite enough of Stanley Cup pressure, thank you very much, and that from now on he would be doing his skating in the more salubrious climate of the Swiss Alps.

Early in September, only days before training camp was to open, Bernie Geoffrion, a fifty-goal scorer, a regular with the greatest Canadiens team ever, was named coach. "A dream come true," he said, beaming, but on the night of December 13 he was to resign. "I'm sick and tired of them. Guys coming in at two or three in the morning, laughing and joking around. They're not acting like professional athletes. I'm not going to stick around and let everyone in Montreal blame me for what's happening. . . ."

Geoffrion named names, too.

"Larouche walking through the airport, smoking a cigar, acting like we won the Stanley Cup when we'd lost a game. I thought Savard would help me. But he's more interested in his horses. I feel sorry for Robinson. How do you think he feels?"

The players, of course, told a different tale. "He flunked out in New York," Shutt said, "he flunked out in Atlanta. Why would he come here, a town like Montreal, where the fans are so demanding?" Where, as yet another veteran put it, "you've got seventeen thousand assistant coaches and the fans are right behind you, win or tie."

Other players, among them honest Larry Robinson, readily admit they came to camp out of condition. With Scotty gone, they grasped that they would not be scorchingly reprimanded for it. Geoffrion, a new boy, was out to ingratiate himself.

"Geoffrion didn't want to push us," Gainey said, "but we needed it."

So faithful Claude Ruel, a former coach and then assistant to Scotty Bowman, stepped loyally into the breach. But come the Christmas break, the team that had lost only seventeen games in 1978–79 and a mere ten the year before stood at an embarrassing 17–13–6.

Something had happened. Something bad.

Where once the players on the other teams, knees wobbly, skated out on the Forum ice determined not to disgrace themselves, now they leaped brashly over the boards actually looking for two points.

"We are no longer intimidated by all those red sweaters," Glenn Resch said.

Bob Gainey agreed. "When you start to slip everybody else in the league sees it, the others catch on. Now even the fringe players on the other teams think they can score here."

Since then, everybody's been taking the pulse, few as knowledgeable as Henri Richard. Richard, who played with the team for a record-breaking twenty years and eleven Stanley Cups, feared the dynasty was coming to an end. "They miss the big guy," he told me.

Sam Pollack.

"Nobody ever saw Sam," Steve Shutt said. "I noticed him in the dressing room maybe two or three times in five years. But you always knew he was out there somewhere. Watching."

Watching, yes, but sometimes to inadvertent comic effect.

"Sam," Doug Riseborough told me, "was very impressed with how scientific football coaching had become, and so, for a while, he tried to adapt their methods to our game. He would wander the highest reaches of the Forum, searching out patterns of play, and if he detected something he would quickly radio Busher Curry, who would be pacing the gangway, a plug in his ear. No sooner would the Busher get Sam's message than he would rush up to Bowman with the words of wisdom. Once, when we were leading the Bruins here, 3–2, with a couple of minutes to go, Sam, watching above, got on the radio to the Busher, who immediately rushed to the bench with the message for Scotty, which Scotty passed on to us. The message was, 'Sam says don't let them score on you.' "

The rap against fifty-year-old Irving Grundman, Pollack's successor, is that he is not a hockey man, he lacks fraternity credentials, but neither did he inherit the team with his daddy's portfolio. The taciturn, driving Grundman is a butcher's boy, and when he was a kid he was up at 5:00 A.M. to pluck chickens in his father's shop on the Main. He became a city councilman and went on to build a bowling empire, hooking up with the Bronfman brothers, who shrewdly took him to the Forum with them. "When I came here eight years ago it wasn't with the intention of having Sam's job. But once I got here I took a crash course with him. Five hours a day every day. He recommended me for the job. Now I'm in a no-win situation. If things go well, I did it with Sam's team. If not, it's my fault. However, we've already won one Stanley Cup, so I'm ahead of the game."

It was also Grundman, obviously a quick learner, who engineered the trade—or theft, some say—that did so much to enable the troubled Canadiens to hang in there in 1980. He sent Pat Hughes and Rob Holland to Pittsburgh for goalie Doug Herron. The season before, the fans, in their innocence, were demanding more ice time for backup goalie Michel Laroque. In 1980 the same fans were grateful that Herron was number one.

Still, Dryden was missed. Bob Gainey felt that it was his retirement that had hurt the team most. "The other teams are
overjoyed. They look down the ice and he isn't standing there
anymore."

Red Fisher, sports editor of the *Gazette,* who traveled with the
Canadiens for twenty-five years, allowed that Dryden used to let
in soft goals if the team was ahead 5–1, "But if they were down
1–0 on the road, he was the big guy. He kept them in there until
they found their legs."

Others insisted that the most sorely missed player was Jacques
Lemaire. Lemaire, hanging back there, brows knit, scowling, as
Lafleur and Shutt swirled around the nets. Certainly he would be
missed in May. Lemaire, the leading scorer in the 1979 playoffs,
accounted for eleven goals and twelve assists in sixteen games.
But the biggest adjustment the team had to make in 1980, according to Larry Robinson, was the loss of Scotty Bowman.
Bowman was feared, maybe even hated, by most of the players,
but he got the best out of them. "With Scotty gone, the fear and
motivation is gone. He's a great hockey man. He made us work
hard. You never knew what to expect."

Something else. In 1980, as all the players were quick to point
out, the team had endured an unseemly number of injuries and,
for the first time in recent memory, there was nobody down
there in Halifax threatening to crack the lineup. The bench was
thin.

Another consideration was that the one superlative defense
hadn't been playing up to par. "In the first half," Shutt allowed
ruefully, "Savard and Lapointe couldn't have made Junior A."

"We can't do it all with one line," Shutt said, and the other
lines were simply not scoring.

But then, on New Year's Eve, there was a miracle at the
Forum. Playing fire-wagon hockey, buzzing around the nets like
the Canadiens of cherished memory, a revived team put on a
dazzling display, beating the Red Army 4–2 in a so-called exhibi-

tion game. Many a fan, his faith in mankind restored, was saying the Canadiens, awake at last, would not lose another game during the rest of the season. Look out, Flyers. Boston beware. *Les Canadiens sont là.*

On New Year's Day, rotund Claude Ruel, mistaken for a buffoon by some, announced, "The past is dead. They are playing a little harder now, with more enthusiasm and pep."

Alas, the past was prologue. The following night *les Glorieux* ventured into Pittsburgh and lost again. They continued to play erratically, but with rather more success than in the first half, before Lafleur sounded off early in February. Some players, he said, were less interested in playing hockey than in drawing their salary. "It's reached a point where some of them don't want to play because they have a little headache. What do you expect a guy like Ruel to do then?" Lafleur also felt that some of the bigger players, say six-foot-six Gilles Lupien, were not doing enough hitting. "I know a number of players who are satisfied with thirty goals, while they could easily score fifty. But they don't because they say then the public and the boss would be more demanding."

By this time I had caught up with the Canadiens myself, determined to stay with them for six games, come to scrutinize the troubled club firsthand; and what follows is in the nature of a concerned fan's journal.

February 7, the Forum, Canadiens 4, Rockies 3.

Good news. Savard and Lapointe, coming off injuries, are back together in the lineup for the first time in a month. Bad news. Back and stumbling. Savard, a racehorse owner and proprietor of a suburban newspaper, is wearing a helmet for the first time this season. And Lapointe, as everybody knows, is having marital problems. The first period is largely smash-and-grab, the sort of play that is giving hockey a bad name, but, at the period's

end, the Canadiens lead 3-2. A disgruntled journalist, rising
from his seat in the press gallery, observes, "Will you look at
that. I mean, they're playing the Colorado Rockies. The most
compelling man on the team is their coach." Don Cherry.

In the second period, the Canadiens stumble badly. From
Doug Harvey to Gilles Lupien, I note, is not so much a fall as a
suicidal leap. Lupien treats the puck as somebody else might
being caught with another man's wife. No sooner does it connect
with his stick than he shoots it blindly out of his zone, as often as
not onto a waiting Colorado blade. Lafleur scores twice. Mario
Tremblay once, his first goal in ten games.

February 9, the Forum, Canucks 4, Canadiens 3.

"Look at those menacing black uniforms," somebody in the
press box exclaims as Vancouver skates out on the ice.

"Yeah, but that's all they've got."

Tonight it's enough to beat the disorganized Canadiens, their
play distressingly tentative. Once more the team squanders a
two-goal lead, characteristically provided by Lafleur and Shutt,
and stumbles through a punk second period. Lapointe separates
his shoulder once more, and will be out again, possibly for another month. "He has to be thinking about something else out
there," a reporter observes sadly.

The unnecessary loss is a bummer flying into Boston for a
Sunday-night game. On our chartered flight, the subdued players
sip their beer morosely. I sit with Doug Riseborough, a scrapper
on ice, who turns out to be most engaging. "That game was
given to them," he says. "A lot of nights what's missing with us
is the concentration. It's just not there."

As we check into the hotel in Boston, after 1:00 A.M., three
garishly made-up hookers, their smiles menacing, are fluttering
around the registration desk, eager to begin negotiations.

"How would they know when we're coming in?" I ask one of
the writers.

"They're always in touch with the sports desk. They ring me

all the time in Montreal to find out when a team is flying in and where they will be staying."

When Frank Mahovlich was still with the Canadiens, one of his teammates connected with a groupie in a hotel lobby, but unfortunately he was slated to share a room with still another player. Instead, he got Mahovlich, who had a room to himself, to switch with him. Settling in with his girl, the player dialed room service. "I want two rye and ginger ale. Room 408. Mr. Mav'lich."

"How do you spell that, sir?"

"M, A—M,A,V—no, no—M,A, H—H,V—oh, fuck it. Never mind."

In the morning, I meet Bob Gainey for breakfast.

"We don't seem to want to do it this year," he says, "or have the ability to do it all the time." He invokes the Cincinnati Reds. "You can hold on to it for so long, then it slips away. But we still have the potential," he concludes wistfully.

Toe Blake is padding up and down the lobby, mingling with the players. It's been a long haul for Toe, working in the mines in summer in Falconbridge when he was playing with the Punch Line, and then coaching the greatest Canadiens team ever, its total payroll $300,000. A long way from there to here. Now traveling with today's *Glorieux*, disco-smart in their Cardin jackets, ostentatious fur coats, suede boots; a team representing a total payroll estimated at $3 million. "When I was playing in this league," Toe says, "I worried about my job. Even the stars worried. If you went sour for five games, maybe even a couple, down you went, but now . . ." Today's average player, he acknowledges, is a better skater, but he misses the passing and the playmaking of the vintage NHL years. In that feathery voice of his, Toe laments that even on the power play forwards tend to shoot the puck into the corners, rather than carrying it over the blue line. "If I were still coaching I'd bring back puck-handling. I wouldn't want them to throw the puck away. Look at the Rus-

sians. They're skating all the time. That's their secret." Neither
is Toe an admirer of the slap shot. "Dick Irwin used to say it
doesn't matter how hard you hit that glass or the boards, the
light won't go on."

The team bus is due to leave for the Garden at 5:00, but come
4:00 Lafleur is pacing the lobby, enclosed in a space all his own.
Doug Herron, whose wife gave birth to a baby girl the day before, will be in the nets. "I know I'm ready," he says. "But sometimes you've got it, sometimes not."

February 10, Boston Garden, Canadiens 3, Bruins 2.

In the first period, the surging Bruins outshoot the Canadiens
8–4, and the difference is Herron, who makes some spiffy stops.
Fifteen long minutes pass before Montreal has its first shot on
the Boston nets. A goal. Engblom. Trooping out of the press
gallery everybody agrees that if not for Herron we could easily
be down three goals. Like Dryden, he is keeping them in there.

In the second period, Boston outshoots Montreal again, 12–8,
scoring twice. Both goals come on two-on-ones. Savard is caught
up the ice on one, Robinson on another. An overworked Robinson is not making many end-to-end rushes this season. He can't.
Poor Robinson is playing forty minutes a game, maybe more,
and seems to be out on the ice every time I look down. "Last
season," Toe says, "Larry wouldn't be out there for more than a
minute, maybe a minute and a half, and then in would come Savard and Lapointe, but now . . ."

Finally, the Canadiens surface with what was once their traditionally big third period. Napier, who some observers thought
would help us forget Cournoyer, ties the game with his first goal
since December 23. Then Lafleur sets up Larouche for the winning goal with a pass from the corner that I can only call magical.

On the chartered jet back to Montreal the players are in high
spirits, a smiling Lafleur drifting down the aisle, serving beer.
These are a classy bunch of athletes, not the sort to goose stew-
ardesses or embarrass other guests in hotels. The French- and

English-speaking players mingle easily; they don't drift off into separate groups.

February 14, the Forum, Canadiens 5, Nordiques 1.

Suddenly, the others are scoring. Mondou, Jarvis, even Chartraw. And of course Lafleur is there, with a goal and two assists.

"What you are really seeing," a bemused French Canadian sportswriter tells me, "is a battle between two breweries." Molson's owns the Canadiens; Labatt's, the Quebec City Nordiques. "Loyalties are split in the province for the first time," he adds, "and we will have to wait and see which brewery improves their beer sales most."

A couple of days after the game, Ruel announces he will wait until the season is over before deciding whether to continue coaching. "The decision is mine," he says.

The players are fond of Ruel, but not intimidated by him. This is now a matriarchal society, Ruel fussing fondly over his charges rather than threatening them. But he remains a joke to some of the writers. At a practice, coaching the team on two-on-ones, he bellows at the lone defenseman, "Each guy take a man."

During his previous short-lived stint as coach, Ruel was standing behind the Canadiens bench in the Boston Garden when a brawl broke out among the fans. Clearing the aisle behind the bench, enthusiastic cops shifted Ruel out with all the troublemakers. "I de coach," he shouted back at them unavailingly. "I de coach."

Now that so many Europeans were playing in the NHL, a writer asked Ruel why he didn't scout the Swedes and the Czechs during the off-season. "Nutting," he shot back, "would make me cross the Athletic Ocean."

February 16, the Forum, Canadiens 8, Penguins 1.

One of the season's rare laughers. Mondou scores twice and so does Lafleur, now only a point behind Marcel Dionne in the race for the scoring championship. It is Lafleur's 399th goal.

It is announced in the dressing room that our charter will not be taking off tonight as expected. Instead, we will be leaving for Buffalo at 10:30 tomorrow morning.

At the airport, Sunday morning, everybody is reading *Dimanche-Matin*, wherein Maurice Richard, who ought to know about such things, observes in his column, *"A lui seul, Guy Lafleur vaut le prix d'entrée."*

10:45. Still no plane. "Hey," one of the players asks, "do you think Scotty's behind this?"

"Damn right."

This will be the team's first trip to Buffalo. In two earlier games against the Sabres, both in Montreal, Scotty has failed to appear behind the bench. Montreal won the first meeting, 6–3, but was routed the second time out, 7–2. "Is there anything personal against Scotty in this game?" I ask.

"Aw, he won't be wearing blades," Robinson replies.

I catch up with Scotty in the somewhat frenetic Buffalo dressing room just before the game, and we retreat to his adjoining office.

"I have no ax to grind with anybody, except Sam," he says. "Sam duped me. Sure, I was offered what they called the GM's job for the year following this one, but I would have had to serve on a five-man committee. I wouldn't have had the right to make trades. Would Sam have taken the job under those terms? I have nothing against Grundman, but Sam looked after himself. Well, that's the name of the game." He sneaks a glance at his wristwatch. "Last summer, at the individual awards dinner, not one Montreal player mentioned me. They miss Dryden, you know. He was a great goalie. He very rarely had two bad games in a row. Well, *we're* second overall, you know."

February 17, Buffalo Memorial Auditorium, Canadiens 2, Sabres 2.

Bowman is not behind the bench, but he was carrying a walkie-talkie in the dressing room, so I suspect he is in direct touch with Roger Neilson. Surprisingly, Laroque is in the Montreal nets. It turns out to be a boring, defensive game, possibly a dress rehearsal for the playoffs, scoreless going into the third period. In the third, both teams collect a couple of goals, but Lafleur fails to earn a point, and now trails Dionne by three.

In Landover, Maryland, a couple of nights later, the Canadiens were defeated 3–1 by the Washington Caps, the latter's first victory over Montreal in thirty-four games. Once more Lafleur, still looking for his 400th goal, failed to earn a point. The next morning it was reported that he had bruised his knee, and would be out for another game. But a few days later, after Lafleur had missed his third game in a row, the club allowed that he was suffering from a contusion of the knee, along with stretched ligaments. He wouldn't be in the lineup for at least another week, but there would definitely be no surgery, trainer Yvon Belanger said.

"I hate to think where we'd be without Lafleur," Toe Blake had allowed earlier. "Maybe even worse off than the Leafs. He's one of the all-time greats. Bobby Orr was the best for ten years, the best I've ever seen, in fact, but after Guy has played for ten years, I might just change my mind."

Lafleur, who was then earning a rumored $350,000 a year with the Canadiens, told me that he could easily get $1 million elsewhere. Possibly in New York. "Why don't you leave, then?" I asked.

"A friend once told me, better to be a king in your own country than a valet somewhere else."

The next season was the shortest ever for a suddenly vulnerable, clearly perplexed Lafleur, who missed twenty-eight games and, for the first time in seven years, failed to challenge for the scoring championship, or to net the magical fifty goals. Poor Guy. Essentially a private man, in 1981 he also became the stuff of gossip columnists and public scolds. Beset by marital conundrums, as well as highly publicized income tax troubles, the once seemingly indestructible player was out of action nine times, either ill or injured. Coming off his last injury—a minor one, a charley horse—he was, according to reports, exhilarated by his best practice of the season, and then he was obliged to endure yet another round of bargaining with obdurate income tax officials. Depressed, he met new teammate Robert Picard for dinner at Thursday's, a singles bar on Montreal's modish Crescent Street. They had a few drinks and wine with dinner, which Guy followed with a couple of Amarettos. Afterward, they repaired to Le Saga, a disco bar, to meet another friend for a nightcap. Lafleur left at 2:00 A.M., alone, in his Cadillac.

"Don't drive," Picard pleaded, reaching for his car keys. But Lafleur insisted, with some heat, that he was just fine.

Maybe fifteen minutes later, out on the highway, Lafleur fell asleep at the wheel. His car plowed through sixty feet of fence and a light standard. A metal plate shattered the car's window, trapping him between the door and the steering wheel. The light standard, a veritable spear now, sliced his ear. An inch or two more to the right, and he would have been impaled.

An off-duty Mountie, who just happened to be driving past, promptly removed Lafleur from the wrecked Cadillac and rushed him to the hospital, where he underwent surgery to his ear but was otherwise pronounced healthy. On balance, he was lucky to escape with his life. Very lucky. But he was never the same player again, losing speed, and showing his vintage form only in increasingly rare bursts.

The same was true of the Montreal Canadiens.

In 1980, they were eliminated by the Minnesota North Stars in the second round of the playoffs.

In 1981, they went down to the Edmonton Oilers, losing three games in a row.

In 1982, they were humiliated in the first playoff round by the Quebec Nordiques, and in 1983, they were knocked out in the first round, yet again.

General manager Irving Grundman was fired.

Coach Bob Berry was also fired and then rehired by Serge Savard, the newly appointed general manager.

Morenz. Richard. Beliveau. Lafleur.

The Montreal Canadiens, a proud dynasty now in sharp decline, are not, as tradition surely demanded, counting on a magical Québécois skater to renew their dominance of the league. Somebody now playing out there in Thurso or Trois-Rivières or Chicoutimi. No, sir. Today *le Club de Hockey Canadiens* is looking to an aging commie—Vladislav Tretiak, goalie for the Red Army—whom they devoutly hope to sign following the 1984 Olympic Games in Sarajevo.

Ça, alors.

North of Sixty

THAT INDISPENSABLE WEEKLY *THE YELLOWKNIFER* ONCE
ran the following small ad by a new settler:

LAWN MOWER for sale. Like new. Reason for selling. No
grass. Or would consider purchasing lawn.

Yellowknife, out there in the Northwest Territories, some
272 miles south of the Arctic Circle, may be a tacky little town.
Functional here, downright sleazy there. With a new alumin-
ium-sided courthouse that looks like the ultimate Greyhound bus
station. An ugly main street. Restaurants that serve unspeakable
food. Mobile-home settlements here, there, and everywhere.
But, for all that, Yellowknife is also absolutely wonderful.

Dug into the oldest rock in the world, the Precambrian Shield,
Yellowknife rides a basement 5,000 feet deep that is seamed with
gold. It lies on the northern arm of the Great Slave Lake, the
gateway to waters that abound in northern pike, Arctic grey-
lings, walleyes, whitefish, and lake trout. Yellowknife, legendary
Yellowknife, can also lay claim to the only golf course in the
world whose clubhouse once literally flew off to war, as well as a
band of Indians who earn their living providing a delicacy for the
Jewish Sabbath table.

The Yellowknife Golf Club, a typical act of north-of-sixty de-
fiance, has no grass, but is rooted in sand and rock. Until 1947, it
was also without a clubhouse. Then an American DC-3 transport

crash-landed on the course, sluing through the jack pines just short of the airport. It was immediately converted into the golf course's first amenity. It filled that social office until 1952, when an American order recalled DC-3s everywhere. Along came some USAF personnel to screw an engine onto the clubhouse and fly it into battle in Korea. *Is it a bird? Is it a plane? No, it's Yellowknife's flying clubhouse.*

There is now a fish plant, run by Dogribs, on the shores of the Great Slave Lake, for which the enterprising Indians net white-fish and pike.

"What do you do with it?" I asked.

"Oh, we ship it to the Jews in Chicago, who use it to make what they call gefilte fish."

Eschewing summer, the blackfly season, I first flew into Yellowknife in the late winter, starting out of Edmonton, traveling with Pacific Western Airlines—PWA—which northerners have dubbed "Pray While Aloft" or "Probably Won't Arrive." I flew into town forearmed with a pocket-size wind-chill chart, which warned me that starting at fifteen below zero, given a wind of twenty-five miles per hour, the flesh may freeze within one minute. I was also toting copies of *Northern Survival* and *Down But Not Out,* the former insisting that "everybody who travels on land in the Arctic or barren lands should be able to build a snow house," and the latter that if our plane went down, "mice and lemmings were edible and should not be overlooked by the survivor." Considerably sobered, I called for the stewardess. "Have you any cognac?"

"Sorry," she said, "but we only serve hard liquor."

Like, I was soon to discover, Hudson's Bay Overproof Rum, which is only available in the NWT and is still traditionally offered as a first drink to unwary visitors, a test of any southerner's fortitude. In Canada's ten provinces, I should point out, liquor is a government monopoly, available from provincial liquor stores. But in Yellowknife the bustling liquor store is privately owned by the good Messrs. Eggenberger and Pollack, who also run the local dairy. "Those guys have got us by the short and curlies," I was told. "You know, from the cradle to the grave."

A prominent sign in the liquor store reads:

YOU BREAK IT,

YOU PAY FOR IT.

Lowering into the airport, I immediately noticed the bush pilot operators' sheds. Wardair, Ptarmigan, Gateway, NWT.

Not only was there a last frontier on the continent's frost-encrusted roof, but also the ultimate pony express. Appropriately grizzled, idiosyncratic bush pilots who fly out of Yellowknife, Tuktoyaktuk, Gjoa Haven, Fort Good Hope, and Cambridge Bay, among other places. They fly charters, taking off into the barrens on floats or wheel-skis, but primarily on instinct, an uncanny ability to read the tundra. The first time I took off with one of them out of Yellowknife, driving into the seemingly endless barrens, across Hudson's Bay, bouncing over Baffin Island, dipping through the bleak and intimidating mountain passes of the eastern Arctic, finally coming down in Pangirtung, I flew forewarned.

"You taking off with Daryl today?" I was asked.

"Right."

"Well, you needn't worry. He's one of the best around."

I nodded, appreciative.

"How come, you'll want to know. Well, I'll tell you. He's the only bush pilot in Yellowknife who can drink scotch standing on his head."

"And when did he last manage that?"

"Four o'clock this morning."

Actually, before attempting the postage-stamp-size strip in Pang, we had to put down in Frobisher, in deference to a partial whiteout. Daryl strode into the air terminal and returned to report, "Nothing's flying."

The man in charge of our shivering party, big Stuart Hodgson, then commissioner of the Territories, cuffed Daryl on the shoulder. "Yeah, but you'll get us through, you bastard, won't you?"

Flying on memory, a third eye, and a hangover, a grudging Daryl finally landed, bouncing, then skidding to a stop just short of a sheer mountain wall. Only after we had all emerged shakily from the plane did a delighted Hodgson ask me, "Did you know that this flight was against regulations?"

"No. Why?"

"The runway," he said, heaving with laughter, "is four hundred feet too short for the Grumman."

Inhabitants of the Territories, or north of sixty, as many of them prefer, dismiss the rest of Canada (and, indeed, the world) as "the outside." The Territories cover roughly a third of Canada, more than a million and a quarter square miles, and from subzero end to end there are but 40,000 frostbitten, stubborn people: a third Eskimo or Inuit; about a third Indian and métis; a third white. A good many of the whites, and an increasing number of the Inuit, are civil servants, government men more than once removed from the gray proprieties of distant Ottawa. Until 1969, the Territories' Eskimos were known to their Ottawa bookkeepers by no more than an identification disk, a sequence of digits. In 1969, Commissioner Hodgson decided this was undignified. So he dispatched one Abraham Okpik on a two-year mission through the bitterly cold, vast land to offer surnames to his people, any surnames they chose, which accounts for the fact that a celebrated Yellowknife hooker is known as Sophie Football.

If the northern civil servant is a special breed, so was the Territories' scholarly supreme court judge of the Seventies, the late Mr. Justice Morrow of Yellowknife. Morrow, packing his court party and survival kit on board an aging DC-3, regularly carried Her Majesty's justice to even the most remote settlements of the high Arctic. Among the court party, when I traveled with it, was chief federal prosecutor Orville Troy, who used to sport a T-shirt with ASS embossed on it. ASS for Arctic Secret Service. "The Arctic Secret Service is so secret," he confided to me, "that you may be a member and not even know it yet."

Once, after a tire flattened on a strip that was no more than a cleared icefield, the court party's resourceful pilot pumped it full and, in the absence of a proper repair kit, pissed on the puncture, freezing it closed immediately before takeoff. Another time, bound for yet another distant settlement, the pilot informed the judge that the weather was closing in; they would have only an hour on the ground or, conversely, could be stuck there for a week, maybe ten days, before the skies cleared again. The judge, improvising, shed his sealskin parka, hurried into his robes, and announced that court would be convened on board. The business on hand, an Eskimo divorce case, was heard in the cabin of the DC-3 with the engines shut off, the temperature rapidly sinking to thirty degrees below zero. Mr. Justice Morrow had flown 1,500 miles just to hear the divorce petition, but, as a matter of form, first asked the applicant if there was any possibility of a reconciliation.

The Eskimo, eager to please, grinned shyly. "Sure. Why not?"

"In that case," the judge asked, "where is your wife?"

His manner rueful, he explained his wife was in yet another settlement, 1,200 miles away.

Teeth chattering, the judge pronounced, "We'll be back in the spring."

In the old days when the bush pilots still flew planes with open cockpits through the subzero weather, there were C. H. "Punch" Dickins and Max Ward. Dickins holds a number of Arctic records and Ward is now president of Wardair, Canada's largest international charter airline. Whiskey Papa, or Welby Phipps, has also retired. Daddy Ho Ho, or Bob Engle, today runs his own airline, a burgeoning business. And so now there are Dunc, Charlie, Jim, Pete, Gene, and many more who come and go, drifting from settlement to settlement. Some are known for their proficiency in flying the barrens, above the tree line; others for their ability to read the almost equally confusing bush country. At least one, Rocky Parsons, is reputed to be very good on the ground. "If you're going to go down," I've heard it said again and again, "you want a pilot who can live off the land. You want Parsons. He'll keep you alive for weeks." Another, Dunc Matheson, is known as the best damn navigator north of sixty. "Equipment, hell. Give him the sun or stars and a piece of string and he'll find his way anywhere."

The trade, a risky one, makes natural provision for survival of the fittest.

"Whatever you do," I was warned, "never fly with anybody who hasn't been working the country for more than five years. If he's made five and survived, he's got to be safe."

"Or overdue?"

"You believe it."

There is also a certain snobbery attached to the trade, the bush pilots knowing and recognizing each other by the craft they fly. This one can't be trusted in an expensive twin-engine job, that one is too clumsy to be allowed floats. All of them are obliged to land on makeshift airstrips in remote settlements, rough clearings on the ice, the so-called runway lit at night by no more than fires set off in oil drums. The worst that can be said for a pilot is that he has no feeling for his plane. He doesn't merely scan his instrument panel, taking it all in with a knowing glance, but is obliged to contemplate each dial individually. And the worst that can be said for a plane is that it is unforgiving.

The bush pilots, an undoubtedly intrepid bunch, are far from foolish, and what they dread most is a whiteout. To be caught in a whiteout, one of them explained to me, is like flying through a bottle of milk. There is absolutely no horizon. And on occasion, even the most experienced bush pilot, riding into a whiteout, wheeling and turning, his sense of gravity lost, is inclined to doubt his instruments and fly upside down into the ground. Inevitably, it happens two, maybe three, times a winter, and then the army comes in, the whole town is organized, everybody who possibly can taking part in the search-and-rescue mission. Nurses, garage mechanics, clerks, volunteering to fly the tundra, secured by straps, suspended from the open underbelly of a four-engine Hercules, tears freezing on their faces as they scan the glittering snow for signs of a camp or wreckage. Smoke. A flare. The glint of the sun on a snapped wing. "Even if you know where the plane is," a search officer told me, "it is very difficult to spot on the barrens or in the bush." There are further complications. Aside from a survival kit, each pilot carries an ELT, a primitive battery-run radio that is supposed to be set off on impact, emitting a signal that can be readily picked up by a high-flying, radar-equipped RCMP airplane. "The problem is," the search officer said, "once a plane goes down, every bush pilot from here to Frobisher Bay decides to test his own ELT, giving it a hard whack and setting it off. We pick up signals everywhere."

One bush pilot, in the late Fifties, survived for almost sixty days in the barrens before he was rescued. Others, like Jim McAvoy's brother, have yet to be discovered. He went down years ago, but to this day, between jobs, McAvoy takes off into the barrens, still searching. The other pilots shake their heads—it's hopeless, utterly hopeless—but nobody says a word to McAvoy. Besides, the next time it could be you.

Stunted jack pines and mean scrub stands of spruce, sufficiently hardy to take root in the Precambrian Shield, line the approach to feisty Yellowknife, capital city of one-third of Canada, its population roughly 10,000. Once a tent city, no more than a mining camp, Yellowknife is now civilized, which is to say Colonel Sanders has come. There is also a legion hall, an Elks, and even an

Odd Fellow's Lodge. There are not only Anglican and Baptist churches, but also a place of worship for those who practice the Baha'i World Faith. There's the Hudson's Bay store, without which no northern settlement would be complete, and of course there are the bars. The Hoist Room, La Gondola, the Snowshoe Lounge, the Trapline. On a Saturday afternoon in Yellowknife, the bush pilots and miners drift between the coffee shop in the seedy Yellowknife Inn and the smoke-filled bar in the squalid Gold Range, where they shoot the breeze over the traditional "two and a juice": two glasses of draft beer and a jug of tomato juice to serve as a mixer. The talk tends to be about jobs available and, naturally, the weather, every northerner's most immediate concern.

On my most recent trip to Yellowknife, a summer fishing expedition, I was glad to see the town's spirit hadn't faltered. The federal government in distant and sometimes utterly daft Ottawa had just awarded the town $40,000 worth of fireworks to be set off on Canada Day, July 1. The locals, instead of rising to cheer, were rolling about with laughter. Reason for laughter: no darkness.

Although the sun shines only tentatively for six hours a day during the punishing winter months, Yellowknife provides twenty exhilarating hours of daylight and four hours of twilight during summer. Late in June, on the weekend of the Midnight Sun, there is the annual Folk on the Rocks Festival out on Long Lake, when fiddlers out of Tuktoyaktuk, Indian drummers out of Fort Rae, and Eskimo throat singers roll into town, all of them more enthusiastic than talented. Then, on June 21, the very Night of the Midnight Sun, the Yellowknife Golf Club, its present clubhouse securely anchored, starts its annual tournament at midnight. Royal Canadian Golf Association rules are followed with one important modification: "No penalty assessed when ball carried off by raven." And there are ravens, ravens everywhere. The big black bold birds are omnipresent in Yellowknife. Perched on powerlines in the chill of winter. Diving down on garbage pails, three or maybe four of them rocking the pail until it topples and they are free to scavenge.

Until 1960, there was no road out of Yellowknife. Weeks before the Mackenzie Highway system, the 947-mile winding link with Edmonton, was completed, a visiting reporter asked an old settler what he would do once the road was ready. Without hesitation, he replied: "Drive the hell out of here." But he is still there, of course.

When its first mile of road was completed in 1944, and two cars were brought in by river barge, they managed a head-on collision within a week. Now there are miles of paved roads and even rows of parking meters on Franklin Avenue. A few years ago, Chief Arrowmaker, a Dogrib, was brought before a magistrate for failing to feed the meter. Outraged, he protested, "I can't read the white man's symbols."

"If you can drive a white man's machine," he was told, "you should be able to read his symbols."

"And not only that," Arrowmaker continued, fulminating, "but this is my land anyway."

Who the land actually belongs to—Indians, métis, Eskimos, or white men—and whether the once contemplated construction of a $7 billion natural-gas pipeline would destroy the environment beyond repair, was debated at the Mackenzie Valley Pipeline Inquiry, conducted in the Northwest Territories from 1974 through 1977 by Mr. Justice Berger.

Fred Andrew, a Slavey trapper, told the inquiry, "I have heard that the pipeline is to go, I can't say anything . . . [but] this is our land, we worry about fires, forest fires, but still the fires keep catching on. Since I recall, I hear that people keep their money in banks. The Indian people don't do that, they go out in the land and kill their meat. . . . We make our living off the land. If we don't have any rabbit or moose or fish, we don't have anything. I have nothing. . . . We don't write, we use our heads, we use our heads the right way. I have been to the white man's land,

and there to go to the bathroom I have to pay ten cents . . . and now, they go all over our land, and they are not paying."

There will be no pipeline, but even so the native way of life seems doomed. Gone, already, are the legendary dog teams, displaced by snowmobiles. Eskimo lads from the Arctic coast, educated by missionaries, or in schools provided by the government, have lost their traditional skills. And now, ironically, it is the RCMP that runs special classes to teach them how to hunt caribou or seal.

Yellowknife took its name from a band of Indians, a branch of the Chipewyans, who used to inhabit the region and were known to early explorers as Yellowknives or Copperknives, so called for the weapons they fashioned from local copper deposits. For years the ferocious Yellowknives lorded it over the neighboring Dogribs. Then one night, as the Yellowknives lay ravaged by a smallpox epidemic, the Dogribs fell on them, decimating the tribe, survivors fleeing across the Great Slave lake, south to Snowdrift.

The white man was no more than an occasional interloper until 1934, when gold was discovered, and the Old Town, as it came to be known, began to take shape on the steep sides of the huge central rocks. Those, those were the days of the notorious Rex Café, cat and gaming houses, and log-cabin banks, and then the raw mining camp began to attract those characters who have since become part of the capital city's heritage. Among them, Burial Smith, town drunk and undertaker, who used to barrel through Yellowknife in a van that served as both a taxi and a hearse, a sign prominently displayed in the window: $15 lying down, $2.50 sitting up. Smith, who unfortunately could not abide corpses, took to guzzling embalming fluid as well as other potent brews. As no graves could be dug into the permafrost in the wintertime, he was obliged to estimate the coming season's losses in summer and, anticipating, dig the necessary holes. "There used to be a saying here," an old resident told me, "that if you died during the winter, they would sharpen your head and drive you in with a sledgehammer or, if you were a crooked bastard, they'd simply screw you into the ground."

If Burial Smith is no more, another character, the mysterious Tom Doornbos, lingered well into the Seventies. A septuagenarian when I encountered him, Doornbos could still be seen prowling the streets, his shabby coat ankle-length, a tattered briefcase always to hand. Years ago, before plumbing came to Yellowknife, Doornbos used to wander the same streets wearing a yoke, vending buckets of fresh water. He was rumored to have fled Amsterdam following a stock-market scandal, and as he wandered through town, he also scoured the streets for old bits of linoleum, string, bent nails, anything. Then, shortly after World War II, when there was a temporary shortage of nails, Doornbos shuffled into Walt England's hardware store and sold him a bucket of invaluable nails, all of which had been straightened out. He had, by this time, begun to acquire lots in and around Yellowknife, and is rumored to have died fabulously rich, a large landholder, but nobody ever really knew for sure.

As late as 1960, the population of Yellowknife was no more than 3,000. Then, in 1967, a sea change occurred, after which nothing was the same any more in Yellowknife, not to say the entire NWT. In 1967, big, incomparably ebullient, and plainspoken Stuart Hodgson, the newly appointed commissioner, lifted the territorial government out of Ottawa, where it was traditionally ensconced, and flew it en masse into Yellowknife. "I'd only just started the job in Ottawa," he said, "when I realized you simply cannot walk into an office here—two thousand miles from where all the action is—take off your southern coat and put on your northern coat. . . . Now when the people of the North are cold, I'm cold also; when their basements are flooded, so is mine."

Hodgson, a former West Coast union organizer, was affectionately known as Oomemak, or the musk ox, to the Eskimos. He carried the government to them, flying into even the most remote settlements at least once a year. A hellraiser, a mover, as deeply involved with the North as he was impatient of the traditionally vacillating bureaucrat. Descending into a settlement with his attendants, Hodgson would call a community meeting, demanding that the Eskimos state their grievances. Once, he told me, a disgruntled Eskimo trapper stopped him as he left a meeting hall. "How come," he asked, "my 'rats [muskrats] were only worth a dollar each this year?"

"Well now," Hodgson began, "after you come in from your trapping in the barrens, we ship your 'rats to Montreal. You know Montreal?"

The trapper shook his head, no. Drawing a map in the snow, Hodgson explained that it was a big city in Canada.

"I understand," the trapper said.

"Good. Well, from Montreal, they send your 'rats across the big sea to a city called Paris in France." He drew another map in the snow. "You understand that?"

"I understand."

"In Paris, there is a house called Dior and they create fashions for the ladies and, if they feature furs, you are paid lots of money for your 'rats. You understand what I'm saying?"

"Yes. I understand."

"But if they do not use furs, we can't get you much money for your 'rats. Last year they did not include furs. You understand?"

"Yes."

"Good."

"But how come my 'rats were only worth a dollar each this year?"

If furs continue shaky, gold has enjoyed a revival. Yellowknife's Great Consolidated Mining Company, as well as the neighboring Giant Yellowknife, extract something like half an ounce of gold out of a ton of pulverized rock, working either end of a seam that passes directly under the town. Once, however, the seam was much richer. According to the town's first newspaper, the six-page mimeographed weekly *Prospector,* the first gold brick poured in the NWT was cast as the Great Con on Monday, September 5, 1938. "Weight of the history-making brick was 72½ ounces." A later issue of the *Prospector,* December 15, 1938, announced on the first page, FIRST WHITE CHILD BORN IN YELLOWKNIFE. It was a girl, Margaret Karin Lundquist. The same issue of the newspaper proclaimed, IT'S HERE!, *Stella Dallas,* at the Pioneer Theatre, with Barbara Stanwyck. It also revealed RADIO TELEPHONE LINKS NORTH WITH OUTSIDE. "Commercial radio-telephone service between Yellowknife and the outside is now in operation . . . from Yellowknife to any part of the world. . . ."

Now, of course, Yellowknife has its own radio station, CBC-TV via satellite, as well as the weekly *Yellowknifer.* Even more important, possibly, are the militant *Native Press,* published by the Indian Brotherhood, and, out of Frobisher Bay for distribution throughout the entire NWT, the Eskimo newspaper, *Inukshuk.* Both native newspapers feature an uncommonly large proportion of stories on alcoholism, the most serious social problem in the Territories. A recent *Inukshuk* headline ran: DRUNKS HAVE FORGOTTEN CHRISTIAN GOD. "A drunkard, according to Anglican Archdeacon Whitebread, will not get into heaven. He was speaking at Alcohol Education Day. . . ."

The sales of alcohol in the NWT are prodigious, and no large northern community, including Yellowknife, is without its de-intoxication center. And so, ten years ago, two imaginative government officials, Jake Ootes and Art Sorensen, came up with a grabber, *Captain Al Cohol Comics,* which warned unwary northern readers that LIQUOR DOESN'T MAKE HEROES! BOOZE IS FOR BUMS! Captain Al, who enjoyed superhuman powers until he was tempted by booze, which rendered him into a blundering fool, was featured in four stirring comic books, which have since become collectors' items. He was to be followed, Ootes told me, by yet another problem hero, Corporal Clap. Alas, the corporal never surfaced, and even Captain Al was banned. Native groups adjudged him a racist, fair-skinned and fair-haired, although most of the people in the north were native. So, in the end, the delightful captain was killed by bureaucracy, not booze.

But booze remains an enormous problem.

Once when I was visiting Yellowknife, vast herds of caribou were reported in nearby Snowdrift. The Indians were potting them by the hundreds, shipping planeloads to market in Yellowknife, netting as much as $1,200 a flight. But no sooner had the cash been turned over than yet another plane was chartered to fly from Yellowknife and return laden with $1,200 worth of liquor. The hunt would not resume until all the bottles were gone, $1,200 changed hands again, and more liquor was sent for. Then, too, to enter the Yellowknife Inn on any day of the week is to elbow your way past knots of despondent Indians and Eskimos, some of them teenagers, most of them drunk, all of them seemingly waiting for somebody or something never to arrive.

For all that, whatever its problems, wonderful, demented Yellowknife has more spirit than any other town I know of in Canada. Take the referendum, for instance, called some years back to determine whether or not the town wanted home mail delivery. Yellowknifers voted a resounding "No," even though winter temperatures can plunge to forty below zero, if only because during the long dark months many of them get to meet each other only when they pick up their mail at the post office. And then, a miner, stopped outside the post office by an inquiring photographer from the *Yellowknifer* and asked what social facility, presently missing, would most enhance the quality of life in town, promptly replied: "A whorehouse."

Language
(and Other) Problems

ALL THE INSTRUMENTS OF AUTUMN 1982 AGREED THAT WE
were in for an unusually punishing season, even for Canada. In
September, with 1,388,000—or some 12.2 percent of the labor
force—already without work, Prime Minister Trudeau warned,
some might say redundantly, "It's going to be a long cold winter." Only a week later the meteorologists were heard from,
merrily predicting COLDEST WINTER OF CENTURY. The April
eruption of El Chicón volcano in Mexico, thrusting 10 million
tons of volcanic ash into the stratosphere, could lower winter
temperatures in Canada by five or six degrees. My God, even
our astrological chart was a bummer. Sunspots and the unfavor-
able position of the planets promised intense cold and more snow
than usual, especially in Quebec, where just about everything
was already out of joint anyway.

Increasingly daffy Quebec, where one day the ebullient Government House leader, Claude Charron, was booked for shoplift-
ing at Eaton's, a downtown Montreal department store, and the
next, Parti Québécois supporters, far from being appalled,
sprang to his defense, many of them ceremoniously tearing up
their Eaton's credit cards. Eaton's, they charged, was a notorious
anglophone institution, its head office in Toronto. In fact, as a
fulminating reader wrote to the *Journal de Montréal,* the emporium had contributed to Quebec's "dechristianization" years ago

by not closing on December 8, Feast of the Immaculate Conception. In the more thoughtful *Le Devoir,* a sociologist, pondering the problem, declared that Eaton's was actually a snare laid for unwary Québécois, tempting the innocent to pilfer, if only because of the absence of sufficient staff to attend to sales. This sin of omission, however, could not be stretched to cover the case of the thirty-five-year-old House leader. Charron, far from seeking help from a sales clerk, had slipped into a $120 tweed jacket and concealed it under his overcoat. He was brought down after a mere three-block chase, literally tackled in the snow. "Quebecers," notes *A Cultural Development Policy for Quebec* in one of its more pertinent passages, "are less successful than the inhabitants of other Canadian provinces at keeping themselves in shape, even artificially."

Since then two other possible causes for Charron's shopping lapse have been offered. Not necessarily related, they are homosexuality or the Liberals.

In May, several months after his resignation from the provincial assembly, Charron published an autobiography, *Désobéir* ("To Disobey"), blaming his misadventure on an inner conflict spurred by his "homosexual dissidence." Not so, protested Cultural Communities Minister Gerald Godin. As he saw it, the Liberals, who had been hounding Charron, were clearly to blame for his colleague's fall from grace.

More embarrassments were to follow.

In June, fifty-six-year-old back-bencher Gilles Grégoire, co-founder of the PQ, as well as the man credited with giving the party its name, was convicted of contributing to the juvenile delinquency of seven young girls, one of them a mere twelve-year-old, by committing immoral sexual acts with them. Grégoire, who has refused to resign from the legislature, is appealing his sentence of two years less a day.

Then, at a press conference in Paris, Inter-Governmental Affairs Minister Jacques-Yvan Morin surfaced with a notion so goofy it prompted even Premier Lévesque to a fit of giggles. In the future, Morin mused, Quebecers would hold dual Quebec-French citizenship.

Meanwhile, in the absence of King Canute, our ever-watchful minister of education, Camille Laurin, tries to hold back the tidal wave of English engulfing the world. Out there in Chateauguay, where French Canadian parents wished their children to begin studying English as a second language in grade one, starting with a weekly forty-five-minute class, the minister of education threatened legal action. Ironically, it was the English-speaking who benefited under a perverse provision of the 1981 Quebec Public Education Act. They began their French studies in kindergarten, but the French-speaking were not allowed to study English until grade four, and even at that, leading educationalists described the level of instruction as tragic. The prohibition was put in force, according to officials of the Ministry of Education, because the teaching of a second language in the very early grades could have a detrimental effect—on the evidence, he might have added, for the French-speaking, but not English-speaking, students. Luc Larivée, chairman of the Montreal Catholic School Commission, did not agree. "The problem," he said, "is political, not pedagogical."

The problem, Prime Minister Trudeau has said, is that "in a fit of cultural paternalism, all the Cambridge and Harvard graduates in the PQ cabinet have decided that, after them, French-speaking Quebecers would have no more need to use English, or to run the risk of thereby losing their Quebec souls. In the meantime, our anglophone fellow citizens in Quebec and elsewhere have studied their French and are now beating us at our own game: bilingualism."

Another embarrassment.

In Quebec City itself, it had to be allowed that the undisputed stars of the provincial capital's erratic hockey team, the Nordiques, were—in Camille Laurin's new nomenclature, about which more later—not authentic Québécois, but merely ethnic or neo-Quebecers. I speak of the three Stastny brothers, Peter, Anton, and Marian—defectors from Czechoslovakia. In an interview with the *Montreal Gazette,* the darlings of Quebec City's hockey fans allowed that—though they found the town friendly—they were not *tout à fait* happy there. Because of Quebec's language laws, Marian's six-year-old son, Robert, had been expelled from an English elementary school in suburban Ste.-Foy. His daughter, Eva, also obliged to study at a French school, was taking private English lessons.

"To survive in North America," Marian said, "you need to speak English. Almost everything is done in English."

Rising to the story in Montreal's *La Presse,* sportswriter Réjean Tremblay complained that the *Gazette* had manipulated the brothers "to better misrepresent and better smash the Quebec people."

A colonized people.

"We are nothing more than an internal colony," Premier Lévesque has said, "which lives at the will of another people."

If that's the case, then what came next was clearly the ultimate outrage.

Protesting a rollback in wages, Quebec's civil servants gathered in the snow outside the Legislative Assembly in Quebec City and spitefully unfurled that fabled banner of imperial insurrection, the Canadian flag. The next day these same pranksters, authentic Québécois even on the egregious Laurin standard, outdid themselves. Crashing a press conference called by Finance Minister Jacques Parizeau, they didn't chant imprecations, neither did they heave rotten tomatoes. Instead, they surrounded the rattled minister and belted out the Canadian national anthem in French:

> "O Canada! Terre de nos aïeux,
>   Ton front est ceint de fleurons glorieux . . ."

In this through-the-looking-glass province that I call home . . . treason.

It was Finance Minister Parizeau, I should point out, who granted Quebec's civil servants a hefty increase in wages on the eve of the referendum on sovereignty-association, in 1979. Not exactly marching orders, but certainly a timely reminder of PQ beneficence. Now, however, the till was worse than empty. When the PQ formed the government in 1976, Quebec's accumulated deficit was $4.9 billion. By the summer of 1982 it had grown to $10.1 billion, with a further $3 billion deficit anticipated in the autumn budget. This, even though the PQ, strapped for funds, had already obliged Quebecers to fork out more for gasoline than anybody else in the land, as well as paying the highest personal income tax in Canada. Anybody, for instance, who earned $40,000 a year paid nearly $3,000 more to the tax collector if he was rooted in Quebec than he would if he lived in Ontario. Naturally, this made it increasingly difficult to recruit executive talent from anywhere else in Canada into Quebec.

Quebec boasts a civil service that has swollen by 243 percent over the past decade, a payroll that now runs to a whopping $11.5 billion, just about half the entire provincial budget. The province, Prime Minister Trudeau noted in a speech delivered in Montreal in December 1981, has "created a new bourgeoisie in the public and para-public sector, which hastened to grow wealthy at the expense of the working classes by having itself paid, out of public taxes, salaries higher than those in other provinces." Though Quebec's population, he said, is 27 percent smaller than that of Ontario, its school system costs $400 million more to administer than that of Canada's largest province.

Look at it this way. *La belle province,* with a population of 6.23 million, requires 342,000 public or para-public employees, while the state of California, with roughly four times the population, hires only 320,000 state workers. To be fair, we do enjoy an all-but-comprehensive health plan here, so the Quebec figures take in all the doctors and hospital staffs in the province. It also includes the overworked officers of a relatively new agency— something unique—the Commission de Surveillance de la Langue Française. The commission has been put in place to enforce the French Language Charter, Bill 101, which, among other things, has made English-language, or even bilingual, commercial signs illegal here.

Early in December 1982, characteristically vigilant officers of the commission—or the tongue troopers, as they have come to be known here—descended on a jewelry store in Hull and warned the proprietor that unless he immediately removed a subversive sign, offensive to the collectivity, from his window, he would be fined $1,000. The sign read: "Merry Christmas."

Item: In the summer of 1980, sixty-seven-year-old Marie-Marthe Larose died of cancer of the esophagus after a two-month stay in the intensive-care unit of St. Mary's Hospital in Montreal. Following her death, her husband praised the competence of the St. Mary's staff in a letter to Dr. John Keyserlingk, who was in charge of the unit. Dr. Keyserlingk, incidentally, is a graduate of Collège Brébeuf, he is married to a French Canadian, and the first language of his children is French. But eighteen months after the fact, the late Mrs. Larose's daughter Hugette filed a complaint alleging that her mother "didn't die in French." Consequently, the doctor and three nurses, also bilingual, were summoned to appear before a closed-door hearing of the language commission early in March 1983. The commission ruled that Madame Larose had been treated by nurses who spoke "little or very little French" during 34 percent of her final two months in the hospital, or, looked at another way, that she had died only 66 percent in French.

What was singular about this episode was not the charge, but that the doctor in the case actually knew the name of his accuser.

For it is in the nature of Bill 101 that in true Star Chamber tradition anyone can file a complaint, retaining anonymity. The accused has no right to confront his accuser.

There will, however, be no substantial modifications of Bill 101, Premier Lévesque has said, because requests for change reflect a "nostalgia for the privileged past," a failure of those dubbed anglophones—or *les autres*—to adapt to the "new reality of Quebec." Most of the approximately 1.2 million anglophones in Quebec live in Montreal; in fact, *les autres* make up something like 35 percent of the two million population of that once charming, but now sadly diminished, city. Bill 101 will remain in place, according to Premier Lévesque, until such time as the real Québécois "have more security in our own institutions."

Meanwhile, the government has not been idle. Confronted by more than 200,000 without work in Montreal, unemployment running to 15.9 percent in the province as a whole (the highest in Canada after traditionally impoverished Newfoundland), it has surfaced with an ideologically acceptable make-work program. It has ordained that as of January 1, 1988, the estimated 200,000 STOP/ARRÊT road signs in Quebec will be replaced to read ARRÊT only. This, even though as recently as 1977, Premier Lévesque pronounced just such a plan ridiculous, saying, "It would make us a laughingstock."

Well, maybe not in a province where it had already been solemnly ruled that there would be no more hamburgers served, only something called "hambourgeois"; and where the importers of Harris tweed were ordered either to come up with a French equivalent name for its product or to import no more.

The truth is, Quebec hasn't been quite the same ever since the separatist Parti Québécois, led by Lévesque, surprised themselves more than anybody, riding into power in the election of November 15, 1976. The PQ charged into office riding a protest vote. The preceding Liberal government of Robert Bourassa had already alienated English-speaking voters, especially immigrants, with a tough language bill of its own, Bill 22, an ill-advised attempt to outflank the PQ. Bourassa called an unnecessary election, thinking that he could defeat the PQ one more time; Lévesque would then retire, and the party would be diminished as a serious threat. He was wrong on all counts. The PQ, which was elected with 41 percent of the popular vote, winning 70 seats out of a possible 110, displaced a government that had come to be held in contempt by most Quebecers, separatist or not. Shrewdly, the PQ chose not to run on its traditional independence platform in 1976, though it was always there, the sustaining floor of their political structure. Instead, they seized the day, promising an electorate weary of strikes, corruption, and ineptitude *un vrai gouvernement* to be followed by a referendum before any move toward independence.

Immediately, Montreal became the center of the battleground, still lacking sufficient sympathy in those days only because President Carter had failed to stand at the psychological wall that divided the English from the French—say, St.-Denis Street—and proclaim, *"Moi aussi, je suis Montréalais."*

Even so, we had never walked so tall. Pollsters tested our temperature on the hour, and there was hardly a taxi driver or bartender who had not had his in-depth views sought out by hungover foreign correspondents on the fly, fresh from Belfast, en route to Beirut. Suddenly, we were a real trouble spot. Edge City.

Here, we didn't sneak into print by seizing a hundred pounds of heroin, worth untold millions on the street. Or by grabbing a cache of cocaine landed by glider in a remote cow pasture. When the incomparable Quebec police pounced, it was the stuff that deserved to make headlines the world over. One night a friend phoned me from Beverly Hills to say he had read in the *Los Angeles Times* that the police had seized 15,000 Dunkin' Donut bags in Montreal. Hard put to contain his laughter, he asked me if it was true.

"Damn right it is," I said.

"Why?"

"Because they weren't bilingual."

It's one of many Canadian ironies that ostentatiously rich Toronto, the hotbed of English Canadian nationalism, could easily be mistaken for American. But Montreal, at the time, was still unique among North American cities, a place to be cherished. Look at it this way. Our favorite little restaurant in those days was called Le Pickwick, its cuisine indubitably French, its décor Dickensian. We also boasted, as *The New Yorker* once noted, something called the Notre Dame de Grâce Kosher Meat Mart. And the majority of marchers in our annual St. Patrick's Day parade are French-speaking, even if they are named Ryan or Bourke: Jean-Guy Ryan, Euclid Bourke. The first time I met René Lévesque, he protested, "Don't give me that shit about this being a cosmopolitan city and how we're going to spoil all that."

Of Quebec's population of 6.23 million, almost 5 million are French Canadian. Their culture, Lévesque and other PQ spokesmen insisted, was incredibly vibrant on the one hand, yet desperately in need of protection on the other. It's very, very confusing, even to somebody who lives there. Anyway, no sooner did the PQ establish itself in office than its grim ideologues were threatening to take down all the city's bilingual signs and put up in their place French-only signs, hardly a life-enhancing act. Oh dear, oh dear, those were indeed days to try the souls and property values—often interchangeable—of English-speaking Montrealers. No time for sunshine patriots or real estate developers. There seemed to be more "For Sale—*A Vendre*" signs than impatiens on the lawns of the privileged suburb of Westmount, traditional preserve of the rich, and rare was the West Island home that couldn't be had at a bargain price. The value of property in largely anglophone Westmount plummeted an estimated 30 percent in fifteen months, and, according to CanaData, new con-

struction business in Quebec fell 43 percent in the first five
months of 1977, as compared to the same period the previous
year. No sooner did young graduates pick up their degrees in
dentistry or engineering than they booked a flight out of town.
Many bank accounts were cleaned out and safety-deposit boxes
emptied, and the border bad towns in Ontario, Vermont, and
New York state were reported to be bulging with freshly stashed
treasure. The Cubans, the Russians, and, of course, the CIA
were rumored to be up to their dirty tricks. A purported agent of
the Deuxième Bureau had his cover blown by the press one
morning, denials grudgingly printed the next. Young families
began to pull out, station wagons west; old businesses were
creeping out of town on tippy-toe. American tourists were hardly
anywhere to be seen in Montreal during the summer of 1977.
Possibly, they were sulking at home because they heard they
were unloved here, or maybe they had been so ill-advised as to
fear French Canadian violence. In any event, the hotels were
hurting. And every morning we opened our newspapers to read
that yet another company had done a midnight flit, its ashen-
faced spokesman announcing without so much as a wink, "The
departure of our head office to Toronto has been on the drawing
board for years and has nothing whatsoever to do with the present political situation in Quebec."

In the absence of Torquemada, Quebec's minister of cultural
development, Camille Laurin, his manner insufferably patroniz-
ing or heroic—depending on where you paid your political
dues—lectured recalcitrant anglophones daily. A fifty-five-year-
old psychiatrist who dyed his hair black, Laurin was primary
spokesman for the controversial Bill 101, which made French the
official language of Quebec, and the province unilingual. Laurin
"relaxed" the unclean at public hearings rather than in proper
autos-da-fé. We were overprivileged and reactionary, he said, and
must begin to think positively, but he also protested that there
was nothing bigoted in the term "Québécois." Anybody who
lived in Quebec, Premier Lévesque said, and paid his taxes here

was a Québécois and, he failed to add, by extension also a Canadian, for a large chunk of our taxes was still paid to Ottawa. What he did add later was even more unnerving. When the premier appointed Robert Boyd head of Hydro-Québec, the largest public utility corporation in North America, he hastily pointed out to the faithful that, in spite of his anglo-sounding name, Boyd was a proper Québécois, that is to say, of French origin, and not one of the oppressors. Or, put another way, in the new order all animals on the farm would be equal unto the Quebec tax collector, but do not ask for too much.

Quebec was seething.

One day late in the spring of 1977, I pulled into a filling station on Lake Memphremagog, in the rolling country of this province's once idyllic Eastern Townships, where for years the descendants of United Empire Loyalists and French Canadians had been farming together peacefully.

"Where'd you get that?" the attendant exclaimed enthusiastically.

He meant the sticker on my somewhat battered 1973 Peugeot station wagon, which read, against a background of merry musical notes, "I'm happy to be a Canadian." I explained that it had been fixed to the rear window late one night a couple of years ago, a prank by a good friend. He hadn't realized then, and neither had I, that yesterday's joke would become today's battle cry.

"Don't worry about me," the attendant said. "I was born right here and I'm not going anywhere. I've got my hunting guns oiled and I'm just waiting for those bastards."

"Those bastards," until November 15, 1976, most assuredly meant the Americans. Our absentee landlords. Since then, however, as far as too many anglophones were concerned, it meant only one thing—those ungrateful, exasperating, and ever-demanding French Canadians (sore losers to a man, brooding ever since they lost the day in 1759 on the Plains of Abraham) who, to our horror, had deposed a Liberal government with the largest majority in the history of the province. Considering that the PQ had been formed only in 1968, it was a remarkable accomplishment. The separatists had endured to form a government out of what Trudeau, only a few years earlier, had disdainfully dismissed as not so much a party as a particle. Some particle.

No matter what happened next, true independence, sovereignty-association, a new constitution, economic civil war, the marines following the route of Ethan Allen's Green Mountain Boys into Montreal, seizing the Seaway, one thing was resoundingly clear: Canada would never be the same again. The real opposition, rather than the floundering Progressive Conservative Party, had been heard from, and they wanted out of this marriage of convenience that is called Canada. Mind you, they wanted out with a favorable property settlement. A little understanding, a lot of alimony. And maybe something like a joint bank account maintained.

The motto of Quebec is *"Je me souviens,"* and what they remember with something like total recall is the British conquest in 1759, and the colony's subsequent abandonment by France until 1967—our Expo year—when General de Gaulle, suddenly remembering his long-lost brethren, sent a chill down Canada's spine by shouting, *"Vive le Québec libre!"* from the balcony of Montreal's City Hall.

Under the terms of Confederation, Quebec was granted control of its own educational system and legal code. But tensions between what Hugh MacLennan, in a memorable phrase, called "the two solitudes" continued to smolder, yielding a good deal of this country's appeal and creative energy, as well as its dark underside, a fearful resentment.

In 1956, Trudeau described French Canadians as "a people vanquished, occupied, leaderless, kept aside from business life and away from the cities, gradually reduced to a minority role and deprived of influence in a country which, after all, it had discovered and explored, and settled. . . ." Since then, of course, he had bet his political life—a wager still on the table, the rest of us serving as chips—on a bilingual Canada. A country where not everybody need speak both languages, but each would be entitled to his own. A society where French Canadians, rather than retreat into a sullen ghetto, the windows slammed shut, the doors bolted, could feel at home from sea to sea. Trudeau, for all his failings, had a dream, and in 1977, it seemed that were it only sweetened by real constitutional change, it was one that most Canadians, English or French, would buy.

There was a snag, however: René Lévesque.

If once French Canada had been leaderless, now it was being pulled in absolutely contrary directions by the two Canadian politicians of size in their generation, one talking to their heads, the other appealing to their hearts. And French Canada, endearingly, supported both.

Just about a year after the PQ had come to power, I asked Trudeau if, fearful of an English Canadian backlash, he felt compromised in how far he could go to accommodate Quebec, being French Canadian himself. Emphatically no, he said, but, come the utterly unthinkable—separation—he would, as he had already stated publicly, resign rather than negotiate. He also pointed out that the PQ never would have come to power had not the provincial Liberal government been so unpopular. So second-rate, he might have added. In that case, I asked, was it not possible, when he and the other so-called Wise Men (Gérald Pelletier, Jean Marchand) declared for Ottawa and the Liberal Party, that they erred in not leaving somebody of stature behind to mind the provincial shop? Going to Ottawa, he said, had been absolutely necessary at the time, if only to convince French Canada that the Québécois were acceptable on the highest levels there, and that it was their country, too.

At that time, not only the prime minister but also the governor-general, the minister of finance, and the minister in charge of federal-provincial relations were Québécois.

Trudeau, soberly optimistic about Quebec and in a fighting mood, was sensitive to criticism that he was too rigid with his own people or that, conversely, as Diefenbaker had once put it, he and Lévesque were peas in a pod. Though he was against special status for Quebec, there was a strong suggestion that he did have a third option, something between separation and the status quo, possibly a constitutional conference; but he was loath to reveal his hole card. "It's because I'm a French Canadian myself," he said, "that I'm so opposed to separatism. Why should we be reduced to a self-inflicted ghetto? And if we become unilingual again, how will we function on this continent?" However, the prime minister professed not to be displeased to see the PQ in office at last. "Better they are in power now than five years from now. The issue has been joined, and Canadians, English as well as French, will now have to make a choice." The PQ, he suggested, rather than those who stood for federalism, feared the coming referendum in Quebec. "Or," he said, "Lévesque wouldn't be delaying; he would be holding the referendum right now."

In 1964, speaking out against traditional French Canadian nationalists, René Lévesque complained, "Our élites scorned or disregarded the economic role of the state. In their eyes, the state had only one role: to act as a kind of insurance company and supplier of technical services to the large corporations. It was a colonial regime, supported by *rois nègres*, which sustained an economic system where Quebec was absent."

Lévesque did not become a separatist until 1967, when, with the Liberals in opposition again, he walked out on the party to form the PQ out of two separatist groups, and thus bestowed on French Canadian nationalists what they had lacked until then: credibility and a celebrated presence.

Where Trudeau is admired, Lévesque is loved. Through him, the Québécois undoubtedly rediscovered their pride and surprising muscle, and, understandably, this proved very heady stuff. The government elected on November 15, 1976, did not mince words. The reconquest, stated the first published draft of their language bill, has begun.

Shortly afterward, working on an article for the *Atlantic,* I phoned Quebec City, trying to reach Claude Morin, then Lévesque's minister of intergovernmental affairs.

"Where are you calling from?" his secretary asked.

"Lake Memphremagog. The Eastern Townships."

I could have said Canada, but I did not wish to be unnecessarily provocative, so I said, "It's still in Quebec, my dear."

Lévesque, enormously sensitive to criticism in the United States, had protested that American journalists hearkened to Ottawa's sweet talk, but never sought him out. Some tried, but not all got to see him. Possibly, like me, they found him impossible to reach. Three weeks of negotiations with his office, many a phone call unreturned, failed to yield an interview.

Meanwhile, Jacques Parizeau, Quebec's portly minister of finance, added a grace note of his own to the heat of our pre-referendum days, saying he didn't mind all the anglos fleeing Westmount, it would make the mansions there cheaper for his chums when it came time for them to move in, administering social democracy *de haut en bas.* And Jean-Pierre Charbonneau, a purist among PQ back-benchers, argued that it made no difference if the anglophones tried to adjust. "They could all be bilingual tomorrow morning, but this wouldn't change the fact that they think and live in English."

So far, it was not an offense to think in English here, but, like all English-speaking Quebecers, I had my nightmares. I saw my nine-year-old being tossed into the unilingual slammer, having copped three years for eating alphabet soup whose letters were proved to be without accents *grave* or *aigu.*

Treason.

"What is it you really want," I asked Gérald Godin, "a new marriage contract?"

Godin, a seemingly amiable poet and publisher, had unseated former Liberal Premier Robert Bourassa in his own riding. "Yes," he said.

"Then why are you asking for separation?"

Godin and I, along with Michel Tremblay, Quebec's most celebrated playwright, had just appeared on a TV talk show together. "You can't be a Québécois, thirty-four, and intelligent," Tremblay had said, "and not be a separatist." In an interview with the *Canadian*, he had added that he could not forgive the English. "They never respected us. Never. For me it isn't a case of economics or statistics. Just a lack of respect. And I don't mean the English of Toronto or Calgary, but the English of Quebec. They lived here, a minority, but didn't respect the majority enough to learn its language."

The PQ's language legislation, Bill 101, was something the English-speaking people of this province had, to some extent, brought on themselves by the infuriating refusal of so many in high and influential places to learn French. The truth is that for years in this society, which has been called a vertical mosaic rather than a melting pot, it was the WASPs who were at the pinnacle and the adorable, saucy French Canadians who were expected to tote the bales. Through all the years of my boyhood here, hardly a French Canadian (or a Jew, for that matter) could be seen in the exclusive WASP dining and country clubs. McGill University, an anglophone citadel, was insultingly indifferent to the French Canadian society that surrounded it, and maintained a quota on Jewish students.

So there was a vengeful side of me that clapped hands each time the PQ minister of retribution, Camille Laurin, lectured the WASPs on their need to cultivate manners more appropriate to a minority; a part of me that responded with pleasure when I saw, on televised newsclips of the language-bill hearings, that they had swiftly grasped lesson number one, how to smile ingratiatingly and make noises calculated to please, latter-day Stepin Fetchits, even as they were seething inside. Oh, how the mighty had fallen. Once indifferent to anything but their own appetites and undisputed right-of-way, they had belatedly learned to speak up for the rights of the individual in a civilized society. Oh yes, yes indeed, those same pillars of the Protestant community who for years would not suffer a Jew to sit on their stock exchange or teach in a school system that was common to both of us had now learned to plead for their children's right to be taught in English.

But, having savored their discomfort, I was fearful that what we were really seeing was not the coming of justice but rather one form of intolerance displacing another. A bill to certify the supremacy of French here was one thing, but it was something else again to agree that the existence of a thriving English-speaking minority was a menace to the very survival of the French language and culture in Quebec.

Québécois fears, clearly stated, were twofold. If the language of business within the province did not become indisputably French, the anglophones would continue in their dominant role. If immigrants were allowed to educate their children in the language of success in North America, the French would eventually become a minority at home, and their culture would gradually fade away. Legitimate concern was one thing, cultural paranoia another. No matter what the PQ legislated, the language of international head offices would continue to be English, as a committee of the PQ's own creation discovered, when it embarked on a European tour. Obviously head offices here should be bilingual, but Quebec, like it or not, was an island in an English-speaking sea, and it was folly to pretend that the province could be complete unto itself, as a country its size easily could be in another Europe. And while it was acceptable that future immigrants to Quebec, *warned ahead of time,* would have to educate their children in French, it was a cruel breach of faith to impose this on immigrants already landed here.

A clause in the proposed language bill, which called for "francization" of all businesses, was to be enforced by language inspectors. For those of us who were raised in Quebec, familiar with its petty officials, this seemed a clear invitation to zealotry or corruption. One manner of inspector, pinched and officious, his shoulders salted with dandruff, could disqualify a Greek restaurant if he heard a scalded kitchen hand curse in his native tongue. But even more commonplace would be the fat, incomparably good-natured official, spiritual brother to our sticky-fingered fire and meat inspectors, who would go out to three-hour lunches with clothing manufacturers, taking a thick envelope under the table to pronounce a cutting-room floor linguistically pure.

As we continued to drink together after the TV show, I suggested to Gérald Godin that if I were in his boots I would negotiate with Ottawa now, from a certain strength, as I expected the PQ could not win a majority in a referendum where the choices were *unambiguously* stated. The Québécois were simply too conservative to opt out. Godin disagreed. Then, as I drove back to our cottage on Lake Memphremagog, my station wagon broke down on the highway and a police car pulled up behind me. While I sat with the young French Canadian cop, waiting for a tow truck, the chat turned to politics, and I asked him what he thought of the present government.

"I saw that bunch on TV on November 15," he said, "you know, in the Paul Sauvé Arena. Some of those guys were wearing overalls. What do you call them—Oshkosh, Bigosh? Others had long hair or beards. Listen here, you work, I work. Those bastards don't work."

The Péquistes were also dubbed "those bastards," on the eve of the election, by Charles Bronfman, addressing four hundred Jewish community leaders in Montreal. He warned his audience, "Make no mistake, those bastards are out to kill us," and he added that if they were elected, against his advice, he would pack his toys and quit the province. His toys, far from negligible, included the head offices of Seagram (Canada), and Cemp, the Bronfman family investment trust, its estimated worth $800 million, as well as the Montreal Expos, founded a year after the PQ, but still last in their league.

I am assured that a prescient Hasidic rabbi immediately rose to protest. "If you leave, Mr. Bronfman, what happens to the rest of us? After all, we haven't all got private 707s, or whatever, at our disposal."

On second thought, after the election, a rueful Bronfman decided to stay put after all, leaving the Expos in place, if not the real head office of Seagram, which, without benefit of a public announcement, was eventually moved to Kitchener-Waterloo in Ontario. And, to his credit, Lévesque responded to Bronfman's outburst with panache. We are all just a little overexcited right now, the newly elected premier said. But, obviously a baseball buff, he also allowed that the Expos might benefit from new management.

Mind you, overreaction to the PQ's triumph was not confined to Jews. The distinguished, if aging, Canadian historian Donald Creighton wrote, in an intemperate article in *Maclean's,* entitled "NO MORE CONCESSIONS, If Quebec Goes, Let It Not Be with Impunity," that for thirty-three years, "Quebec has been playing the politics of blackmail." They are to be appeased no longer. If they go, let them leave Confederation as they entered it in 1867, without the District of Ungava, the northern and larger half of the province, once part of the Northwest Territories; and "minus, of course, the territory of Labrador," which was awarded to Newfoundland in 1927. *Les maudits Québécois* would also have to concede a St. Lawrence Seaway corridor, to be under joint Canadian-American control. There would be no more bilingualism in the rest of Canada. Or garlic in salad dressing. But Creighton, not totally blinded by rage, did stop short of demanding that Lévesque and his cabinet be hanged.

Among other mad and foolish things, there sprang up in Montreal itself a movement for an eleventh province that would save anglophone areas of Quebec—Westmount, Montreal's West Island, the Eastern Townships—for Canada, creating something of a Palestinian state on our own west bank, as it were.

Some of the French were also overreacting. Or talking nonsense.

In the county of Hull, an especially deep PQ constituency group, taking the long view, resolved that the new country of Quebec should adopt a pacifist foreign policy, which is to say, Americans could relax, we were not about to reclaim Louisiana or other territories first discovered by the French.

And in a silly attempt to patch together an instant mythology, the search for usable heroes led the PQ shamelessly to dust off a statue of Maurice Duplessis, hidden in a government warehouse for years, and plunk it down in a prominent position right in front of the Assembly. Ironically, Lévesque had come into politics in the first place to fight everything the wretched Duplessis had ever stood for. At the time, he referred to the generation that had endured *la grande noirceur,* "the great darkness" of Duplessis, as one that had been "cursed" and "damned." But Duplessis had also been a nationalist, his government highly autonomist in style, and that's why his memory was being burnished.

Meanwhile, on the highest levels of political action on both the separatist and national-unity fronts in 1976, a humiliating common denominator—symbolic of the crux of the real Canadian dilemma—prevailed. Given a spot of trouble in the northern dorm, even the most promising lads in the branch-plant school had to report, cap in hand, to the principal's office. No sooner had Lévesque been elected, independence his long suit, than he got a shave and a shoeshine and revealed where our true dependence lay. He flew down to New York to sup with the bankers there, attempting to reassure them in an unfortunate speech that, while separation was inevitable, the Québécois, unlike the Cubans, would be well-behaved neighbors. We wouldn't pick our toes; we wouldn't nationalize American holdings. Shortly afterward, a jaunty Prime Minister Trudeau pinned a carnation to his lapel and hurried down to Washington to tell some senators, and an even larger audience of page boys, that though the lads in the French sixth form were being obstreperous, Quebec would certainly not separate.

Anglophone Canadians and Québécois, equally concerned about their future, were obliged to watch their leaders, speaking in another country, making their positions clear to us for the first time since the November 15 election.

Though I didn't vote for them, I welcomed the victory of the PQ in November 1976. After years of dithering, it promised that the real issue that divided this drafty house against itself would at last be joined. The long and wasting quarrel between two founding peoples, begun on the Plains of Abraham, would finally be settled one way or another. Or so it seemed.

Furthermore, fair-minded federalists had to allow that it looked as if we were going to get an honest government, something of a departure in this traditionally patronage-ridden province. An administration led by intelligent social democrats, some of Quebec's brightest and best, among them graduates of Harvard, Cambridge, and the London School of Economics. The immensely popular Lévesque, Parizeau, Claude Morin, Jacques-Yvan Morin. Lévesque was magnanimous in victory, immediately reassuring English-speaking Quebecers that they were welcome in the province, an integral part of its history. His government, he said, would be judged on how it treated its minorities.

Everybody applauded.

But the old entertainer, we were to discover, could play many a contradictory tune. In an angrier mood, leading into the referendum, he pointedly evoked memories of the Sixties. Exploding mailboxes in Westmount. Terrorist bombs in the stock exchange. The October Crisis. "I will not be responsible for what happens," he warned, "if the English continue to oppose the true aspirations of the Québécois."

The Péquistes, we soon learned, were unfortunately arrogant. The very name Parti Québécois, which Lévesque once had the good taste to object to, suggested that anybody who was not of it was of necessity against Quebec, beyond the pale. The more militant Péquistes were also in the tiresome habit of branding those Quebecers who had gone to Ottawa—numerous civil servants, Trudeau, and the Québécois members of his cabinet—not as ideological opponents, in honest disagreement with them about the direction this country should take, but as traitors pure and simple. *Fédérastes, vendus.* This officious line, gathering all virtue onto itself, was nowhere more in evidence than in the lean and hungry figure of Camille Laurin, minister of cultural development. His proposed language bill, he argued, was absolutely necessary if the French were to claim their rightful place in the economic sun. But more than three hundred francophone business leaders, who had already claimed that place, signed a letter objecting to the bill, saying they found some of its clauses "almost odious." While they were in fundamental agreement that French must become the undisputed language of the province, they feared that if the bill were adopted without making adequate provision for the teaching of English, "We French-speaking people of North America will quickly fall into functional illiteracy." Laurin immediately snapped back that these businessmen were the lackeys of the English establishment. This brought the editor of *Le Devoir,* Michel Roy, into play. He reproached Laurin for the narrowness of his vision. "On one side there are good Quebecers, those who share his convictions; on the other side are the bad Quebecers, who, daring to utter a few reservations, are therefore in the pay of the enemy."

Even so, early legislation introduced by the PQ was very good indeed. A government-backed, no-fault automobile insurance program. An enlightened land act to protect arable green areas from rampaging developers. Quebecers were promised a referendum in which we would respond to a clear-cut question on whether or not we wished to separate from the rest of Canada. And then we finally got to see Dr. Laurin's long-debated Bill 101, which turned out to be vengeful and mean-minded in its particulars. "The English in Quebec is like a fox in the hen coop," Dr. Laurin said. What we needed, he added, was a shock.

We got it.

Bill 101, which ran to nearly forty pages in the statute books, declared French the only official language in Quebec, with a stroke reducing some 20 percent of the population to second-class status. The bill put an end to a 200-year-old convention in Quebec, which gave equal legitimacy to both English and French; it also violated Section 133 of the British North America Act, which guaranteed the use of English in both the courts and the legislature. At the constitutional conferences of 1864-67, the Fathers of Confederation solemnly ruled to maintain forever English and French in the parliaments and courts of the federal government and Quebec. Speaking for the government, George Etienne Cartier said, "The English minority of Lower Canada [Quebec] also had to be protected with respect to the use of its language, because in the local parliament of Lower Canada the majority will be made up of French Canadians. The members of the [1864 Quebec] conference wished that this majority not be able to decree the abolition of the use of the English language in the local legislature of Lower Canada, any more than the English majority of the federal legislature can do so for the French language."

Bill 101, William Johnson wrote in the *Toronto Globe & Mail,* "rang the death knell of a bicentennial way of life in which two languages, French and English, were established." The government of Quebec, he added, supports the great injustice of Bill 101 "even now when the myth of an endangered French Quebec has ceased to be credible except to the severely credulous (between 1976 and 1981 the English-speaking population of Quebec declined by 90,600 while the French rose by 268,700)."

There will be no more question, Camille Laurin declared in his white paper on the French language, of a bilingual Quebec. Then, justifying his disestablishment of the English language, he wrote: "English predominates clearly in the general communications at work: 82 percent of all communications are carried out in English in Quebec as a whole." But this, William Johnson wrote, was not the case. Far from it. Citing the 1971 findings of the University of Montreal's Gendron Commission on the state of the French language in Quebec, Johnson proved how the slippery Dr. Laurin had distorted the statistics. "The U of M survey," Johnson wrote, "found that at work communications of francophones were 87 percent in French, while anglophones communicated 82 percent in English. [Dr. Laurin's] white paper took that 82 percent and simply applied it to all Quebecers. So did English become the language of work, according to the white paper. And so the Charter of the French Language was passed to save the French language. . . . [But its] chief effect, despite the rhetoric, has been to oppress the non-francophones."

Bill 101 ruled that any company with more than fifty employees would in future require a "francization" certificate to prove that it conducted all internal business in French, even if there was not one French-speaking employee on the premises. As a result, there was some fancy footwork in the needle trade. Some companies cut off employment at forty-nine and hastily incorporated another label.

Bill 101 led to the creation of the Commission de Toponymie, which promptly began to rename towns, rivers, and mountains, especially in the Eastern Townships. So, Tea Table Island was reborn Ile Table à Thé; Bunker Hill became Colline Bunker; and Molasses Lake, Lac à Mélasse. The bill also meant that come 1981 all English, or even bilingual, commercial signs would be illegal.

In January 1983, in the little border town of Degelis, motel keeper Louiselle Laforge was ordered to appear in court in Rivière-du-Loup for what now amounts to exhibitionism here.

Displaying English signs. "Please," she protested, "let me keep my three small English signs to attract tourists from Maine and New Brunswick. I promise you that no one will be hurt if they see the words OFFICE and BAR OPEN on my motel."

Inspectors from the Commission de Surveillance de la Langue Française had already dismantled a big, naughty $4,000 sign whose three-foot-high letters winked LICENSED DINING ROOM. A spokesman for the commission stated that Mrs. Laforge's faith in the English sign was a delusion, "a typically Québécois reflex" that had no basis in reality. American tourists, in fact, preferred French signs.

"If that's the case," the motel keeper responded, "why has my business dropped by more than half since they took away my big red English sign?"

Closer to my home in the Eastern Townships, one of my favorite bars, the Thirsty Boot, has had more than one threatening visit from the tongue troopers. They want the sign changed. Last time they turned up, the proprietor wasn't there. Turtle, the bartender, phoned him at home. "They're here again. What should I do?" he asked.

"If you can't throw those bastards out yourself," the proprietor replied, "I'm sure there are guys sitting at the bar who will do it for you."

To appreciate the enormity of Bill 101, it must be understood that if something similar were legislated in Ontario or Nova Scotia to preserve the purity of English there, it would mean that no more Châteauneuf-du-Pape or Pouilly-Fuissé could be imported, unless it was labeled in English. It would be illegal for a restaurant menu to offer pâté or filet mignon. Nouvelle cuisine would be new cooking and croissants would be called crescents. There would be no boutiques. The language would be cleansed of such impurities as *tête-à-tête*, *parvenu*, and *chemise*.

Bill 101 ruled that wherever a child came from—abroad, or even from another Canadian province—it had to be educated in French, unless one of its parents had been to an English school in

Quebec. In some cases, the children of English-speaking parents who had been educated outside Quebec were allowed a three-year period of adjustment before their children were plunged into French schools. This, however, did not apply to the children of Greek or Italian immigrants in Montreal, and soon an estimated 1,400 children were illegally attending English schools, under the threat of compulsory expulsion. Yet another clause of Bill 101 compelled all non-francophone professionals who were candidates for any of the thirty-nine Quebec professional corporations to take French proficiency tests, which led to a *cause célèbre,* i.e., a celebrated case.

Between 1976 and 1981, 532 nurses and 265 registered nurses' assistants (RNAs) failed, without arousing comment, a language proficiency test that required a literary and metaphorical knowledge of French. Then, late in 1981, Joanne Curran, a bilingual working-class girl, scored 85 percent on the oral exams, but failed the written test by eight points. She lost her job as an RNA at Santa Cabrini Hospital in Montreal. But the scrappy Miss Curran, who hardly fit the PQ stereotype of "white Rhodesian"—of anglophone riches and arrogance—took to the French TV talk shows, arguing her case fluently. Fair-minded French Canadians, of which there are many, were outraged. For the first time, it seemed, they grasped the real iniquities inherent in the details of Bill 101. Lysiane Gagnon wrote in *La Presse,* "I'd bet a year's salary that a good number of francophones would flunk this test." Even Pierre Bourgault, a well-known separatist intellectual, called the tests "stupid and inhumane, a scandal." A far from contrite Camille Laurin haughtily suggested that the Office de la Langue Française might lower the passing mark for RNAs "because they have less schooling than nurses who take the exam." Furthermore, he noted, Miss Curran hadn't scored 85 in the French oral test, as she claimed, but only 82. So there.

Miss Curran, who had only begun to fight, published an open letter to Dr. Laurin in the *Gazette.* Setting out that she was for the predominance and protection of the French language in Quebec, she claimed, nevertheless, that she was a victim of the law, "of the most pure and narrow-minded of bureaucracies. I am a victim, Dr. Laurin, of what I consider to be racial discrimination. I am a Quebec citizen who, like thousands of others, must now prove that she belongs in Quebec society."

Even before Bill 101 became law, the Sun Life Assurance Company—never a model corporate citizen of Quebec, its investment in the province minimal—abruptly announced the removal of its head office, a Montreal landmark, to Toronto. Other corporations, emboldened, sniffed the wind, adjudged it tribal, and were soon tripping over each other in their eagerness to flee Montreal.

Come 1979, we had become a city where you wakened each morning to count your losses. The moving vans were everywhere. Farewell parties had become the new rule. Why, they were all but dancing on the grave here. Wray's downtown funeral parlor had been born again as an insufferably modish disco. Where many a good man had been laid out, the mindless did now cavort.

We had learned to walk on tippy-toes in Montreal, whistling in the dark even as we awaited fresh pronouncements from the PQ. What we had not been prepared for was a stab in the back. It came on September 25, 1979, when the *Montreal Star,* this city's anglo guiding light for 110 years, consulted first principles—its ledgers—and decided to call it quits. It is worth noting that the lead story in the *Star*'s business section on that fateful Tuesday was headed BUILD OUR CITY. "The development of Montreal," it noted, "will have to be achieved by people committed to Montreal—people whose future and whose heart are in Montreal and not elsewhere."

Yes, indeed, but another story lower on the same page told a more telling tale. "Montrealers who have moved to Toronto in recent years have formed a club in that city—called the Montreal

Club—as a gathering centre to keep abreast of what is happening in Montreal and to pick up a bit of gossip about other Montrealers now in Ontario. . . . As one former Montrealer, now an executive in Toronto, put it: 'Sometimes I think it is easier to find someone you know in Toronto than walking along St. Catherine Street.' "

On Tuesday, September 25, I had picked up what I did not yet suspect to be a collector's item, the *Star*'s ultimate edition, at a newsstand opposite the Montreal Press Club in the basement of the Sheraton–Mt. Royal Hotel. A blue-bordered box on the front page enriched me with a hitherto unsuspected fact:

MONTREAL

Montreal
has more city squares
than any city
in North America.

5:00 P.M. it was, and, as had long been my habit, I had come to join a few irreverent cronies at the Press Club bar to guffaw over the day's inanities committed by oafs in office everywhere. I should point out that at this hour the bar is usually attended by only a handful of resolute drinkers, and so I was understandably astonished to find the club surging with reporters, many of them men and women I had never seen before. They were in a febrile state.

"What's going on?" I asked one of the regulars.

"Haven't you heard? The *Star* folded this afternoon."

Automatically, I glanced at the front-page headline of what was to be the last *Star* ever to flicker over Montreal. EXPOS SURGE FROM BEHIND TO STAY ON TOP.

"Who ever would have thought," a wag at the bar said, "that the *Star* would have folded before the Expos?"

"Those bastards," somebody else said. "Only a month ago they assured us there would never be only one English-language daily in Montreal."

Between 1976 and 1981, according to Reed Scowen, a Liberal, an estimated one hundred major head offices quit town, accounting for a loss of 14,000 jobs and, incidentally, a virtual collapse of the real estate market. In the same period, the anglophone population of Montreal dropped 11.8 percent, some 94,-565 people, many of them recent university graduates, tooling down the 401 to Toronto or points farther west. For the most part, however, English-speaking Quebecers were quiescent on the introduction of Bill 101. Anticipating rules not yet in place, many rushed to oblige, old and long-established firms dropping compromising apostrophes. Eaton's, for instance, sanitized itself, the Quebec branches of the department-store chain becoming Eaton. Steinberg's, one of the largest supermarket chains in the province, was reborn Steinberg. Such ready compliance, both public and private, was prompted by only a few drops of goodwill and, to come clean, buckets of guilt.

After all, if Bill 101 was unarguably repressive in some of its particulars, French Canadians, it must be said, were not acting vengefully without cause. There were real grievances. Historical grievances. For years French Canadians had been treated as second-class citizens in their own country and even their own province. Before the emergence of Trudeau, there were very few French Canadian or even bilingual civil servants in Ottawa, and the French-speaking were obliged to deal with their own federal government in a language many of them didn't understand. In downtown Montreal, unilingual clerks in Eaton's, and other department stores, were often gratuitously rude, imperiously demanding that French Canadian customers speak English—or do without service. Montreal offered few corporate positions, in the higher reaches, to French Canadians. Or law partnerships in the most influential firms. Or seats on the stock exchange. In those days the rulers of St. James Street, who controlled the levers of financial power in the province, maintained a strictly WASP preserve. But it is also fair to point out that French Canadians were held back by their own educational system. Antiquated and church-ridden, emphasizing family verities, it eschewed materialism and its rewards: a spiritually praiseworthy but, alas, impractical stance, which left the financial fields to be plowed by the uncultured anglophones. The anglophones didn't protest, no sir, they rubbed their hands together gleefully, putting French Canadian shoulders to wheels they spun for the anglos' fun and profit.

So there is another way of looking at Bill 101.

Anathema to English-speaking Quebecers, the bill has undoubtedly helped to bolster a still fragile French Canadian pride. The midnight flit of so many head offices from Montreal, a drain on the economy mourned by the English-speaking, has been a source of joy to many French Canadians, not all of them separatists. Of course, to militant separatists the departure of so many *maudits anglais* from Montreal is not only a pleasure, but also offers real political advantage. In the future, they feel, they will be able to say to those timorous French Canadians who argue that should Quebec separate there will be a disastrous run of English capital from the province, look here, my little chickens, the English have already flown the coop, you have nothing more to fear. And meanwhile, should there be another referendum, a good many nay-sayers had already voted with their feet. But even many of the French Canadians who consider René Lévesque to be a somewhat dotty romantic, and the economic policies of the PQ deplorable, are secretly pleased. And why not? Thrust aside for so long, they have leaped eagerly into the vacuum created by the PQ. Suddenly, they have been given an edge. Suddenly, traditionally closed WASP brokerage and law firms are stumbling over each other to recruit French Canadian partners. Suddenly, the largest independent brokerage house in the province is entirely French Canadian: Geoffrion, Leclerc Investments.

Possibly, a Jewish analogy would best serve to explain the situation.

Many Jews in Israel and the diaspora who find Menachem Begin's policies insufferable, his claims to what he calls Judea and Samaria specious, nevertheless experience a secret gut pleasure when that hot and uncompromising old man reminds the President of the United States, "The Jews bow only to God."

Similarly, French Canadian businessmen in Montreal who take Camille Laurin to be a zealot, and Bill 101 an affront to individual liberty, are very pleased to have somebody stick it to the English. Which is exactly what Camille Laurin did in his long-awaited report that preceded the referendum.

A Cultural Development Policy for Quebec, published in 1978, starts out by cheerfully dismissing the rest of Canada as an entity "which sometimes claims to be a 'nation' and carries on to divide Quebecers into racial categories: the authentic Québécois, Anglo-Saxons, and ethnic or neo-Quebecers." A crippling Canadian presence, it complains, imposes upon Quebec "restrictions that become shackles when it attempts to develop its own values and cultural endeavors." This, incongruously enough, at a time when the prime minister of Canada was a Quebecer, as was the minister of finance and also, for what it's worth, the governor-general; and when there was hardly a separatist theater group, painter, composer, or writer in Quebec that wasn't on a Canada Council grant or fettered to such federal cultural institutions as Radio-Canada or the National Film Board.

Any reference in the report to "so-called" Canadian culture is pejorative, describing it as pseudo-American, or without "cultural personality"—which is to dismiss arbitrarily the work of Robertson Davies, Northrop Frye, Alice Munro, Margaret Atwood, Christopher Plummer, the late Glenn Gould, Mavis

Gallant, Margaret Laurence, Morley Callaghan, and, come to think of it, Bobby Orr and Wayne Gretsky. But, happily, the report finds that the indigenous stuff amounts "to an outpouring of works of art that is proof of Quebec's genius."

The report, pondered and debated for months by the brightest and best Dr. Laurin could gather in conclave, abounds not only in chauvinism, but also in banalities and bromides. Both sex and age, we are earnestly told, are the result of natural laws. "We do not choose our sex, we do not choose to grow old." Women, we are assured, "are people," but this daring notion is not qualified by any scientific data. In Quebec, as elsewhere, the report claims, children make great demands on adult energy. And again, without documented support, we are asked to swallow whole the notion that "adolescents make up a large proportion of the population."

All these "brief yet thought-provoking" *pensées* came in Vol. I, the real illuminations saved for the heftier Vol. II, in which it is revealed, "Books have been one of the most important vehicles of culture for centuries, and will continue to play this role for some time." Then, after pages of complaints about the smoking and drinking habits of Quebecers, Dr. Laurin, no ordinary psychiatrist but a thinker who can see around corners and then some, ventures that "alcohol becomes all too often a prop, a stimulant or an escape."

Two weeks before the referendum, Prime Minister Trudeau spoke out at a dinner in Quebec City. For thirty-six of its first one hundred years, he was swift to point out, Canada had been governed by French Canadian prime ministers from Quebec. In the tradition of Laurier and Louis St. Laurent, he added, he had gone to Ottawa to insist on the right of Quebecers to play their larger role in Canada. "We have resolved to say NO to those who wish to tear down the house, to those who want to uproot us from this country which is ours, this country we discovered, colonized and explored. . . . We want to say NO to those who think Quebecers are not smart enough . . . to defend themselves both in Quebec and on the national scene."

The referendum question, alas, did not ask Quebecers whether or not they wished to be independent. Instead, after being extensively tested for acceptance in private PQ polls, it argued for permission to negotiate the nebulous concept of sovereignty-association. The question ran:

"The government of Quebec has made public its proposal to negotiate a new agreement with the rest of Canada, based on the equality of nations; this agreement would enable Quebec to acquire the exclusive power to make its laws, levy its taxes and establish relations abroad—in other words, sovereignty—and at the same time, to maintain with Canada an economic association including a common currency; no change in political status resulting from these negotiations will be effected without approval by the people through another referendum; on these terms, do you give the Government of Quebec the mandate to negotiate the proposed agreement between Quebec and Canada? Yes. No."

Put plainly, the PQ wanted to leave home, but, like many another middle-class kid in this brave new world, only on condition that it was promised a regular allowance. The PQ was willing to say goodbye, if the rest of Canada would kiss it on both cheeks, guaranteeing both its currency and its passports.

Ridiculing the question in his Quebec City speech, Trudeau called it the ultimate cowardice, "because it does not have the courage to put the simple question, Do you want to separate from Canada, YES or NO?" Instead, having led Quebecers to the nationalist well, it refused to drink the water. The PQ, Trudeau said, is ambiguously "asking us to decide and vote on a question which puts our destiny in the hands of others. Because, in the referendum, they have promised not to make Quebec independent unless the others are willing to accept us in association."

Actually, the question was artfully composed to appeal to many in Quebec who were not separatists. If you vote no, Lévesque told them, the province will be without bargaining power. Ottawa will trample all over us. But when the people finally went to the polls on May 20, 1980, 59.5 percent voted no and 40.5 percent voted yes. Even putting such a candy-coated question, separatists failed to eke out a yes majority strictly among French Canadians in the province. We were into a new situation. Not only the English opposed what René Lévesque had called the true aspirations of the Québécois, but also the French. Ardent PQ supporters who had thrown themselves enthusiastically into the campaign, working incredibly long hours without pay, were understandably depressed. The government, shorn of its primary purpose, began to drift.

Soon after their defeat in the 1976 election, the all but discredited provincial Liberal Party elected a new and surprising leader, a highly respected intellectual, and former editor of *Le Devoir*, Claude Ryan. The fastidious Mr. Ryan promptly began to clean the stables, alienating many a former party boss, the traditional dispenser of patronage. He led the "no" forces in the referendum campaign, and after his triumph it was assumed, even by many a disconsolate PQ supporter, that he would certainly be the next premier. But there was something about the unforgiving, obdurate Ryan that suggested should he be elected there would be no more cakes, no more ale. So come the next election, on April 13, 1981, Quebecers, having admonished the PQ, reelected the still immensely popular René Lévesque to office, providing him with eighty seats, the Liberals with only forty-two. A little more than a year later, Ryan resigned, to be replaced by interim leader Gérard D. Lévesque, who was appointed to serve until a new leadership convention could be held.

But the second PQ government, forewarned by the electorate not to flirt with separation anymore, cut down to a train without an engine, as it were, began to come untracked rather early. To begin with, there were proliferating economic problems not entirely of their own making, but clearly exacerbated by an administration made up of ideologues, many of them former academics, whose stance was snobbishly antibusiness. Then the PQ became accident-prone. And, suddenly, *les autres,* quiescent for such a long time, turned very hot indeed, their anger fed by an accumulation of irritating and unnecessary affronts. There was the issue of the signs. The Joanne Curran case. Then, without warning, the Montreal telephone directory dropped all English-language listings of provincial government services, a hardship for many old people. And, even more ominously, the dreaded Camille Laurin was preparing an education bill that threatened to shut down some English-language schools and shift the control of others into French hands. Foolishly, the PQ had cashed in and spent a valuable emotional resource: anglophone guilt. Now they were working on a large overdraft. Only six years in office, they had demonstrated that, given a chance, they could be far more intolerant than the English had ever been. Moderate anglophones, once inclined to give the PQ the benefit of the doubt, now saw the government as resolutely racist. But if the mood had changed, the fundamental disagreement over what the real issue was remained the same. As far as the English-speaking were concerned, it was their democratic right—after all, they were Canadians as well as Quebecers—to conduct their affairs in their own language. To post bilingual commercial signs, to run their own school system. But to the PQ, the use of English, far from being a civil right, was a privilege. A minority privilege. Even Claude Ryan, then still leader of the Liberal Party, warned, "Those who continue to hope for equal status for those languages [English and anything other than French] are dreaming."

Lévesque, responding to a brief put to him by the Alliance Québec, the newly constituted if somewhat muted voice of English Quebecers, turned down every one of their requests for moderation. Alluding to what he saw as the continuing fragility of the supremacy of the French language in Quebec, he noted that he did not share the group's concern about the future of their community. But the justification for Bill 101, that because of the declining French birth rate the French language was threatened, was not borne out by the evidence. In 1961, the mother tongue of 64.9 percent of Montrealers was French, and in 1981 the percentage had grown to 68.4. In the province as a whole, over the same period, it had moved from 91.4 to 93.4 percent. Furthermore, a 1982 federal study, written for the Office of the Commissioner of Official Languages, noted that since 1976, the proportion of Montrealers whose mother tongue is English had shrunk from 22 percent to 18 percent—from 607,505 to 520,590. One in seven anglophones had left Montreal since the PQ came to power. In the province as a whole, the number of those whose first language is English fell from 800,-680 to 706,115—from 13 percent of Quebec's population to 10.9 percent. That "the risk of oblivion is not negligible" for anglophone Quebecers was the verdict of the author of the study, sociologist Gary Caldwell. Caldwell, incidentally, is a member of the Quebec government's own institute for cultural research, and is a longtime supporter of the PQ.

Certainly, Jewish Quebecers, long uneasy with the new nationalism, have begun to quit the province in considerable numbers. By 1981, the Jewish community, once 119,000 strong, had been reduced by at least 15,000, some say much more. Among the first to pack their bags were young university graduates, most of them bilingual, and not all of them fleeing their mothers. They felt unwanted. Mel Himes, a political science professor at Dawson College in Montreal, said, "The Jewish community is . . . dying. [It] still hasn't come to grips with the trauma of its young people leaving."

It didn't help matters when the most rigid defender of Quebec's nationalist flame, the St.-Jean Baptiste Society, was heard from. The society felt that something more should be done to honor the memory of one of its philosophical progenitors, the late Abbé Lionel Groulx. Groulx, who once said, "Who knows if our former nobility doesn't owe its decay to the mixture of blood which it accepted too easily, and sought too often."

Groulx died in 1968. Ten years later, the centenary of his birth was celebrated with essay contests and a stamp issued in his honor, but in 1981 members of the SSJB began to lobby for a proper monument to be erected. In his day, the Abbé Lionel Groulx was an enthusiastic admirer of Mussolini. "Happy," he once wrote, "are the peoples who have found dictators." He also fancied himself an expert on the Jewish psyche. But, speaking in his defense on a French TV program, François-Albert Angers, a spokesman for the SSJB, said the abbé, far from being anti-Semitic, merely noted well-known characteristics of Jews. Among them, obviously, the foibles outlined by the abbé in a letter written in 1954. "We must also consider his innate passion for money. A passion often monstrous and one that removes all scruples from him. He will do anything for money. And so we find him at the bottom of every shady affair. . . . He shows no moral scruples in business, in the professions. . . . His lack of discernment makes him a crushing conqueror."

A year later—in November 1982—a *Toronto Star* reporter uncovered the PQ's ethnic list, a catalogue, labeled "confidential," of 750 ethnic community leaders and 250 ethnic organizations, mostly Jewish, Greek, or Italian. The list, compiled in 1979 and used as a guide in the heat of the referendum campaign, was really, on balance, not so much sinister as silly, but both sides overreacted. The list, charged a Liberal member of the legislature, Harry Blank, "smacks of the KGB," while Lévesque dismissed the fuss over the issue as "a tempest in a teapot."

Comments on the names featured in the ethnic list ran from "right-wing extremist" through "fanatic" to the ultimate calumny—"opposed to Quebec nationalism." Religious belief or racial origin was attached to each name. In my case, for instance, the tag read "of Jewish origin," which certainly let the cat out of the bag, so to speak. The *Gazette* ran the complete list under the head "Who's Who in the Government's List of Ethnic Leaders," and any prominent Montrealer who was not included felt slighted. Michel Beaubien, author of the document, denied that it was meant as a blacklist. Rather, as if to resolve any doubts about his own foolishness, he said that it was "designed to expand awareness of the milieu, especially on the socio-political level." Lévesque, on reflection, conceded, "In some cases, it's a rather repugnant work."

An obviously weary and short-tempered Lévesque now had more important problems to cope with. He had been badly out-maneuvered in the seemingly endless constitutional bickering between federal and provincial governments, a debate that finally ended with the patriation of Canada's constitution, the symbolic severing of the last lingering colonial cord. In the process, Lévesque lost something long cherished by every previous premier of Quebec, the province's traditional *de facto* veto on constitutional matters.

Before the constitution even came home the St.-Jean Baptiste Society was heard from again. In full-page newspaper advertisements and posters, it branded as traitors all Quebec members of Parliament who had voted to patriate the constitution. "Remember each one of them," it enjoined the faithful. "Today they have the upper hand but tomorrow you will, and you will make them pay for their treason."

Our very own constitution came complete with a Canadian Charter of Rights and Freedoms. The Canada Clause, Section 23 of the Charter, ruled that anyone who has been educated at the primary level in English or French in Canada may send his children to either English or French schools. This ruling, which contradicted Bill 101, was swiftly tested in the Quebec Superior Court, where, contrary to Bill 101, it had already been ordained, according to the British North America Act, that English as well as French was a language of the courts and legislature of Quebec.

In a landmark ruling, on September 8, 1982, the Quebec Superior Court pronounced, this time in language that roused the flagging spirits of all English-speaking Quebecers. Chief Justice Jules Deschènes ruled that the Canadian Charter of Rights and Freedom took precedence over Bill 101. In fact, he said, the Quebec government's argument to the contrary "demonstrates a totalitarian concept of society to which the court cannot subscribe. The human person is the highest value we know, and nothing should be used to help reduce the respect it is due. Other societies put the collectivity above the individual . . . [but] this conception of society has not yet taken root here—even if certain political initiatives seem at times to be courting it dangerously—and this court will not honor it with its approval. Every individual in Canada and Quebec should enjoy his rights in their entirety, be he alone, or a member of a group; and if the group has one hundred members, the hundredth has as much right to benefit from all his privileges as do the ninety-nine others. . . ."

The court ruling had an immediate effect on no more than an estimated 300 schoolchildren, but even so Education Minister Camille Laurin said that the cabinet might consider withholding subsidies from schools which accepted pupils not eligible under Bill 101. A week later he decided to appeal the decision. Judge Deschènes's legality, he said, is one that "takes precedence over legitimacy, rights and collective interests of a people."

By the end of 1982, the PQ had trouble, trouble everywhere. Forced by ever-worsening economic conditions to legislate a rollback in the wages of public servants who had done so much to thrust the party into office in the first place, the government was threatened with a long and wasting succession of illegal strikes. One of these strikes, by 70,000 teachers, provoked a brutal back-to-work law late in February 1983. Bill 111 called for union leaders to be fined $10,000 for every day the strike continued; furthermore, the accused were to be presumed guilty unless they could prove their innocence. Individual union members were to be fined as much as $100 a day, and the unions themselves faced a penalty of from $5,000 to $50,000 a day. Outraged, and swearing vengeance against the PQ, the teachers drifted back to work.

Pierre Bourgault, a sort of nationalist conscience, leader of a militant separatist party long before Lévesque hammered together the PQ, wrote, "I see people, a lot of people, who just a few months ago swore by the name of René Lévesque, and who now have become so angry at him and his government that they throw out their Parti Québécois membership cards, they shout 'betrayal,' they swear never to be taken in again, they almost cry in anger when they contemplate the lost dream." He was talking, he said, not about militants, but about the backbone and heart of the PQ, a party whose following had dropped 18 percent according to the latest surveys. Lévesque, he wrote, "wants to go home so badly. I don't blame him. He's tired; he's exhausted and he has lost. He doesn't know how to win again. His party is in disarray and his government doesn't know which way to go. He has no more trump cards. No more imagination. No more ideas. He knows it and he wants out."

Then a ghost of independence dreams past surfaced: Francis Simard, one of the men responsible for the October Crisis of 1967. Sentenced to life for murder in May 1971, but freed on parole in March 1981, he called a bizarre press conference a day after the publication of his book, *Pour Finir avec Octobre*. The conference, appropriately enough, was held at the headquarters of the St.-Jean Baptiste Society. Simard, formerly a member of the FLQ cell that kidnapped Labor Minister Pierre Laporte, murdering him twelve days later, declared that the murder was not accidental, but had taken place because the group wanted to show the world that they were serious. A tough decision, he allowed, but "a decision of sincerity and conviction." The death, he added, was "rapid," because the FLQ wanted to be humane.

. . .

A poll, taken early in 1983, revealed that if an election was held immediately the PQ would lose badly, even though confronted by a Liberal Party led by an interim leader. Six years after the PQ originally came to power, only 19 percent of Quebecers said they would vote for them again.

"No independence," Pierre Bourgault wrote in the *Gazette*, "no social democracy, no dream. I am angry—and very sad."

But René Lévesque, just possibly on his way out, had already achieved something like *de facto* separation for Quebec. Repressive language laws, once in the statute books, were unlikely to be revoked even by a Liberal government, terrified of being labeled the running dogs of the English-speaking minority. Head offices, once uprooted, will never return to Montreal. The young, having set themselves up in Toronto or the West, will be coming back only for funerals. English-speaking Quebecers will continue to quit the province. The most ambitious of the new immigrants will naturally want their children educated into the North American mainstream (that is to say, in English), so they will settle elsewhere in Canada. Montreal, once the most sophisticated and enjoyable city in the country, a charming place, was dying, its mood querulous, its future decidedly more provincial than cosmopolitan.

O Canada

THE REST OF THE WORLD CAN RELAX. CANADA, FADING badly in the ninth inning, has taken a raincheck on the twentieth century.

In 1904 our prime minister, Sir Wilfrid Laurier, promised (scout's honor) that the "twentieth century shall be the century of Canada." A later prime minister, William Lyon Mackenzie King, doing his utmost to keep undesirables (that is to say, Jews) out of the country during World War II, failed to turn the trick. Trudeau has managed, as advertised, to keep this bickering country intact, but only just. Then, at the Progressive Conservative Party convention in Ottawa in June 1983, the leadership candidate with the most impressive intellectual credentials, John Crosbie, finally threw in the towel. He wrote off the twentieth century, a false start, but declared that the twenty-first could still belong to Canada—provided the delegates voted for him.

Promises, promises.

The thing is that looking ahead into the twenty-first century, bristling with nuclear arms, even Lloyd's of London might not offer a completion guarantee on it. Innocent Canada could be the only bidder. Be that as it may, in another time in that steaming convention center, those 3,000 delegates, the very soul of small-town Canada, would have roared back their approval, even as Canadians once took Laurier's promise for redeemable currency. But, as we all know, Crosbie failed in his leadership bid, the prize going to Brian Mulroney, who may very well be our next prime minister.

Mulroney, if he wins the job, will have his work cut out for him. For these days disenchanted Canadians no longer believe in anything, least of all themselves. This endearing northland, perennially richer in promise than in fulfillment, is not merely ailing, it's in real danger of flying apart. It sometimes seems the center, maybe even the periphery, won't hold. Out there in Tuktoyaktuk, Inuvik, and Aklavik, the Inuit and the Indians, yesterday's enemies, have come together to ask for something like self-government in the vast Northwest Territories. A special status for the branch of the branch plant. An American manufacturer, typical of a dastardly breed that would turn a profit on a neighbor's misfortunes, has brought out "The Canadian Civil War Game." The Russians, we have come to realize, play better and more exciting hockey than we do. And if this seems unimportant, imagine, if you will, a team of spunky Chinese, lugging their own tattered equipment, coming off the anti-imperialist sandlots of Peking, a real Red Machine, to beat a major-league all-star team again and again. Our dollar, worth $1.03 U.S. as recently as 1977, has diminished to eighty-one cents. Put plainly, everywhere you turn there is trouble.

The Inuit and the Indians claim to be a colony of white Canada, making no distinction between English and French obloquy. The Québécois, who insist they are North America's oldest colony, *les nègres blancs d'Amérique,* protest that they have been shamelessly exploited by English Canadians. But, hold on, English-speaking Canada's aroused nationalists shout, no, no, *we* are the colony, America's patsy, our economy run as a branch plant.

If there's some truth in all these accusations, there is also a good deal of hyperbole. We are, above all, a nation of injustice collectors. In an adolescent society, where the verities come in convenient halves only, and absolutely nobody is responsible for his own failures, round and round we go. It's a dizzying and depressing time, this country, like Stephen Leacock's famous horseman, riding off in all directions. Without much faith in its own future.

Flying from Montreal to New York, I often run into lawyers and accountants, bent over portfolios, and again and again they tell me, "None of our clients are investing at home any more, certainly not in Quebec. We're putting up office towers in Atlanta and shopping plazas in Houston, and my God, just look around New York, the Canadians are building everywhere."

There are some large ironies involved here. After nine brief months in opposition in 1979, the Liberals, restored to office in Ottawa in 1980, established a National Energy Program (NEP) and a Foreign Investment Review Agency (FIRA), an attempt—long overdue, as some saw it—to regulate rampaging American investment in our country. These measures were prompted by pressure from the New Democratic Party (NDP) and the Committee for an Independent Canada.

I last talked with one of the committee's spokesmen, Mel Hurtig, in 1977. Hurtig thumps the nationalist drum out of a small publisher's office in Edmonton. On one wall, a huge map of Canada swarmed with colored pins, denoting any city or town where Hurtig had been invited to speak. The opposite wall was plastered with newspaper clippings about Hurtig, enshrining the pages of any publication, however humble, that had been good enough to mention him. Hurtig argued that at the time about $665,000 in Canadian funds left the country every hour of the day—80 percent going to the United States. Foreign ownership in Canada, largely American, exceeded $100 billion. A breakdown of foreign investment in Canada, he said, showed manufacturing to be 60 percent foreign-dominated. Oil and gas 90, aircraft 92, computer 91, electrical 88, tobacco products 90, machinery 78, petroleum refining 99.9, mining 64, rubber 93, auto 97, chemical 89, mineral fuels, 81, and smelting and refining 85.

Even if these figures were not absolutely accurate, it was obviously a sorry state of affairs, strongly in need of corrective measures. But the pleasures of living in a branch-plant economy, largely those of a kibbitzer, were not to be sneezed at. If, for instance, there was a war in Vietnam, we could, even while we did piecework for the Americans in private, plead for peace in public. We delighted in lecturing the other America on its treatment of blacks, even as we kept them out of here. But there were also problems in being a branch plant. Dividends earned on Canadian wealth were invested or spent out of the country. Indigenous capitalists, a sentimental bunch, tended to store their profits in offshore Bermuda, which at least shared some of our British traditions, but the ugly Americans clipped their coupons at home. Something else. Too many of our natural resources were being railroaded south, creating no jobs here. Decisions involving our industries were being made outside of the country, the head office's priorities, not a community's dependency on the branch plant, being the primary consideration. Beyond that there was the question of pride. We were not, as the Québécois once put it, *maîtres chez nous.*

So, in 1973, urged on by the NDP, Trudeau formed Petro-Canada, our very own oil company, and the president thereof had the *chutzpah* to tell Exxon that if it wanted to sell off its Canadian operation, Imperial Oil, we were interested, if the price was right. Then, in 1980, NEP and FIRA were put in place. We would remain the hewers of wood and drawers of water, the nationalist prophets maintained, unless we had the courage to curb the voracious American appetite. Yes, possibly, but only two years later NEP, which was supposed to make us self-sufficient in energy by the year 2000, was under attack almost everywhere, and the Liberals were back-peddling on FIRA. Ottawa, having taken one step forward, was now taking two steps backward.

The problem was that, riding the Seventies energy boom, the economic nationalists did not anticipate a worldwide recession and an astonishing drop in the demand for oil and gas, nor that the crybaby Americans, declaring Ottawa's new NEP rules unfair, would pack up their drilling equipment and go home. Not for the first time, what our well-intentioned prophets also failed to understand were their own profiteers. Which is to say, it was not only the Americans who were pulling out. There was now even a huge and continuing flight of indigenous capital to the more permissive south.

John Crosbie bit the bullet at the Conservative Party convention.

The only candidate sufficiently intrepid to offer specific policies to the delegates, he dared to invoke a return to continentalism. He insisted that Canada, with a modest population base of 24 million, must openly welcome foreign investment. "In an increasingly hostile, uncertain and protectionist world economic environment, Canada must seek a new partnership with the United States—as a foundation of our future growth and security." He also pointed out that past high tariffs had left Canada with too many fragmented and inefficient firms, "structured to produce a wide range of goods solely for the Canadian market, goods that were now produced more inexpensively in the newly industrialized countries."

A couple of years back, in the Mount Royal Club, a preserve of Montreal's most important corporate executives, I asked one of this country's leading politicians, then still a corporation president, if in fact our businessmen were not too sheltered from punishing trade winds by government grants and protective tariffs. We were in one of the club's private dining rooms. He asked the waiter to shut the door. "Look here," he said, leaning closer, "if the guys in this club had to compete, really compete, say in New York, ninety percent of them are so incompetent they couldn't even find work."

In this country, where a Rotarian-like faith in our importance was once the rule, everything is now being questioned.

During the Tory convention in Ottawa, I took time out for lunch with a mandarin who had accompanied Prime Minister Trudeau to the Big Seven's economic conference in Williamsburg. "How do we really stand internationally?" I asked.

"The truth is," he said, "we don't count for anything. We're tolerated only because of Trudeau."

When I last saw Trudeau, I inquired whether our largest problem was not that Canada, then 115 years old, was still more geography than nation, its loyalties fiercely regional rather than national.

"We haven't accomplished that many great things as a nation," he said. "When we look at the great things we've come up with, what have we got?" He paused; he shrugged. "Expo '67."

Canada is enduring bad times. Soul-searching times. Unemployment has risen to 12.4 percent, 1.5 million Canadians are without work. The number of people going on welfare, after their unemployment insurance ran out, tripled in 1983.

There is no solace to be had anywhere, even in the world of sport.

Going into the 1983 baseball season, Dave Stieb, the rock on which the pitching staff of the hitherto inept Toronto Blue Jays was built, announced that he wanted to be traded. "I get no recognition up here," he said. "In the States, I could get into those contracts and make more money off the field than on it." Furthermore, he declared that he didn't care for Toronto fans or their stadium. "I personally don't mind pitching in cold weather, but suppose we had a World Series in this stadium in the kind of weather we get in October. What would that be like?"

O.K., O.K., but hockey is supposed to be our game. We invented it. Once more, however, in 1982 the dazzling Russians came over to skate rings around just about the best the National Hockey League has to offer. They have now thrashed various NHL combinations in six series since 1972, and given a shot at it, they would most likely abscond with the Stanley Cup as well. Our Holy Grail, *our manhood,* an exhibit in the Kremlin.

Worse news. Four of the leading fourteen scorers in the NHL in 1982 were foreigners—Swedes or Czechs. Tiger Williams, of the Vancouver Canucks, wasn't pleased. "We got commies, we got Swedes, and we got Indians. I'm the only white people we got."

Then, in June 1983, for the first time in history, the premier player picked in the NHL draft was not a native son with boils on his neck, missing three front teeth, but *a clean-cut American high school kid,* Brian Lawton.

There are problems in television as well. Tit-content problems.

The Canadian Radio-Television and Telecommunications Commission (CRTC), after considering many hotly contested applications, awarded licenses to several groups to introduce pay television in the spring of 1982, on condition that their schedules offered viewers 50 percent Canadian content. The largest and potentially most profitable franchise went to a group called First Choice, and their first choice, proclaimed in coast-to-coast newspaper ads, was Playboy Films. First Choice, our joy their first consideration, promised to help thaw out those long cold Friday nights ahead of us with what they called adult erotic films. They were no such thing, outraged feminists complained. Rather, they were prurient soft-core porn that could easily harden as satiated viewers demanded more, more in succeeding winters. So the CRTC, guardians of our cultural integrity, summoned the president of First Choice to a two-hour meeting. First Choice claimed they would coproduce with Playboy, making some of the films in Toronto. Furthermore, the films would be introduced by 1982's Playmate of the Year, Newfoundland's very own Shannon

Tweed. But the hardball players of the CRTC would not be put off with dusty answers. What they wanted to know, *make no mistake about it,* was how much Canadian content there would be in the Playboy Films and what, moreover, would be the nature of that content. Put another way, would Canadians yet again be relegated to fill the office of script assistants, grips, and gofers, or would we see our very own bare-breasted girls jiggling right up there on screen for once?

Even before the Playboy issue exploded, yielding the first good laugh of the winter, the Federal Cultural Policy Review Committee, which spent three years and $3 million traveling across Canada, published a 400-page report. Apart from a time-honored plea for the government to spend more money on culture, the report was surprisingly bold. It recommended that the once justifiably renowned but now moribund National Film Board should get out of production and be turned into a training and research center. The Canadian Broadcasting Corporation, it proposed, should drop commercial advertising. It should continue as a TV broadcasting outlet, but with its own production limited to the news. All other program material should be bought from independent producers.

Mind you, not all the cultural news out of Canada is grim.

In 1982 yet another committee, this one made up of dedicated academics, scholars beyond reproach, deliberated behind closed doors, emerging to pronounce that from this day forward, thirty Canadian novels were to be considered classics plain and simple.

If I can be pardoned for tooting my own horn here, I am proud to say the cultural court ruled that I had committed one-thirtieth of Canada's classics. That's official, yes, but if on reflection not all that impressive, I am bound to remind you that I come from a country inhabited by a mere 24 million people. Furthermore, that I didn't apply myself to Talmudic logic as a boy for nothing. Which is to say, had I, for instance, been born in Great Britain or the United States, I might, on a per capita population basis, have contributed three British or ten American classics to the world at large.

2

IN 1965, WHEN MIKE PEARSON WAS PRIME MINISTER OF Canada, he visited LBJ in Texas. His party landed on a runway right on the ranch. "The rambling old ranch house," Pearson wrote in his memoirs, "was surrounded by planes, jeeps, trucks, communications towers, and security people, with the Pedernales River running past the front door. President Johnson and Lady Bird were awaiting our arrival. As we mounted a little podium before a battery of TV cameras, the president . . . welcomed me very warmly and greatly enlivened the ceremony by ending his remarks: '. . . and we are so happy to have Mr. Wilson with us.' "

Two years later, during Canada's Centennial Year, LBJ repaid the visit, stopping at the prime minister's summer residence at Harrington Lake. When he arrived ahead of the president, Pearson has written, security people were all over the place, "on rowboats, and in the bushes with their walkie-talkies. . . . I went into the house and up the stairs. At the top a hard-faced chap said: 'Who are you? Where are you going?' I replied, 'I live here and I'm going to the bathroom.' "

In larger terms, it's no more than some room upstairs, in the North American attic, a place to be ourselves, that Canadians claim to crave, but even if we were granted that breathing space, free of both economic and cultural pressures from the United States, I fear all we would do is continue to squabble endlessly, each province shrieking me, me, me! Certainly we don't seem to be up to anything more edifying these days.

Newfoundlanders bitterly protest, with considerable justice, that they were short-changed in a deal which enables Quebec to resell to the U.S., at a huge profit, Newfoundland electrical power routed through *la belle province*.

Quebec, rolling about in self-pity, like an elephant in a mud puddle, blames Ottawa every time it rains on Sunday.

Ontario expects the rest of us to maintain high import quotas on manufactured goods in order to protect its own inefficient industries.

Then there's the West.

If, in this perpetually bickering country, as René Lévesque has put it, Quebec is nothing more than an internal colony, which lives at the will of another people, then out there in the alienated West, they are peering through the other end of the telescope and what they see are perfidious frogs. A French Canadian plot. For as long as they can remember there has been a French Canadian prime minister, and now the ministers of finance and energy: both out of bloody Quebec as well.

At the Tory convention, in Ottawa, more than one seething, potbellied western delegate, grim-faced under a plastic Stetson, told me that Trudeau was a communist, but one of them, who undoubtedly had his sources, assured me that he was really a mole planted in Ottawa by Moscow. "Didn't he visit China even before he got elected?"

Yep.

"You think he had to travel that far for egg rolls?"

Nope.

Trudeau and Lévesque, ostensibly at odds, the delegate confided, were actually in cahoots. "If we don't watch it, fella, our kids will have to parlez-vous if they want work. You better believe it."

Pierre Elliott Trudeau, now sixty-three years old, went to Ottawa as an MP in 1966, and has been prime minister of Canada for the last fourteen years, save for nine months following the general election of 1979, when Joe Clark formed a shaky minority government.

Acknowledging that interregnum recently, Trudeau told me, "I enjoyed my sabbatical. I was in opposition just long enough to refresh myself."

Swept into office in 1968, he seemed to begin as a star without a vehicle, for Canada was fragmented even then. Everybody's darling he was, the national savior. Utterly different from any Canadian politician who had come before, he was seen as the strong man who could save the nation, keeping Quebec in confederation.

Over the years, Trudeau has shown a weakness for windy technocrats, smug futurologists who were not only often wrong, but expensively wrong to boot. Economics has never been his strong suit. Coming into office, he seemed disdainful of the Liberal establishment, too fastidious a man to soil his hands with patronage, but he soon learned how to ladle it out to old cronies like a traditional machine pol. Take Gérald Pelletier, for instance, one of the two other "Wise Men" who accompanied Trudeau to Ottawa. Pelletier, since serving as secretary of state, has fallen on one soft pillow after another. Paris, New York. Once ambassador to France, then ambassador to the UN.

In his long and exciting years in office, the often refreshingly candid Trudeau has also said many rash and foolish things. In 1971, he did not endear himself to the unemployed in Victoriaville, Quebec, by telling them they were now "in the front ranks of the new leisure class." Then, once pressed for action by apprehensive farmers with full silos out west, he told them, "Well, why should I sell the Canadian farmer's wheat?" But, for all his mistakes, Trudeau must be accounted one of our most intellectually impressive and forceful prime ministers. Where fifty-four years of squabbling and six previous prime ministers had failed, Trudeau succeeded. He had actually brought home a constitution, ramming it through Parliament and Westminster. However compromised and short of its original intentions, the constitution, legal in both official languages, included a charter to protect the basic rights of all Canadians. True, Quebec had dissented, its legislature melodramatically flying its flag at half-mast the week the Canada Act came home, but home it was at last, in spite of René Lévesque. Trudeau had also brought many a distinguished

French Canadian into federal politics, rooting them in positions of power, and his years in office had been enriched by a vision, his impassioned struggle for a civilized, bilingual country. He did keep Quebec in confederation. Impatient with emotional nationalism, whether out of Quebec or English Canada, he had reminded his countrymen, "Men do not exist for states; states are created to make it easier for men to attain some of their common objectives."

But now the long and controversial Trudeau era was winding down. "I can't say for sure," he told me, "but I certainly do not plan to run in the next election."

He had, to say the least, become an unpopular leader, abominated in the West, a target for all the media trendies who had once embraced him as *nonpareil.* The Gallup Poll showed the stumbling Liberals backed by only 34 percent of the electorate, the Progressive Conservative Party leading with 50 percent, the rest of the vote going to the New Democratic Party.

John Roberts, minister of the environment, acknowledged, "We're treading water, manning the bilge pumps. It's *fin de régime* time here."

An astonishing state of affairs, considering that the Liberals, in power for an incredible forty-one out of the last fifty years, had come to take office as their heritage and to look on elections not as a time to choose, but as an opportunity for the rest of us to applaud.

Many people felt, I suggested to Roberts, that the Liberals had simply stripped their policy gears and were now being caught trying to coast uphill. They had run out of ideas.

"Sure," Roberts allowed, "but so have the other guys. At the moment neither party has a clear idea of objectives. It's difficult to see, for instance, how anybody can restore all those lost jobs."

I had met with Roberts early in January 1982, when Joe Clark was still the Tory leader or, as he saw it, prime-minister-in-waiting with only one hurdle or minor inconvenience to surmount. On January 29, in Winnipeg, Tory delegates were to vote on whether or not to call for a leadership review (that is to say, another convention) or to continue with Clark at the helm. The Tories were then so close to power it was assumed that Clark would pass the test, however grudgingly endorsed, and then lead his troops back into office.

At the time, the Liberal grip slackening, many an Ottawa footnote was enduring a slippery transition period. Civil service mandarins, once enamored of Trudeau, were now, without even pausing to clear their throats, doing their utmost to establish distance between them. Mind you, they had failed Trudeau at least once before.

When the Watergate tapes revealed that former President Nixon had referred to Trudeau as "that asshole," the immediate retort from Ottawa, as quoted in the *New York Times,* was "no comment"—an endorsement less than ringing, it seemed to me.

Now, however, careers were at risk. We weren't talking about old-fashioned abstractions like loyalty, but fundamentals, the serious stuff Ottawa men were prepared to die for: indexed pensions. So civil servants no longer dined out on Joe Clark jokes, but were at pains to say the Tory leader wasn't such a twit, really, but a decent fellow, in spite of his obvious intellectual shortcomings. Still, they stopped just short of outright endorsement. After all, Clark's spluttering car could still be forced off the road in Winnipeg.

3

IT CAME AS NO SURPRISE, REALLY, THAT THIS COUNTRY that invented pablum, and provided the world with its first factory chickens, should also offer Joe Clark as prime minister.

There never was a more ordinary Joe.

The largely unknown Clark, after only three years as an MP, emerged as Tory leader at the convention in 1976, winning the job on the third ballot, everybody's second choice. The next day's headline in the *Toronto Sun,* one that would continue to hound him, read JOE WHO? Then, once Canadians had seen more of the thirty-seven-year-old leader, he was adjudged a wimp. Clark, who had come out of Bow River, Alberta, had failed law school, dabbled in small-town journalism over two summers, and, for the rest, spent all his adult life in politics, a backroom boy grimly determined to become prime minister one day. Once elected leader, he slipped on one banana peel after another. Setting out on what was meant to be a prestige-bolstering world tour, he promptly lost his luggage. Inspecting an honor guard, he stumbled right into a bayonet. Out in India, surveying a wheat crop ripe for harvesting, he asked, "And what season of the year would it be here?"

Like the prime minister himself, Clark had marital problems. His steely young wife, Maureen, would not answer to her married name, but insisted on being called Ms. McTeer. Like Margaret Trudeau, she was outspoken, once imploring reporters to "stop crapping all over my husband." Actually, in the months following his election as Tory leader in 1976, Clark was more pitied than scorned by the press corps. Many reporters, who felt there should be *some* alternative to Trudeau, spun out entire columns of celebration of the fact that Clark, speaking in Toronto or Calgary, had made complete sentences.

Though his fumbling and obvious lack of stature hardly helped, Clark was really undone by the emergence of Quebec as the major issue in Canada. After the 1976 Progressive-Conservative convention it was Clark who was riding high, very high, and the Liberals, in office since 1963, who had been reduced to a chilling 29 percent in the polls. The Liberals, with power their only unbending principle, and their support shriveling, were even talking of dumping Trudeau. Then, presto! On November 15, 1976, René Lévesque and his Parti Québécois rode into power, set on independence for French Canada. Quebec. The heartland.

Ironically, even as Trudeau was faltering, set to topple, his nemesis René Lévesque, thrust him stage center again. A majority of Canadians took another look at Trudeau and decided he was needed. Badly needed.

The truth was, most of us suspected that one day the prime minister would have to sit down to the table for some hard bargaining with the premier of Quebec, and while Trudeau was easily his intellectual equal, Clark, even if he sat on three telephone directories, would still have the fiery Quebec premier looking down on him. Clark was unbelievably inept. In a crucial batch of by-elections, in May 1977, one of the candidates he extended the PC welcome wagon to was Roger Delorme of Terrebonne, Quebec, a former radio hot-liner. Delorme, a real charmer, had already revealed on his radio show that a mere million Jews had been burned in the Holocaust (the other five million, kindling?) and furthermore, ". . . Zionism rhymes with Nazism. . . . I have dealt with Zionists and Nazis and it was the same thing. . . ."

Clark stubbornly refused to disown Delorme, who stood no chance of winning, and thereby failed at once as both opportunist and man of principle. He also suffered the indignity of having his candidate disown him. Clark, Delorme said, was largely unknown in Quebec. "I'm fighting a campaign and I haven't got time to sell him."

Clark, meanwhile, was certainly out there trying to sell himself, constantly on the trot from one end of the country to the other.

In the general election of 1979, at the request of a candidate running behind in a predominantly Jewish Toronto constituency, Clark rashly promised that if elected, he would move the Canadian embassy in Israel to Jerusalem. Elected, albeit to head only a shaky minority government, Clark was immediately threatened with an Arab boycott of Canadian goods, and so he was obliged to renege on his promise, looking silly again. Then, only nine months in office, Clark stumbled into a Liberal parliamentary trap, his minority government falling on a no-confidence vote on its budget. Now Clark not only had to contend with the rising laughter of his enemies, but also with the indignation of his own party. After all those wasting years in the wilderness, he had led them to the honey pot, but not allowed them time to gorge themselves. They would, of course, be unforgiving.

Typical, perhaps, was the story of the Alberta lawyer who had labored for the Tories for two decades and at last, it seemed, was to reap his reward. He was informed by Clark's Ottawa office that he was about to be appointed to the supreme court of his province. Overjoyed, the lawyer sold his partnership in a flourishing practice and invited his cronies to a celebratory dinner. The restaurant he had so discreetly chosen was over the border in Montana, because he feared that everybody, himself included, might have too much to drink, and it just wouldn't do for a man about to become a judge to be seen in his cups. The high-spirited party was well into the coffee and cognacs when a young waiter came to their table.

"Hey, you guys Canadians?"

"Yes. And damn proud of it, too."

"I just heard something on the radio that might interest you."

"What's that?"

"Your government just fell."

In the next general election, in the winter of 1980, Clark promised that if he was reelected he would dismantle Petrocan, the enormously popular government-owned oil company. He would not only dismantle the corporation, but he would hand every elector five shares in it. Considering that the market value of a share was then $10, the truth is Clark was offering each of us fifty bucks to vote for him. Even at that price he lost, and once again editorial writers and cartoonists declared an open season on him. Columnists poked fun at his $200 hair-styling. They were scornful of his mechanical-toy walk and his high-school debater manner of speaking. Even Tories delighted in jokes celebrating his ineptitude.

Question: What were the best two years of Joe Clark's life?
Answer: Grade three.

Depending on where you paid your political dues, he was an admirably stubborn and determined man or uncommonly insensitive to ridicule. But the fact is that he not only persevered, but going into the Tory convention in Winnipeg in January 1982— at which the party was to decide on whether or not to call for a leadership review—he was riding high. His party led the Liberals by a seemingly unbeatable fifteen Gallup Poll points.

Even so, when I caught up with him in his Ottawa office before the convention, he was incredibly tense, bracing himself against the arm of his easy chair, as if we were lurching through bumpy skies at 30,000 feet. Stiff, watchful, he countered questions with rambling rehearsed responses. He didn't even seem to understand his own notion of Canada as "a community of communities." Pressed to elaborate on it, he retreated into foggy generalities, the idea lost somewhere in the middle distance. Surprisingly, however, he did say he was convinced that Trudeau would not retire. "I will be fighting him in the next election." An election he would win, Clark vowed, if only because the Canadian people realized that what they had done to him after only nine months in office "wasn't fair."

A forty-three-year-old man, *a politician,* who expected justice in this world was, to say the least, somebody to be cherished, but he wasn't going to get anything like it in Winnipeg.

Winnipeg.

Arriving late Wednesday night, January 26, I found the airport milling with Quebec delegates for Clark. Most of them, honoring an old tradition, had had their expenses paid. A rough lot, they seemed. One glance at them, in fact, and I grasped that it would be all but impossible to pick up a pool game on the streets of St.-Jérôme or Chicoutimi this coming weekend. Obviously, all the good ole boys were here.

No sooner had I checked into my hotel than I made for the convention center, which had the feel of a forlorn legion-hall dance just breaking up. Big paunchy men wearing western boots, silvery-haired ladies in ill-fitting dresses. Rows of campaign buttons riding every bosom. WE'RE HERE FOR CANADA. SOCIALISM . . . How Do You Like It So Far?

Clearly, this was not the rich, insufferably stylish, and well-connected bunch you meet at a Liberal convention. Nobody here, skating on the thin ice of one perfunctory meeting, called the prime minister "Pierre," or expected to read his own name in the social pages of the *Toronto Globe & Mail* or the *Montreal Gazette* the next morning. These people did not serve on the boards of orchestras or ballet companies, or drink in the VIP room between the acts at the Stratford Festival. They didn't ski on Whistler Mountain, and couldn't tell you about a darling little undiscovered isle in the Caribbean, just the thing for the February blahs. This sour, dissatisfied bunch was composed of small-town insurance adjusters and lumber merchants and accountants and car dealers. They called their wives "Mother," and they vacationed in Winnebagos. They belonged to curling clubs and the Rotary. They had had it up to here with pornographic films playing on the shopping mall, socialist fags running CBC-TV, and those uppity frogs still in office in Ottawa. Usually, nobody listened to them, but now—at last—they were kings and queens for a day. No, three days. Drinking beer out of outsize plastic cups, they were pursued by supplicants for Clark and men who wanted them to vote for a leadership review.

At the opening plenary session on Thursday morning, I didn't even grasp that Clark was on the platform with the other dignitaries until his presence was pointed out. When Guy Lafleur is on the ice you are compelled to watch him, whether or not he's got the puck. When Trudeau enters a crowded room, you know, you know. Joe Clark didn't have it. Obviously rattled, his voice rising, he assured the gathering that this would be the last year of Trudeau's life, then hastily corrected himself, saying political life. But it was too late. The television cameras had caught him, and his latest flub would play on the news that night.

Friday, the day of the vote, started ominously for Clark. An editorial-page cartoon in Canada's national newspaper, the staunchly Tory *Globe & Mail,* showed a resolute Clark preparing to leave his hotel room to make his crucial convention speech, unaware that he had neglected to put on his trousers. Joe, on trial, continued to be a subject of mirth even to his supporters. "Of course I'm voting for Joe," a jovial man at the bar told me. "I've got to support him—he isn't qualified for any other job."

Then, Brian Mulroney's militia, some 250 delegates from Quebec, their expenses also paid, arrived en masse. Mulroney, Clark's archrival for years, held effective control of the Tory party in Quebec. Going into the convention in Winnipeg, Clark had ostensibly won Mulroney's endorsement, but that staged love-in, the two competitors smiling tightly under hot TV lights at the Ritz Carlton Hotel, in Montreal, struck objective observers as just about the warmest since Teddy Kennedy had joined Jimmy Carter on the stage at the Democratic convention in New York. It was also no secret that the Quebec delegates Mulroney held on a short leash would be voting for a leadership review in Winnipeg. Party officials asked some of Mulroney's militia to sign their names three times to prove that they were not impostors or moles from Moscow. Then they were told they couldn't register, because—aw, shucks—the computer had broken down. Mulroney, with a touching concern for the democratic process, protested loudly. His delegates were registered.

Sixty-six point nine percent of the 2,406 registered delegates in Winnipeg voted for Clark, the others demanding a leadership review. A solemn, shaken Clark took to the platform and announced that he was resigning as both leader of the opposition and leader of the party. He called for a leadership convention at the earliest possible moment. He would be a candidate himself, he said, and furthermore, he expected to win.

So the stage was set for another Tory convention in Ottawa, in June, and the anointing of Brian Mulroney, not only as party leader but, the conventional wisdom has it, as the man bound to be our next prime minister. The Tories, persistent anglers, their bait taken by a chub for seven frustrating years, were finally to land themselves a flashing fighting trout.

4

APRÈS NOUS, LOUIS XV SAID, LE DÉLUGE. BUT AFTER Trudeau, until the eclipse of Joe Clark, it seemed that all we would have to cope with in Canada was a slow steady drizzle.

Brian Mulroney, an untested factor, is something else again. Though he has never sat in Parliament, he is, unarguably, the compleat politician. Ironically, he is reportedly better liked by Trudeau than his own possible successor to the Liberal leadership, that brooding elegant WASP in the woodpile, the former minister of finance, John Turner. Mulroney is charming, handsome, shrewd, but also, some say, too clever by half. A slippery fellow.

Mulroney's ancestors, on both sides, came over from Ireland during the potato famine. Now forty-four years old, fluently bilingual, he is the self-styled Boy from Baie Comeau, the third of six children of a Quebec North Shore electrician, with the outlines of a useful myth already in place.

Why, just listen to this.

When Colonel Robert McCormick, once the real boss of the North Shore as well as the *Chicago Tribune,* came to Baie Comeau, the nine-year-old Mulroney would be called upon to sing "Dearie" in his boy soprano. His reward was $50 which he promptly turned over to his mother.

Should a Prime Minister Mulroney bend too readily to American pressures on Canada, the nationalists will say he learned to sing for U.S. bucks before he even knew how to shave. Cartoonists will enjoy a field day. But should he, on the other hand, stand up to the U.S., they will say now there's a man who learned what it really meant to be a Canadian when he was just another shining morning face. He never forgot how he was obliged to ingratiate himself with the Yankee boss of Baie Comeau.

At university—first at St. Francis Xavier, in Nova Scotia, then at Laval in Quebec City, where he studied law—Mulroney made friends who were still with him in his long and circuitous campaign for the leadership. Pat MacAdam, Michael Meighen, Michel Cogger, and Jean Bazin. Mulroney has a well-earned reputation for being fiercely loyal to his old friends, who stuck with him when he was down, if not exactly out, and for remembering his enemies with something like passion. I like that. But should he come to power, it could mean lots of jobs for old cronies whose only qualification is loyalty to Mulroney.

Active in Tory backrooms since his student days, always a glutton for work, Mulroney first made his reputation as a member of the Robert Cliche Commission, an inquiry into corruption and violence in the Quebec construction industry. Then, in a campaign that was ill advised and far too slick, he brashly contested the Tory party leadership in 1976. A surprising second on the first ballot, he finally lost out to Joe Clark. Something he wouldn't forget.

Following his defeat, Mulroney became executive vice-president and then, in 1977, president of the Iron Ore Company of Canada, where he developed a reputation as a master of labor-relations magic. He also bought a mansion in the higher reaches of Westmount. Then Joe Clark, elected prime minister in 1979, was bounced out of office, suckered on a budget confidence vote. Mulroney was quite properly scornful. He didn't mourn. Professing loyalty to Clark, he went out on a cross-Canada speaking tour, suggesting how, come to think of it, he might have done things somewhat differently. Certainly this called for some fancy footwork, but on another, more important, issue, Mulroney showed he was not without principles. While a fulminating Clark led the Tories in a no-holds-barred fight against Trudeau's constitution, Mulroney more or less backed the prime minister. A risky stance. Then, once Mulroney had declared himself a leadership candidate, following the Winnipeg convention, he demonstrated there were some things he would not stoop to in order to win delegates. A desperate Clark, for instance, stopped just short of prostrating himself in an attempt to gain the support of the Parti Québécois. In fact, he became their favorite candidate, Lévesque's potential Ottawa poodle, PQ apparatchiks bending their shoulders to the wheel for him in the boonies. But Mulroney, to his credit, refused to ingratiate himself with the separatists. On the contrary. He made it abundantly clear that they would be no happier with him in office than they were with Trudeau.

Come the showdown at the Ottawa convention in June 1982, Mulroney did not repeat his mistakes of 1976. He led a floor campaign that was a model of political realism. It didn't inspire, there was nothing exalted about it, but it worked beautifully. After the first ballot, he had reduced Joe Clark to a shell-shocked stiff. Cruelly caught by the TV cameras, the former prime minister sat there, eyes empty, mouth open, visibly sustained only by his wife's anger. Maureen had been to see *Rocky* three times and had recommended it to Joe as a lesson in how to overcome. But as Clark watched two other candidates, the trailers on the first ballot, lead their supporters to Mulroney's section of the stands, he knew he was not going to overcome. Though he still led in the actual delegate count, he was dead in the water. On the third ballot, Newfoundland's John Crosbie, whom Mulroney had even more reason to fear, came out low man on the poll and was therefore eliminated. Then, on the fourth ballot, Mulroney took the prize.

But even before the fourth ballot vote was tabulated, Joe Clark, accompanied by Maureen, was to be embarrassed one more time. Starting out on what must have been the longest walk of his life, pursued by TV cameras, he drifted across the milling convention floor, determined to shake hands with his rival before his own defeat was officially announced. But when he arrived, his good-loser smile barely intact, Mulroney wasn't there to receive him. The winner had already ducked under the stands to grab a quick shower and change his shirt before bursting on stage to deliver his victory speech. Even before he had been publicly counted out, Clark learned the first lesson of a defeated politician. If you want to see the boss, phone ahead.

The sadness of the convention, such as it was, lay not in the fall of Joe Clark, but in sour, resentful small-town Canada looking at its own reflected image and finding it unacceptable for high office. They hated Pierre Elliott Trudeau. He talked to them *de haut en bas.* Once, in British Columbia, he had given them the finger. When they had raged at him because the print on their corn flakes boxes was now bilingual, he had shrugged and replied, "Why don't you just turn them around?" Even though he was sixty-three years old, he still did the disco bit with glamorous young things, not the kind *they* married, but the sort whose pictures they saw in classy magazines. They hated that independently rich bastard, who used to be driven to school by a chauffeur, but they also respected and feared him, and were proud to have him represent their country abroad. They did not respect or fear Joe Clark, who was as gauche as they were. Joe, their ordinary Joe, even had to be taught how to use a knife and fork properly, after he became prime minister. Wherever he traveled, advance men advised his hosts that Joe always ate the same thing: steak well done, french fries, ketchup, and a Coke. He was stiff, he was awkward, and, in the end, he was betrayed by his own natural constituency. The delegates wanted to win for once, just once, so they turned their backs on Joe and went for a sweet-talking city slicker, another damn Quebecer, Brian Mulroney, who might very well have been a Liberal. He wore expensive suits and Gucci shoes, and he enjoyed dining at the Ritz Carlton. He had not met his wife at a legion-hall dance or in the parking lot of a Canadian Tire store, but at the poolside of the most exclusive tennis club in Montreal. Mila Mulroney, a mere twenty-nine years old, wasn't your average cloth-coat Tory wife either, but a fetching, intelligent young lady. Foreign-born. The daughter of a Yugoslav shrink, Dr. Pivnicki, head of psychiatry at the Royal Victoria Hospital in Montreal.

The Tories, voting against their natural instincts, weren't even sure what they had thrust into the leadership. In his early days, Mulroney had been branded a red Tory, somebody concerned with social issues, but in his leadership campaign he was labeled a right-winger, and, certainly, the right wing of the party had fallen into place behind him. However, with Mulroney, it was still difficult to tell where he stood on most issues. Tacking, always tacking, he had developed a tendency during the campaign of filling his ideological sails with whatever favorable winds were available, not yet revealing his true course. So, for the moment, the jury was out but hopeful. The press, however, had already made him its darling, even as they once had Trudeau. Though he has yet to be tested in parliamentary debate, he will, many have written, make a great prime minister.

In *Where I Stand*, a book of his speeches published during the campaign, Mulroney came out for everything nice. He was for a new beginning. Giving the people of Canada hope. Higher productivity. A firm commitment to research and development. Tighter control of government spending. Civilized labor relations. And then, worrying some observers, he told a Tory seminar at the Ottawa convention that the Reagan government should be given the benefit of the doubt over its interventionist policies in Central America. This, he added, was our hemisphere, and under his administration, Canada's armed forces would "go first class" and be better allies of the Americans in a number of strategic areas. But it is an earlier speech of his that gives me pause. In a 1982 fund-raising address, Mulroney, like every booster of a Canadian politician who had come before him, said, "This is quite simply the most blessed nation on the face of the earth. There is nothing that Canadians cannot do in a reasonable and thoughtful way once they set their minds to it."

Which is where the rest of us came in, not waving but drowning.

A far more realistic, if less thrilling, assessment of Canada's estate was once proffered by novelist Hugh MacLennan. "Canada's geographical vastness is deceptive," he wrote. "At the moment little more than 4 percent of the whole country is under cultivation; and it has been estimated that only 7 percent ever will be."

This country, 116 years old but still blurry, is like a child's kaleidoscope that remains in urgent need of one more sharp twist of the barrel to bring everything into sharp focus. Making us whole. Something more than this continent's attic, filled with resentful folks, wheat, yearning, resources we have seldom been able to manage to our advantage, and a lamentable tendency to repeat our mistakes.

Item: With great fanfare, Premier Lévesque announced in Paris, in June 1983, that agreement had been reached whereby the French-government-owned Pechiney Ugine Kuhlman group would invest $1.5 billion in Quebec to build an aluminum smelter, creating eight hundred jobs. So far so good. But the kicker is that the Quebec government will fork out one-third of the money, as well as supply electricity for twenty-five years at less than half the going price. Electricity, estimated to make up one-third of the cost of aluminum ingots, usually sells for $21 per 1,000 kilowatt-hours in the U.S., but we will provide it for $10. The real profit, and the jobs, comes not from making ingots, but from the manufacture of finished products. Typically, however, we will end up exporting piles of ingots, stamped MADE IN CANADA, and then importing the finished aluminum goods, mostly from the U.S. "We offer our natural resources, in this case electricity," Nick Auf der Maur wrote in the *Montreal Gazette*, "and get very little in return."

Looked at another way, the PQ has argued passionately for independence, saying Québécois culture will thrive only if Québécois stop serving as the drawers of water in the larger Canadian scheme. And yet—and yet—independence, we have been told more recently, is economically guaranteed by the might of the James Bay hydroelectric project. Or, put plainly, the Québécois will cease being drawers of water for the rest of Canada, only to become suppliers of cut-rate water power to France and, just possibly, New York State as well.

O Canada! O Quebec!

All but the most obdurate Quebecer should grasp that their highly vaunted culture, essentially parochial, has a better chance of surviving on this continent within the confines of Confederation (English-speaking Canadians, many of them bilingual, acting as a buffer) than it ever would should the province separate, finding itself adrift in an utterly anglophone sea. Similarly, English Canadian nationalists, some of them consumed by blinding anti-Americanism, need only glance at the globe to appreciate that if we are bordered on one side by voracious commercial appetite and a culture of a daunting vitality, we look out on the other on the Gulag Archipelago.

For all our difficulties with the United States, real and imagined, we are fortunate in our neighbors. Both English and French Canadians must come to terms with continental realities before the ship of state sinks, a bickering bankrupt. We can certainly negotiate fewer branch-plant humiliations, more independence, but we can't saw the continent apart on the forty-ninth parallel. Or at the Ontario border. And, obviously, we are stronger together.

For all my complaints about the PQ, a nationalist aberration now in sharp decline, I could not live anywhere else in Canada but Montreal. So far as one can generalize, the most gracious, cultivated, and innovative people in this country are French Canadians. Certainly, they have given us the most exciting politicians of our time: Trudeau, Lévesque. Without them, Canada would be an exceedingly boring and greatly diminished place. If I consider the PQ an abomination it's only because, should their policies prevail, everybody in Canada would be diminished. This is still a good neighborhood, worth preserving. So long as it remains intact.

A NOTE ON THE TYPE

This book was set in a digitized version of a type designed by the first William Caslon (1692–1766), greatest of English letter founders. The Caslon face, an artistic, easily read type, has enjoyed two centuries of ever-increasing popularity in our own country. It is of interest to note that the first copies of the Declaration of Independence and the first paper currency distributed to the citizens of the newborn nation were printed in this typeface.

Composed by American–Stratford Graphic Services, Inc., Brattleboro, Vermont. Printed and bound by The Haddon Craftsmen, Inc., Scranton, Pennsylvania.

Designed by Virginia Tan.